W9-CGM-107

STRICTLY KOSHER READING

Popular Literature and the Condition of Contemporary Orthodoxy

Yoel Finkelman

JEWISH IDENTITIES IN POST MODERN SOCIETY

Series Editor: Roberta Rosenberg Farber – Yeshiva University

STRICTLY KOSHER READING

Popular Literature and the Condition of Contemporary Orthodoxy

Yoel Finkelman

BOSTON

2011

Library of Congress Cataloging-in-Publication Data:
A catalog record for this book is available from the Library of Congress.

ISBN 978-1-936235-37-7 (hardback)
ISBN 978-1-61811-002-2 (paperback)

Book design by Adell Medovoy

Published by Academic Studies Press in 2011
28 Montfern Avenue
Brighton, MA 02135, USA
press@academicstudiespress.com
www.academicstudiespress.com

In honor of Mr. Joseph Schorer,
whose mother's blessing came true.

CONTENTS

ACKNOWLEDGMENTS

To Nava, for the endless support and concern, for insisting that "hofesh" not get discarded, and for (almost) always being right. To my children, Elisheva, Shulamit, Eliya, Hallel, and Yeda'ya, for being worthy and occasionally welcome distractions. (I'm very proud of all of you!) To my parents, Rabbi Dr. Eliezer and Marilyn Finkelman, for raising me with their unique combination of Torah, kindness, wisdom, and honesty. To my in-laws, Frieda and Joseph Schorer, for their vision, support, and love.

The beginning of this research was supported by the Moshe Davis Memorial Fellowship from the Institute of Contemporary Jewry at the Hebrew University. In addition, a grant from the Memorial Foundation for Jewish Culture supported some of the ongoing work.

Many thanks to all those who read and commented on drafts or sections of this book, or at least put up with my lengthy conversation about these topics: my wife, Nava; my parents, Eliezer and Marilyn Finkelman; my sister, Svia England; my brother, Yaacov Finkelman; as well as Judith Baumel-Schwartz, Menachem Butler, Kimmy Caplan, David and Sara Eisen, Adam Ferziger, Ari Ferziger, Samuel Heilman, Menachem Kellner, David Fink, Dina Knoll, B. Barry Levy, Eitan Morell, Alex Pomson, Moshe Simon-Shoshan, Marc Shapiro, Jeffery Saks, Malka and David Schaps, David Shatz, Yael Shenkar, Hannah Skolnik, Reuven Spolter, Jeremy Stolow, Kenneth Stow, Chaim I. Waxman, Ari and Naomi Zivotofsky (who lent me that book again and again), and David Zisenwine (I hope that I have not forgotten anyone). Thanks also to Michael Rose for the door-to-door service. I particularly appreciate the efforts of Sharona Vedol, Sara Libby Robinson, Igor Nemirovsky, Kira Nemirovsky, Stephanie Monasky, Adell Medovoy, and Roberta Rosenberg Farber of Academic Studies Press for their interest in the project, encouragement, and hard work.

I presented sections of this book at various academic conferences and other speaking engagements, and I thank my numerous listeners for their comments. Several anonymous referees, including from Academic Studies Press, have offered penetrating criticisms and comments, for which I also offer my appreciation.

Sections of this book have been previously published as: "Medium and Message in Contemporary Haredi Adventure Fiction, *The Torah U-Madda Journal* 13 (2005), 50-87; "Tradition and Innovation in American Haredi Parenting Literature," *Innovation and Change in Jewish Education*, Ed. David Zisenwine (Tel Aviv: Constantiner School of Education, Tel Aviv University, 2007), 37-61; "Nostalgia, Inspiration, Ambivalence: Eastern Europe, Immigration, and the Construction of Collective Memory in Contemporary American Haredi Historiography," *Jewish History* 23 (2009), 57-82; "Relationships Between Schools and Parents in Haredi Popular Literature in the United States," in *Jewish Day Schools, Jewish Communities: A Reconsideration*, Eds. Alex Pomson and Howard Deitcher (London: Littman Library of Jewish Civilization, 2009), 237-254; and "ArtScroll's Empire," *Jewish Review of Books* 4 (Winter, 2011), 12-14. I thank Oxford University Press, Springer, Yeshiva University, and the Littman Library of Jewish Civilization for permission to republish this material here.

PREFACE:
THE GEHINOM TRIO AT SLIME'S BAR

Us versus them. Good versus bad. Torah versus all else. A cute, even humorous illustration in an innocent children's book leaves little to the imagination. A mother wheels her two newborn infants out of the nursery. One turns toward the left, down a path marked "Olam Habah" [the World to Come]; the other turns to the right, down a path marked "Olam Hazeh" [this world].[1]

The picture makes the distinction clear and unambiguous. Down the path to the World to Come, the infant meets observant Jews – men and boys in *kippot* [skullcaps], Haredi [ultra-Orthodox]-style black hats, and Hasidic garb, along with women and girls in modest skirts, long sleeves, and head coverings. Happy, well-mannered young girls sit attentively at the "Living Torah School"; clean-cut young men study with a pious-looking rabbi at the yeshiva; grandparents and grandchildren interact at the "V'Zocher Chasdei Avos [remember the kindness of the parents] Home" for the aged; and mothers and children shop happily at the "Shabbos Kodesh [holy Sabbath] Bakery." A large family sits idyllically around a table in a book-lined dining room, right next door to a catering hall at which a wedding takes place, much to the delight of the attendees. There are no police, but the neighborhood hardly needs law enforcement since people act kindly, feeding the pigeons or helping the elderly cross the street as a driver waits patiently.

A large brick wall separates this idyllic community from the vastly different culture on the other side of town, where non-Jewish or Jewish-but-non-observant citizens live a vicious and unkind existence together with their violent, self-centered, and ultimately unhappy neighbors. Some cruel boys accost a pig-tailed girl in a public school. No classes take place, but several teens, one with bright green hair, smoke and gamble on the roof. Four men slump over tables at "Slime's" bar, drunkenly listening to the sounds of "The Gehinom [hell] Trio," a rock band made up of long-haired, tattooed young men. In homes, those not watching television by themselves fight with their spouses or chase

From Baruch Chait, *The Lost Treasure of Tikun Hamiddos Island*, reproduced courtesy of Baruch Chait and Feldheim Press.

Many middos are acquired as we grow up. We must be very careful to choose a positive Torah environment, which will enhance the development of good middos.

their pets with nasty intent. Several policemen patrol the city, helpless to stop the violence and theft; one policeman guards the criminals in prison. The closest to an act of kindness involves one long-haired man who drags a drunk or unconscious person out of the "Laytzanim [scoffers] Tavern."[2]

Remarkably, one who follows the path to the World to Come receives much of the goodness of this world as well. Nobody seems angry and no one fights or suffers. The poor do not appear on the good side of town, but a sign declares that a "free kitchen for the needy" will take care of them. The physical buildings of the school, the yeshiva, and the old-age home are new and clean, and they are surrounded by clean, well-kept parks and swimming pools. In contrast, on the non-Orthodox side of town, run-down, dilapidated buildings stand in an environment with almost no grass or parks. One who enters the Torah world receives worldly blessings as well.

The miserable people on the wrong side of the wall may not even be fully human, since in one drawing a dog leads a man on a leash into the psychologist's office, and in another corner a red-haired woman dressed in a bathrobe wheels what appears to be a dog in a baby carriage. She is so out of touch with her potential as a mother that she treats her pet as a child. The illustration makes its larger message crystal clear. The world is populated by good guys and bad guys, with nothing in between. The good guys are observant, ultra-Orthodox Jews, and everyone else is miserable, violent, and suffering. A few pages later, the book explicitly states the source of this dichotomy. "Without Torah one cannot fully develop refined middos [character traits]." Non-observant Jews and gentiles have little hope. The author makes his educational message explicit in a caption under the illustration. "We must be very careful to choose a positive Torah environment, which will enhance the development of good middos."[3]

This illustration appears in the second of a four-part series of books for children on improving their characters. Baruch Chait, a well-known Haredi educator and rabbi, authored the book, and Feldheim, the purveyor of Haredi popular literature, distributes it. Sales numbers are not available, but anybody involved in child-raising in the Haredi community in the past decade has heard of or seen the books. Young children, those just old enough to appreciate a picture book, can already begin the difficult work of improving their characters. They can also absorb a worldview that distinguishes sharply between us and them.

Strictly Kosher Reading attempts to make sense of this illustration. Or, to be more precise, it attempts to use the popular literature of the contemporary American Haredi community as a lens through which to examine how this isolationist religious community marks itself as different.

The community's popular literature works hard to present Haredi Judaism as distinctive, to declare Haredi separation, to construct categories of self-understanding that make community members feel different from others. Haredi Jews illustrate their children's books in ways that exaggerate the differences between insiders and outsiders in order to construct a sense of distinctiveness. Without that subjective sense of difference, Haredi Judaism might cease to exist as a distinctive religious sub-community.

Hence, Haredi Jewry spends a great deal of energy examining the "secular" world, and it defines itself through contrast with that secular world. This drawing not only presents the happy observant Jews, but makes sure to contrast them with the unfortunate people on the other side. A negative image of non-Haredi Jews solidifies Haredi Jewry's self-understanding and reinforces its attempts to educate youngsters in Haredi values.

Yet this self-same popular literature also reveals an equal and opposite reality: Haredi Jews and their community are profoundly acculturated and are quite similar to the outside culture that they claim to reject. Acculturation refers to a social process in which an immigrant or minority group adopts patterns of behavior and thought from the majority culture, but without assimilating and losing its distinctive identity and sense of uniqueness.[4] Much of what Haredi popular literature presents as uniquely and distinctively Jewish is, in fact, very similar to non-Haredi American culture and is very different from the texts, ideas, and values of the older Jewish tradition to which Haredi Judaism pledges allegiance. The boundaries that appear clear and unbridgeable in the children's illustration are in fact quite porous. No brick wall separates the good side of town from the bad, not only because good people do live outside the Haredi enclave and because some Haredi Jews misbehave, but because American Haredi Judaism has become profoundly Americanized.

Put in terms of social theory, Haredi popular literature works to construct "symbolic boundaries," i.e. a subjective sense of being different. Symbolic boundaries involve socially constructed categories of collective thinking that allow group members to distinguish between "us" and "them," which in turn enable members of the group to view themselves as separate. Symbolic boundaries combine with other more objective signs of distinctiveness – separate dress, neighborhoods, and schools, for example – to construct Haredi identity in America.[5] That is to say, the brick wall in the illustration may be a fiction, but it is a very important fiction. Popular literature is one location where Haredi culture attempts to define itself as different at the same time as it borrows extensively from the supposedly degenerate culture that surrounds it.

I divide the argument into seven chapters. The first chapter provides background on the Haredi community and its popular literature and articulates the book's method. Chapter 2 addresses boundary maintenance, describing the ways in which this literature both maintains and blurs the boundaries between Haredi culture and general culture. Haredi popular literature blurs boundaries by importing ideas and values from the outside culture, but also maintains those boundaries by insisting that readers rely only on Haredi renderings of those ideas. Haredi literature borrows ideas and genres from outside the Jewish canon, creating a syncretic combination of the traditional Jewish with the contemporary American. At the same time, social and economic forces limit and control which elements of contemporary culture merge with the tradition and which do not. In Chapter 3, I take a close look at the ways popular authors explain, to themselves and their audiences, their seemingly subversive borrowing from general culture. Surprisingly, many authors acknowledge explicitly that they merge Jewish with non-Jewish culture, and these authors work to explain what makes that borrowing legitimate and why it does not undermine the Haredi dogma of a pure and totalizing Torah.

In Chapter 4, I look at a critical element in a group's sense of distinctiveness: history. Individuals and groups define themselves by telling stories about who they are, where they come from, and how they arrived at their current time and place. Haredi history books and biographies ground communal identity in a founding myth: a utopian Eastern European Jewry which has, with difficulty, been transplanted into contemporary America.

In Chapter 5, I take a close look at works of popular Haredi theology and argue that they present a theological picture of the universe, of religion, and of faith that reinforces a sense of isolation and difference. Numerous works attempt to prove the truths of Haredi Judaism. In the process they envision Haredi Jews as skeptical and rational, and they envision non-Haredi Jews as ignorant, at times willfully so. In Chapter 6, I identify the rhetorical strategies that Haredi authors use when they criticize their own community. A healthy and functioning society must identify and try to improve its inevitable flaws, but self-criticism and airing of "dirty laundry" can undermine the community's sense of moral superiority. What rhetorical tools can Haredi authors use to raise issues of concern to the Haredi public agenda without also calling into question the group's sense of cultural supremacy? Chapter 7, by way of conclusion, suggests that all communities construct their identities not so much around pure facts or data, but around narratives and stories. Haredi popular literature offers a glimpse into the narrative around which Haredi Judaism builds itself.

Scholars, laypeople, and Haredi Jews themselves make a serious mistake if they understand Haredi Judaism as a throwback to the past, a medieval tradition transplanted into the present. As much as the community is animated by the spirit of conservatism and by a sense that the past, and only the past, ought to guide the present, in fact this community is dynamic and diverse, struggling to maintain its sense of self even as it takes on forms, ideas, and values from the surrounding community that it claims to reject.

Chapter I:
ARTSCROLL JUDAISM: HAREDI POPULAR LITERATURE IN CONTEXT

Over the course of the 1970s, the Orthodox Jewish publishing house, Feldheim, gradually changed its editorial policy. It reduced its publication of academic and semi-academic books[1] and increased its production of popular works of Haredi ideology. In 1976 a new publisher, ArtScroll-Mesorah, joined the trend, producing the first of its multi-volume Bible translation and commentary.[2] During the decades that have since passed, the amount of Haredi popular literature has grown by leaps and bounds. Publishers such as Feldheim, ArtScroll-Mesorah, Targum Press, CIS, and others produce thousands of volumes written from a Haredi perspective for the consumption of the Haredi public, as well as for Modern Orthodox, non-Orthodox, and in rare cases non-Jewish readers. Precise numbers are hard to come by, but these publishers have collectively produced several thousand titles in the past decades. ArtScroll's website, for example, lists over fifty genres—Basic Judaism, Biography, Children, Crafts, Dating and Marriage, History, Inspiration, Jewish Law, Parenting, Prayer, Psalms, Reference, Repentance and Teshuvah [repentance], Spirituality, Self-Help, The Sabbath, Women's, Young Adult Novels, etc.—in addition to audio books, e-books, software, videos, gifts, and the like. A trip to a Jewish bookstore in any Orthodox neighborhood will reveal a wide selection of books for children and adults, all written in clear and accessible English. By now, ArtScroll may well be the world's largest publisher of English-language Judaica.[3]

Some popular books seem aimed at novices and newcomers: English speakers without extensive Judaica backgrounds who want to learn something about basic Jewish belief, prayer, or practice. Some readers may even become *ba'alei teshuvah* [repenters, newcomers to Orthodoxy]. Those who adopt Orthodoxy as adults may take their first steps in Orthodox practice with the help of one of Feldheim's English-language summaries of Jewish law, may gain their first introduction to a biblical book from an ArtScroll commentary, or may learn about Jewish beliefs from a Targum Press guide for beginners.

But beginners are not the only audience. Outsiders to the Orthodox Jewish community might expect well educated Orthodox Jews to do without this popular literature, since they should be able to access the Jewish tradition in its Hebrew-language original. Walking into any Orthodox school, synagogue, or living room would quickly disabuse them of this illusion. These publishers have captured a substantial percentage of the Orthodox book market, since many highly educated Orthodox Jews prefer to get their biblical commentary or halakhic instructions in a simple, easy-to-read English rather than the dense Hebrew or Aramaic prose of classical Torah literature.

Some genres are more in line with traditional Jewish religious writings of the past, such as works of theology and religious ideology, halakhic [Jewish legal] codes, translations of and commentaries on classical Jewish texts, and liturgical books. But even here, publishers have an interest in making the tradition accessible and easy to understand.[4] The Schottenstein Talmud serves as a prime example. For fifteen years, ArtScroll's international team of Orthodox rabbis labored to produce an edition of the Babylonian Talmud that would transform it from a book closed to all but the most educated into a text intelligible to anyone with even a minimal background in rabbinic Judaism (ironically, including women, whom the makers of this edition no doubt would be happy to continue to exclude). Costing an estimated $21 million to produce[5] and extending to seventy-three volumes, the Schottenstein Talmud seamlessly merges the traditional-looking Vilna page-layout with a newly laid out word-by-word translation, explanations in plain English, and clarifications of key concepts, all accompanied by helpful background material and clear diagrams and photos.[6]

But the Haredi popular publishing industry does not just produce classical Jewish texts like the Siddur or the Talmud. Haredi self-help books, fiction for children and adults, parenting guides, and cookbooks all adapt contemporary, non-traditional genres for the ironic purpose of defending the tradition. Sometimes, the publishers' biggest money makers come from these less religiously weighty volumes, such as Susie Fishbein's series of cookbooks, *Kosher by Design*.[7] These cookbooks combine short religious messages about Shabbat, Jewish holidays, or the Jewish home with easy-to-follow instructions for making gourmet food quickly and easily in one's own kitchen. Like Martha Stewart with a long skirt and *sheitel* [wig], Fishbein makes classy kosher cooking look easy. But she also transmits images of how Jewish women *should* celebrate holidays, decorate their homes, and imagine their roles as mothers and homemakers. All these books, no matter what the genre or format, share Haredi Jewish content in an accessible, popular, and user-friendly print format.

Modern Orthodox intellectuals have attacked these books, at times quite bitterly. According to these critics, Haredi popular literature presents a narrow-minded and dogmatic version of Judaism, selectively citing sources that are compatible only with the most fundamentalist interpretations of the tradition. Oversimplification, ignorance of history, and at times outright distortions misrepresent Judaism's complex and nuanced legacy.[8] I appreciate this critique and agree with much of it. Still, an overly polemical approach can distract readers from other, to my mind more fruitful, questions. After all, much Haredi popular literature does not aspire to reach the standards that the critics set for it. I prefer to understand the phenomenon of Haredi popular literature in the context of contemporary culture and to learn about the complex relations of the Haredi community with its surroundings. I want to articulate the functions that Haredi popular literature plays for the community that produces and consumes it, and to use this literature as a lens through which to examine the construction of contemporary Haredi identity. I want to paint a nuanced picture of the relationship between Haredi Judaism and the culture in which it is embedded.

American Orthodoxy Comes of Age, 1950-Present

The rise of Haredi popular literature did not occur in a historical vacuum, as it was part and parcel of the surprising revival of Jewish Orthodoxy as a whole in the second half of twentieth-century America. Toward the middle of the twentieth century, Orthodoxy was weak and in the process of ongoing "institutional decay,"[9] with observers predicting its imminent collapse and disappearance. The distinctions and differences between Orthodoxy and the American Conservative movement were blurry and unclear, a sure sign that Orthodox identity itself was unclear. Moreover, Orthodox dogmatism and commitment to detailed laws and rituals seemed ill suited for the intellectual openness and personal freedom of modern America. Not only was Orthodoxy small, weak, and ill-defined, but its membership was hardly devout. Most Orthodox laypeople were neither religiously well-educated nor consistently observant. Many were, to use Charles Liebman's term, "non-observant Orthodox" – people who were not themselves observant, but who remained attached to Orthodox institutions more than to those of any other denomination.[10] In many cases, nostalgia motivated these Orthodox Jews much more than ideological commitment or spiritual fervency.

Something changed dramatically in the years after the Second World War, and in the last third of the century in particular. Gradually, the older generation of nominal and non-observant Orthodox Jews died off. Many of their children did not remain in the Orthodox fold, but those who did became increasingly motivated by a spirit of commitment and passion. Holocaust survivors and refugees from Europe came to the United States, and many brought with them a deeply held emotional attachment to the Jewish tradition, a passion for observance, and boundless energy to rebuild what had been destroyed. A wave of *ba'alei teshuvah* did a great deal to boost the self-confidence of American Orthodox Jewry. America may have been the *treyfene medine* [non-kosher country], but a new generation of highly educated, religiously fervent, and religiously energized Jews had appeared, much to people's surprise. Over time, Orthodox rabbis, educators, leaders and institutions paid less attention to the non-observant, and felt the need to respond primarily to the needs of those who were fully committed, or might be convinced to become fully committed, to strict observance. The fuzzy borders between Orthodoxy and the Conservative movement became sharpened as Orthodoxy moved to the right and the Conservative movement to the left. Orthodoxy became if not numerically stronger – Orthodox Jews remain some 10 or 12 percent of America's Jewish population, as they have for some time[11] – then at least emotionally stronger, as well as more distinctive, more self-confident, and more observant.

Orthodox synagogues, elementary schools, high-schools, advanced yeshivas, kollels [advanced yeshivas for married men], colleges, etc., all sprouted up throughout North America. Numerous neighborhoods – from New Square, NY, on the more Hasidic side; by way of Flatbush and Kew Gardens Hills, NY; to Teaneck, NJ, on the more Modern Orthodox side, in addition to similar neighborhoods outside of the New York area – became the geographical locations of intensely Orthodox life. Kosher food became readily available throughout North America, and kosher restaurants sprouted up in every Orthodox neighborhood of significant size, as did gift shops, bookstores, food markets, butchers, bakeries, old-age homes, charities, social-welfare organizations, and more.[12] Together, these institutions helped create Orthodox enclave communities, where Orthodox Jews would live together and mutually enforce one another's sense of identity and commitment. By century's end, predicting Orthodoxy's demise was no longer fashionable. In fact, given Orthodoxy's newfound dedication and passion, predicting its imminent victory seemed more common. "In the struggle for the soul of American Jewry, the Orthodox model has triumphed," said journalist Samuel Freedman, no doubt exaggerating.[13]

Three Camps in American Jewish Orthodoxy

American Orthodoxy grew in several directions, and it might be helpful to divide the growing Orthodoxy into three subgroups: the Hasidic, the Haredi, and the Modern Orthodox. At one end of the spectrum are certain Hasidic groups, such as Satmar or Skver, which minimize acculturation and the infiltration of general culture into their tight-knit communities. Strictly observant not only of halakhah, Jewish law, but of a network of distinctive Hasidic practices, members of this Ultra-Orthodox community diminish their contact with non-Hasidic Jews and with general American culture to the extent that it is possible. The group avoids television and internet, eschews general education, and further reinforces cultural isolation with distinctive Hasidic dress, Yiddish as a spoken language, and their own network of neighborhoods and accompanying cultural institutions. Hasidic Jewry shows signs of some acculturation, but a much more limited acculturation than that of virtually any other group of American Jews.[14]

At the other end of the spectrum are the most acculturated and Americanized group of Orthodox Jews, referred to as "Modern Orthodox" or as "Centrist Orthodox." For them, a thoroughgoing Americanization has led to neat and easy integration into American middle-class culture. While formally committed to strict practice of Jewish law, Modern Orthodox Jews observe many rituals inconsistently.[15] Modern Orthodoxy retains some distinctiveness, with its network of separate schools and synagogues, but Modern Orthodox Jews tend to downplay distinctiveness. The community's members eagerly gain a general education, and their schools work to combine Torah study with a top-notch secular education, whether in the sciences or in the humanities. Modern

Orthodox Jews dress, for the most part, like their non-Orthodox companions. They speak English fluently, and are often functionally illiterate in spoken Hebrew or Yiddish. Broadly speaking, Modern Orthodox Jews, despite their Orthodox lifestyles, are remarkably similar to other white, middle-class, suburban Americans.[16]

But there is also a middle group – which we will refer to in this book as Haredi [sing., Haredim pl.].[17] William Helmreich refers to this middle group as "strictly Orthodox," though in colloquial language they are often called "Yeshivish," (due to the centrality of yeshiva education for men) or "Black Hat" (due to the black fedora hats that are de rigueur for men). On the one hand, they share with their Satmar or Skver co-religionists to the right a measure of isolationism and a stated rejection of American culture as degenerate and incompatible with Torah. Hence, they work very hard to build boundaries, isolating themselves in enclave communities such as Flatbush in Brooklyn or Lakewood, New Jersey. They make sure to dress differently from other Americans – black fedora hats, white shirts, and dark pants for men, and long skirts, long sleeves, and socks for women, as well as hats, kerchiefs, or wigs to cover the hair of married women. These Haredi Jews attend private schools dedicated more to Torah than general education, and they pepper their language with in-group colloquialisms and jargon borrowed from Yiddish, Talmudic Aramaic, or Biblical Hebrew.[18] They create tight-knit communities that reinforce strict observance of Jewish law.

Yet, in comparison to the more isolationist Hasidic groups, this Haredi community garners a more expansive general education, earns higher levels of professional training, and has undergone a deeper process of often unacknowledged acculturation.[19] English, even with the in-group colloquialisms, serves as the vernacular. Many of these Haredi Jews acquire advanced secular education – at a high-school, college, and even graduate level – which enables them to work outside the Haredi enclave, in white-collar professions. Consumption of non-Haredi media is not uncommon, even if it is frowned upon. Haredi Jews work in the American marketplace and are active in contemporary politics. Haredi fashion, even as it maintains its distinctiveness, is influenced by contemporary trends. Haredi youth listen to non-Haredi popular music, and yeshiva students often follow sports closely. And, as this book will show, this Haredi community is grounded in and influenced by numerous American cultural trends, particularly regarding such issues as psychology, the structure of the family, taste in fiction, and the like.

This middle, Haredi group of Orthodox Jews is loosely associated with Agudath Israel, a worldwide Haredi political and social movement.[20] For the most part, this group consists of yeshiva-oriented Jews who trace their roots to the Lithuanian Jewish tradition of intense Torah study, though the Agudah umbrella also includes some of America's more moderate Hasidic groups. Torah study is a central value, and virtually all adult men spend several years in full-time *lernen* [Torah study] in yeshiva after attendance at a Haredi high school. In yeshivas, students spend some ten to twelve hours a day occupied primarily with the study of Talmud. Many students, though hardly all, continue to college, generally part time while continuing yeshiva study. But this college attendance focuses on professional training, and Haredi Judaism does not encourage acquisition of a broad-based liberal-arts education.[21] Though women are considered exempt from the central commandment of Torah study, and are barred from the study of Talmud, the Haredi community educates them in separate-gender schools that combine general education with a truncated Torah education. This frees women up for the professional training that will help them earn a living and support their future families, particularly if their husbands continue to study Torah full time after marriage.[22]

The lines between this Haredi American Judaism, the more isolationist Hasidic groups to the right, and the Modern Orthodox groups to the left are not entirely clear (and one could certainly map the community using other categories). Still, the position of American Haredi Judaism in between the Hasidic isolationism and the Modern Orthodox integration makes this community a prime subject for a study of the tensions between isolation and acculturation. Moreover, by the term "American" I refer to more than just a geographical location. A more open Haredi Judaism exists in other English-speaking countries such as England, and more importantly, American Haredi immigrants to Israel have imported some of the attitudes, sensibilities, and worldview from the New World to the State of Israel. Generally, the ultra-Orthodox community in Israel tends toward greater isolation than that of the American parallel.[23] Yet, Haredi Jews who move from North America to Israel often bring with them the more moderate American Haredi approach, and small pockets of more moderate American-style Haredi Judaism exist in some English-speaking neighborhoods in Israel. (At times, these

American-style Haredim have trouble fitting into the more rigid and more isolationist Israeli Haredi environment.) A significant number of authors of English-language Haredi popular literature currently live in Israel, where they express a more Americanized Haredi Judaism in their writing. By American Haredi I refer, then, not exclusively to a geographic location, but to an attitude, ideology, and mindset, a collection of religious and cultural sensibilities, a set of habits and intuitions, that constitute a Haredi "interpretive community," the center of which is in North America. I examine this community's popular literature within the context of late twentieth- and early twenty-first century North America, even understanding that the periphery of this transnational culture may be geographically located elsewhere.

The Growth of Haredi Orthodoxy

As Orthodoxy grew, its more isolationist, Haredi wing emerged as particularly strong. Reinforced by an influx of devout European refugees who arrived in the United States in the 1940s and early 1950s, these Haredim began urgently building new communities, schools, yeshivas, and institutions. The message of these refugees found a listening ear among an increasing number of native-born American Jews, and over time yeshivas grew, communities expanded, and religious conservatism and halakhic stringency became increasingly influential within Orthodoxy as a whole. The devotion and passion of rabbis, lay activists, educators, and young people brought tremendous energy to Haredi Orthodoxy, thereby making fervent commitment to a strict tradition seem particularly attractive to at least many in the new generation. Modern Orthodox institutions and communities grew, but Haredi institutions and communities grew even more quickly and became particularly strong. Increasingly, Haredi Judaism became the hegemonic voice in American Orthodoxy, as the Modern Orthodox felt self-conscious and increasingly defensive relative to the self-confidence of "the right."[24]

Symbolically, one can trace the beginning of the cultural shift in American Orthodoxy to the publication in 1963 of the first issue of Agudath Israel's monthly magazine, *The Jewish Observer*. Its unapologetic positions gave voice to a conservative, dedicated religious community that was happy to use the tools of modern media to spread its message. The magazine became the voice of a self-confident and energetic Haredi Jewry that was prepared to reach out and use merchandise, popular culture, and popular literature to reach the observant and non-observant public. This book will focus on the ways in which popular literature, like *The Jewish Observer*, offers an intriguing glimpse into the tension-filled ideological and cultural world of that Orthodoxy.

Two cultural ironies about this group stand out. First, Haredi Judaism is both isolationist and acculturated. Despite signs of acculturation, discussed above, American Haredi rhetoric emphasizes the vast difference between Judaism and contemporary culture. "At no time has the contrast between the values Judaism stresses and those of the society around it been more pronounced than today."[25] Haredi culture understands itself to be not only different from contemporary culture, but also superior. Popular authors contrast the "unchanging Torah life-style" to that of the "hollow, aimless modern culture," and they do not tire of criticizing "the moral decay at every level of society."[26] Hence, much Haredi social energy and educational effort focuses on protecting community members from the perceived dangers of contemporary culture.

Second, Haredi Judaism is both voluntary and authoritarian. While the community possesses no formal or legal authority, it does wield quite a bit of informal power over members, who are called upon to willingly conform to strict religious standards and social norms. By law in the democratic West, all citizens may legally live their religious lives as they please, and the community can do little to prevent them from violating communal norms. Moreover, mainstream multicultural American culture offers few barriers to integration, such that the Haredi community maintains voluntary separation rather than having segregation forced upon it; anyone who wants to leave the community can do so.[27] At the same time, the Haredi enclave-community places great stock in rabbinic authority, an ethic of submission, and a doctrine of *da'as Torah*, according to which great rabbis have authority over all significant personal or communal decisions.[28] To maintain a sense of authority, the Haredi enclave creates a broad network of informal sanctions that enforce a strong measure of conformity, since conformity helps support the isolationist group's social cohesion. The Haredi community trains members to live up to Haredi Judaism through a process of potent socialization. A young person who grows up in an intensely Haredi home, attends a Haredi school, associates with Haredi friends, and has as much of his life as possible encompassed by the warm embrace of the Haredi enclave, is likely to identify strongly with Haredi Judaism and may well find abandoning that enclave, or violating its written and unwritten expectations, deeply unpleasant. Indeed, the strongest sanction is the threat of losing one's place in the community, being made to feel less a part or unwelcome.

These two ironies will serve as a backdrop for the central arguments in *Strictly Kosher Reading*. This book argues that Haredi popular literature exemplifies and provides a lens into the challenges that the Haredi community faces in living up to these tension-filled commitments. Popular literature plays a significant role in both isolating the community from what it considers the dangerous surroundings as well as facilitating access to some appealing aspects of general culture. Popular literature helps maintain the enclave's authority by offering appealing and accessible literature which community members can freely choose to read, even as that literature argues for and defends the community's encompassing authority.

Haredi Judaism: Embattled and Thriving

American conditions contributed to the emergence of a self-conscious, devout, and distinctive Orthodox Judaism. The bland, suburban (not to mention white and middle class) "religion of the American way of life," as Will Herberg so aptly described mainstream American religion in the 1950s,[29] gave way, through the 1960s and beyond, to counterculture movements, an appreciation of diversity, and a greater degree of ethnic and religious distinctiveness. A growing atmosphere of multiculturalism emerged, which made it, ironically, increasingly acceptable to stand out. Non-mainstream religious commitments became mainstream. Furthermore, American culture became more socially and sexually liberal, which motivated a backlash among devout religious groups, primarily Christian but also Jewish, which preferred a more conservative stance.

But there were internally Jewish reasons for these developments, as well. Many of the refugees who fled to America during and after the Holocaust came from devout Eastern European backgrounds, and they felt compelled to rebuild something passionate and committed on American soil. And, for American-born Jews, the notion of a strict Orthodoxy seemed an appropriate Jewish response to Hitler's destruction. Furthermore, the 1970s witnessed a dramatic rise in intermarriage and a consequent crisis of "Jewish continuity" among the broader American Jewish population. Orthodoxy, and devout Orthodoxy in particular, could make a strong claim to preserve Jewish identity and combat intermarriage into the next generation.

The growth of American Haredi Judaism serves as but one example that has undermined the more extreme versions of the so-called secularization thesis, according to which modernity leads inevitably to the collapse or marginalization of religion. Indeed, devout religious groups, for the time being, seem to be doing quite well, whether in the United States or in other places around the world. Some suggest that various structural aspects of modern American society help some kinds of religious communities grow. Freedom of religion not only challenges faith, but also creates opportunities for faith. The same people who may choose to opt out of religion may just as well choose a more devout and demanding religion. Social mobility, mass communication, and large urban population-centers might seem to homogenize the population into a single secular culture, as some proponents of the secularization thesis argued, but they also allow like-minded individuals to find one another and create voluntary and distinctive sub-communities. Or, in the economic terms that have become popular, freedom of religion creates an open market of religious ideas and asks faith communities to provide the best possible product in order to attract adherents. The invisible hand of the market improves the product and makes it more compatible with the needs of the population.[30]

Conditions in the late twentieth century also helped produce "a generation of seekers," people who spend their lives searching for spiritual satisfaction and meaning. While some focus on the personal, individual search for flexible and ever-changing coordination between their existential state-at-the-moment and one or another spiritual message, other seekers find what they look for in stronger, more fixed, and less flexible religious traditions.[31] Haredi Judaism constitutes but one of hundreds of devout religious groups that have thrived in America's pluralistic context.

Furthermore, in a pluralistic environment, the numerous "others" – images of what each group does *not* want to be or become – can help the community define itself by defining what it is up against. Organizing a group around a sense of cultural threat or peril helps to galvanize identity and create a feeling of belonging and attachment. The threat can energize community members to respond to the challenges, engage their detractors, and defend themselves. As Christian Smith has suggested, religious communities thrive not so much despite being embattled, but *because* they are embattled.[32] A community may strengthen itself by playing up the differences between itself and the culture around it in order to create a sense of threat and embattlement. And the group might also do well downplaying the similarities between itself and the surrounding culture. As I will argue extensively, Haredi popular literature plays a significant role in maintaining the subjective sense of cultural threat that helps galvanize the Haredi community, much at the same time as the literature works to hide its own absorption of many aspects of American culture.

This is not to deny the reality of separation and isolationism. Haredi distinctiveness exists not only in the minds of Haredi Jews, but in the visible, outward signs of difference and separation from the general culture. Distinctively Haredi neighborhoods, schools, recreational events, music, dress, slang, and the like all create and reinforce the separation, creating what Emmanuel Sivan has called Haredi enclaves that help shield the community from perceived threats. Living together, acting differently, and developing a self-perception as different all help create and construct Haredi identity in the diverse and dynamic environment of contemporary American culture.[33] In the end, Haredi identity is constructed by the combination of symbolic boundaries and material or social boundaries.[34] Haredi popular literature plays a significant role in constructing both kinds of boundaries.

Where Does Haredi Popular Literature Come From?

It is not surprising that popular literature has emerged as an important aspect of Haredi culture in the closing decades of the twentieth century. First, Haredi Orthodoxy's growth created a critical mass of people who could serve as a market for this literature. Producers and authors could potentially earn significant profit. Second, mainstream Western culture was becoming less Puritan, more individualistic, and increasingly sexually explicit, pushing Haredi Jews to create alternatives to Western popular culture, which seemed out of line with their religious values. Third, technological advances made writing, publishing, and distribution cheaper and more efficient, allowing for profitable publishing to a smaller market.

Fourth, popular literature plays important roles in constructing Haredi Orthodoxy's enclave and in socializing people into Haredi commitment. The enclave culture tries to maintain the adherence of members by creating a complete social envelope for the individual, such that he or she will venture outside the enclave as little as possible. As I will argue in Chapter Two, Haredi popular literature discourages group members from extensively consuming secular popular culture by providing a distinctively Haredi alternative. Orthodox Jews of all kinds are often genuinely acculturated, and the same cultural forces that make a genre popular within the general public affect Orthodox Jews as well. They could read general, non-Haredi literature, but from an ideological and religious perspective, Haredi Jews may prefer an Orthodox version of a literary genre, such that it will match their values and concerns.[35] Hence, much Haredi popular literature imitates contemporary literary genres, taking on literary forms that did not appear in traditional Jewish literature – such as adventure fiction, parenting guides, self-help books, and magazines. Imitating these contemporary literary styles and genres blurs the boundaries between outsiders and insiders by borrowing elements of outside culture. But it also helps the Haredi community maintain its boundaries by discouraging consumption of the non-Haredi versions of these books.

Popular literature is only one part of a wider Haredi popular culture, which helps Haredi Jewry create distinctive communities with expansive social capital and a thick cultural atmosphere. Haredi music, computer games and films, recreational activities, summer camps, jargon, and the like contribute to Haredi distinctiveness. Furthermore, a "material Judaism"[36] has also emerged, a Haredi physical culture which includes distinctively Haredi ritual objects, games and toys, formal and casual clothing, decorative arts, food, house wares, buildings and architecture, and even medicines.[37]

These developments within the Haredi community coincided with parallel developments within America's Christian culture, particular its sizable Protestant evangelical wing.[38] Christian popular literature, Christian music, and Christian material culture helped define and strengthen America's devout evangelical population during the last third of the twentieth and beginning of the twenty-first centuries. Exponentially larger and more influential than the Haredi community, evangelical Christianity was growing, along with the market for mass-produced evangelical Christian products. Similar products had existed in America for well over a century, but as evangelical Christianity grew in numbers and cultural power, the objects produced and consumed were transformed from "Jesus junk" to commodities of higher quality and sophistication.[39] The network of Christian bookshops expanded rapidly as the market for Christian books skyrocketed beginning in the late 1960s. The 1980s also witnessed (no pun intended) a massive growth in Christian rock music, as well as the first "crossover" Christian musicians – such as Amy Grant and Stryper – who had their music appear on the non-religious music charts. Through the 1990s, the American Christian book and music market continued to expand.[40] While we know very little about the economics and market aspects of the popular Haredi market, some of the economic dynamics of the two markets are similar.[41]

It is probably too simple to suggest that this Christian market directly influenced Haredi Jews. More to the point, some of the same forces that propelled this Christian literature and culture were propelling their Haredi counterparts as well. In the 1970s and 80s, numerous middle-class baby boomers were raising families, and many wanted a religious tradition into which to raise them. Many, though hardly all, desired a strong and demanding religion. In particular, they responded to a growing sense that so-called traditional religious values were being undermined by the 1960s counterculture, the outlawing of prayer in public schools, the Equal Rights Amendment, unwholesome television, gay rights, and what they perceived as a broader political and cultural assault on religious and family values.[42] Popular literature and culture became effective ways of transmitting religious values and messages to believers and to the next generation.

In both evangelical Christian and Haredi popular-culture markets, another dynamic factors in. American freedom of religion creates a competitive market for religious ideas and practices. Marketing becomes critical for religion, following the principles of supply and demand. At the level of demand, urban or suburban middle-class religious people whose lives and pocketbooks are integrated into the American economy find their religious lives wrapped up in the consumption of material goods such as books. This creates a market for religious goods and services. On the supply side, producers can earn significant profit by providing those goods and services to potential consumers. Under these conditions, those religious groups that market themselves successfully, succeed; those that do not, fail. Those religious groups that produce well-marketed products have a better chance of garnering adherents. Those adherents then become an expanding market for similar products. Religious commodities grow following an evolutionary pattern of survival of the fittest.[43] As we shall see in coming chapters, this gives the consumers enormous, albeit indirect, power in determining the path that religion takes, for laypeople determine which religious organizations to join and which religious products to buy. American Christians and Haredi Jews discovered simultaneously that they could use the tools of mass-market consumer products, popular media, and user-friendly literature to help spread the Good News to believers and potential believers. In the process, they discovered that they might even make a few bucks. Religious popular culture was inevitable for Christians, and to a smaller degree for Haredim as well.

Granted, tens of millions of evangelical Christians serve as a market for religious consumer-products, while there are only a few hundred thousand Haredim.[44] Haredi popular culture has come nowhere near the evangelical expansion into every possible sub-community and market. Would-be Haredi gatekeepers may get upset that Haredi music borrows too much from contemporary pop and rock music, but there still are no Haredi skateboard ministries or "professional wrestling" circuits, as there are in Protestant circles. In part, Haredi culture is less expansive than its evangelical counterpart because evangelicals attempt to insert themselves into so much of American culture out of a desire to transform that culture into something more Christian. Haredim, who make no claim to want to Judaize America, confine themselves to narrower cultural pursuits.[45] Still, in both cases a combination of religious fervor and a desire to earn profit pushes a religious community in a consumer-centered culture to express its religiosity and reinforce in-group solidarity through the merging of religion and popular culture.

Characteristics of Haredi Popular Literature

What are the characteristics of this Haredi popular literature? First, the material produced by ArtScroll, Feldheim, Targum Press, and other publishers is popular literature. Unlike the dense prose of halakhic responsa and Talmudic novelae, this literature is easy to read, designed by authors and publishers to reach a maximal audience within, and sometimes outside of, the community.[46] Indeed, much of the English-language Haredi literary output of the past half-century has been involved in making dense and difficult classical texts accessible to anybody, whether through translation or easy-to-read commentaries. The most obvious example is ArtScroll's massive and impressive Schottenstein Talmud, which elucidates the opaque Talmudic text in a relatively easy to read, user-friendly fashion. Other genres, such as self-help books or fiction, also make for light and accessible reading.

ArtScroll, Feldheim, and Targum Press tend to produce inspirational literature, whether meant to inspire non-Haredi Jews to join the Haredi fold or to inspire currently Haredi Jews to be more passionate about their observance and commitment. Not accidentally, jacket covers and blurbs state explicitly that reading these books will make readers more happy, energetic, and fervent about themselves and religion: "The messages will linger long in the heart;" "You will emerge the richer for it;" "You will make wiser choices."[47]

As popular literature, these works tend to focus on the ongoing concerns of daily life. Contemporary halakhic popular literature, for example, tends to organize information around the realia of day-to-day life. Works such as *The Shabbos Kitchen* or *Children in Halachah* summarize older halakhic material and organize it based on the concrete conditions of contemporary nuclear families.[48] In contrast, ancient halakhic literature, such as the Talmud, offers a loose, associative organization. Even in the Middle Ages, when halakhic material became structured into codes – such as Maimonides' *Mishneh Torah* – works were structured to a greater degree around the internal logic of halakhic legal categories and less around the day-to-day experience of the lay person. The tendency to structure books around the reality of life is even more prevalent among the non-traditional genres of Haredi popular literature. For example, self-help books and parenting guides focus on the immediate tasks and petty frustrations of suburban social life, such as relationships between spouses or bedtime routines for children.

As we shall see in coming chapters, Haredi publishers want not only to spread Torah, but to earn a profit in doing so. They may publish seemingly subversive literature and play with the edges of Haredi legitimacy in hope of gaining publicity, but publishers still function as gatekeepers, assuring that works that emerge from under their hands are adequately Haredi, if for no other reason than to brand their company properly and not to alienate potential buyers.[49]

The creation of ArtScroll's subsidiary, Shaar Press, exemplifies this tension, suggesting that ideological motivations are inextricably tied with the desire to earn profit. The publishing and business infrastructure of ArtScroll-Mesorah and Shaar Press are the same, but as part of its branding strategy, ArtScroll wants to maintain a reputation of ideological purity. When it feels that a work might sell, but that it might also violate the sensibilities of the more isolationist segment of the Haredi community, it publishes the book under the imprint of Shaar Press, branding the product as a more open, "modern," work, one that has (in the words of the imprint's self-description on book dust jackets) "its compass set on the eternal verities of the Jewish tradition," but which may "sometimes [be] controversial."

We should not assume that Haredi popular literature opposes or contradicts Haredi elite culture. Much of the history of the study of popular religion has assumed that the "small tradition" of popular religion necessarily conflicts with the "great tradition" of elite religion. More recently, scholars and historians of popular religion have identified less confrontational relations between popular and elite religion. In the case of American Haredi Judaism, popular and elite religion live together comfortably, with little tension.[50] In part, this relative harmony stems from elite rabbinic overview of popular literature, both in the form of *haskamot* [approbations] commonly printed in the front of popular literature and because publishers are unlikely to violate standards dictated by great rabbis. But the harmony also stems from the power that "the masses" have over the rabbis. When religious identity is voluntary, as it is in the Haredi enclave, leadership has little interest in alienating the masses by attacking popular religion.[51]

Interestingly, not all authors of Haredi popular literature identify fully with the Haredi community. Haim Perlmutter, for example, who has authored a series of books designed to ease the study of Talmud, identifies as a devout religious-Zionist.[52] Similarly, one of Feldheim's particularly popular books, *Nine Wonderful Months: B'Sha'ah Tovah* – a book which shall occupy us in Chapter Two – was authored by a husband-and-wife team of religious-Zionists, Baruch and Michal Finkelstein. But the literature remains Haredi in a very important sense. Publishing companies have strict but unstated criteria for what they are willing to publish and what they are not. Publishers reject or modify any book that might not be deemed adequately kosher, that might interfere with the branding of books as appropriate for any Haredi home. A reader can rest assured that the contents of a book published by a Haredi label do not violate the accepted norms of the Haredi book market, even if the author is somewhat of an outsider. A non-Haredi author who writes a book that meets Haredi market standards can publish with these publishers; a non-Haredi author who does not, must find another venue.

Take the example of Shmuel and Judy Klitsner, a married couple who identify with the liberal wing of Modern Orthodoxy. In the late 1980s, the couple, together with a third associate, co-authored a young-adult novel, *The Lost Children of Tarshish*, about a group of Jewish children stranded on an isolated island – a kind of Jewish response to *Lord of the Flies*. After publishers insisted that they revise the book to eliminate female characters – an island of unsupervised co-ed young adults would be too racy for Haredi standards – the novel was published by the Haredi CIS publishing company. Yet, decades later, when each one of the couple published a book of decidedly non-Haredi biblical exegesis, they did so outside the Haredi market, one with the Modern Orthodox Urim Press and the other with the non-denominational Jewish Publication Society.[53]

How This Book Looks at Haredi Popular Literature

Strictly Kosher Reading will use Haredi popular literature as a lens through which to examine the tension between isolation and acculturation in American Haredi culture. To do so, I pay close attention to the canon: that collection of texts that Haredi Judaism considers normative. Canonical texts matter a great deal in the Haredi community,[54] not only due to the centrality of Torah study in Haredi Judaism, but also because Haredi Judaism's official ideology claims that the canonical texts of the tradition dictate and determine proper behavior and ideas. Yet, as the sociological and anthropological truism suggests, lived religion does not always conform perfectly to the texts which are said to be normative. Concrete individuals and communities live their religion while embedded in cultural and material contexts that may promote a religious practice that pushes against the canon. In the context of American Haredim, popular media are a wonderful tool with which to examine a nexus of Haredi values that do not derive directly from the formal Jewish canon of texts, but emerge as a syncretic combination of the tradition with themes from contemporary self-help and popular inspirational spirituality.

In order to get at these complexities of Haredi popular literature, I adopt an eclectic method, borrowing from several different disciplines. At one level, social historians teach us that a community's literature serves as a lens into the reality of that community in its time and cultural context. Intellectual historians take that further, asking readers to compare the texts of a given culture at a particular time to those of the same culture at earlier times, and then to speculate about the social, economic, intellectual, or political reasons for changes in ideas and values over time. Both social and intellectual historians treat texts as artifacts of an existing culture.

At another level, critical approaches in culture studies suggest that a simple historical method can be oversimplified and naïve. Texts do not only reflect an existing reality; they are also ideological, working to alter reality by forming the attitudes and practices of readers. As such, what they depict may be quite different from current reality. I will attempt to combine these two approaches, examining how Haredi popular literature reflects an existing and quite real cultural experience on the ground. At the same time, I will also try to point to ways in which popular literature works to help form and modify reality.

Some research within media studies suggests more detailed categories in which readers can think about how popular cultural texts both reflect and work to alter reality. We must account for the role of market and economic forces in the production and consumption of culture. More specifically, producers of popular religious culture want to present God's truth to readers and consumers, but they also want to accomplish the more prosaic tasks of selling products and earning profit. At times, the two goals work hand in hand, but at other times God and Mammon, profit and prophet, do not live together quite so harmoniously, with producers of religious goods treating God's word as another commodity to be sold to the highest bidder. The distribution of religious popular culture into a free market of goods and ideas suggests that consumers have quite a bit of power in indirectly determining how the religious marketplace constitutes itself. The invisible hand pushes the market to produce primarily what the community is willing to buy, rather than what official ideologues declare valuable.[55]

I adopt this eclectic set of approaches because I want to contribute to a richer explanation of the complex relationship between Haredi popular literature, the community that produces and often consumes it, and the general culture in which Haredi Judaism is embedded. In this, I draw more on various academic works, such as those of Kimmy Caplan or Jeremy Stolow, than on the Modern Orthodox polemics against "the ArtScroll phenomenon." Still, this analysis seeks to challenge some aspects of Haredi self-understanding, and even suggests places where Haredi authors and publishers misrepresent things that they do. Some Haredi readers may not recognize themselves in this analysis. Indeed, the suggestion that Haredi Judaism might be colored by the historical, cultural, and market conditions of contemporary America is anathema to Haredi self-understanding. As one popular work explains,

> Chareidi ideology is a value system that is derived from and mandated by the Torah and dates back to the point in history when the Torah and the Jewish People were initially unified. Consequently, the mannerisms and socio-political perspectives of the chareidim are a direct outgrowth of that value system and not the other way around – as the social scientists would have us believe.[56]

According to this Haredi author, the Haredi community constructs its ideals from the top down. Judaism has always placed certain values at the top of its axiological hierarchy, and the contemporary Haredi community, like good Jews throughout history, attempt to live up to those values. The tools of social, historical, or cultural analysis will prove irrelevant to the timeless Haredi example. Yet, as I will argue, Haredi popular literature often reflects ideas very different from those expressed in the works of Jewish tradition, even those canonized by Haredim themselves.

My interest in the relationship between Haredi popular literature and the traditional canon pushes me to focus almost exclusively on texts and the ideas expressed in those texts, unlike many other studies of popular religion that focus also on objects, commodities, events, festivals, fashion, and consumer products in the broadest sense.[57] I compare the content of Haredi popular literature with the canonical tradition to which Haredi Judaism pledges allegiance. Further, I pay particular attention to genres of contemporary literature – such as self-help books, fiction, diet guides, parenting guides, magazines, and history books – that differ from the canonical genres of the tradition. These newfangled genres highlight more directly the acculturation and the discontinuity between contemporary Haredi Judaism and the tradition that it considers normative, as both the medium and message hint at historical change. I want to understand how Haredi popular literature understands the ideas and concepts it has inherited from the canon, and how it creates a syncretic combination of contemporary media, ideas, and values with those of the past.

Other scholars have examined English-language Haredi popular literature's role as outreach literature and examined the way it influences readers outside the Haredi camp.[58] Yet, due to my interest in Haredi Judaism's attempts to construct symbolic boundaries – the community's attempts to make members feel different from others – I pay more attention here to the function of this literature *within* the community. In some cases, works of Haredi popular literature are addressed to insiders. A work of popular halakhah, for example, with over 400 pages explaining the intricacies of the laws of blessings, assumes that readers already care about the minutiae of the topic.[59] But much Haredi popular literature presents itself as focused on outsiders. The accessible English-language format provides an introduction to aspects of Judaism for those who had not been lucky enough to receive an Orthodox religious education. Yet, as Hendershot points out regarding evangelical popular culture, we should not assume that works ostensibly written for outreach purposes are necessarily consumed or meant to be consumed exclusively by outsiders.[60] For reasons to be discussed below, it seems likely that much of the outreach-oriented literature is in fact read, and meant to be read, by insiders as well. Due to my interest in in-group self-understanding, I will examine this literature primarily in terms of the internal Haredi discourse of which it is part.

My focus on texts and their content means that I am particularly concerned with what these works ascribe to Judaism and general culture, what they prescribe as valuable for Jews, and what they proscribe as negative and prohibited. But we still know next to nothing about what concrete readers do with this literature. That is, I want to know what is "encoded" in these texts, though we still know very little about how readers "decode" them. Reception studies would examine not only what these works appear to be doing for the community, but what readers themselves understand as they read and how they incorporate popular literature in their identity-construction and day-to-day lives. As has been the case with studies of consumers of popular culture in numerous contexts, such an analysis – certainly a desideratum – would undoubtedly reveal more nuance and might complicate some of the generalizations I have made about Haredi identity.[61]

Moreover, my analysis focuses on this literature as a collective social and cultural product, rather than as works of individual authors. The efforts of authors are embodied within a larger cultural industry that includes publishers, editors, booksellers, buyers, and readers, who may share a collective sense of values, propriety, and concerns. While individual authors are, of course, important, the broad similarities between a great many Haredi popular works suggest that individual authors work within the confines not only of the Haredi power structure, but also within hegemonic Haredi assumptions about truth and values. These works are unconsciously constructed not only by the fingers and the keyboards of the authors-as-individuals, but by the collective, unselfconscious understandings of what matters. And that collective unselfconsciousness is a cultural product more than an individual one.[62] But this "collectivist" approach should not obscure the tensions between the different players within the Haredi publishing industry. Contrary to a popular stereotype, Haredi Jewry is not monolithic. Authors, publishers, editors, booksellers, buyers, and readers may have different interests and agendas, both ideological and financial. We should not lose track of the differences between these players and the ways in which those differences play out within the literature.[63] Furthermore, Haredi popular literature includes a great deal of dispute and internal disagreement. These disputes point to the fissures within the socially constructed Haredi community. Different voices emerge – voices of men and women, of more conservative and more innovative authors or stakeholders, of those with differing political-cultural stances, of those who stand to make a profit from differing positions. Juxtaposing and comparing those different voices can help create a more subtle picture of the internal discourse of Haredi Jewry.

By making my method explicit, I hope to explain why I think this book can help explain the inner workings of Haredi acculturation. Still, Strictly Kosher Reading is an example of engaged scholarship. I make no claim to strict objectivity or to an outsider's perspective devoid of interest. I am a Modern Orthodox Jew, one committed to a different kind of Orthodoxy than the one offered by the books I am studying. I began studying these works in part in order to understand my own Modern Orthodoxy and the ways in which it differs from the commitments of my coreligionists to the right. In that sense, just as my analysis of ArtScroll books revolves around the ways in which they construct "others" against which to define their own identity, I, in my personal religious life, use Haredi popular literature to define an "other" for myself, to understand what I am not. With that, I have made every attempt to treat the subject of this study with honesty and fairness.

***

"There are many good reasons for studying popular [literature] .... The best, though, is that it matters."[64] In today's economy, popular culture saturates life. It can change people's ideas, worldviews, and practice; it can provide outsiders with a lens into the workings of a given community or subculture. It helps to construct contemporary life, at the same time as it offers a window into contemporary life. This book offers a close reading of a series of Haredi popular texts, juxtaposing them with traditional sources on related topics and with the Haredi social and cultural reality within late twentieth and early twenty-first century America. These readings should provide a window into a complex and tension-filled world of the Haredi encounter with contemporary America and its culture. We begin, in Chapter 2, with several descriptions of how this literature creates a syncretic whole by combining aspects of the Jewish tradition with aspects of general culture. The chapter offers a discussion of the functions that syncretism plays in constructing the boundaries of American Haredi Judaism.

Chapter II
"Ancient Wisdom": Haredi Popular Literature and General Culture

Haredi popular literature provides a fascinating lens through which to examine the cultural dynamics of the religious community that produces and consumes it, as the literature weaves its way between isolation from what it considers a dangerous general culture and a parallel attraction to aspects of the same culture. A close examination of that literature provides insight into the mechanisms that help the community negotiate those tensions. In particular, we can compare Haredi popular literature to its parallels in non-Haredi popular literature and to the canonized texts of the Jewish tradition, and we can thereby gain a clearer understanding of how modernity and tradition are interwoven in the lives and ideas of these devout contemporary Jews. On the one hand, this literature declares that "Torah values are diametrically opposed to those of modern secular culture."[1] On the other hand, these books often express ideas that are influenced by if not borrowed from the contemporary culture that Haredi Judaism claims to decry.

This chapter will point to three interrelated ways in which Haredi popular literature works to negotiate this paradox, to facilitate both isolation and acculturation, and at times to disguise that acculturation. The first is coalescence; the second, filtering; and the third, monopolizing. By "coalescence," I refer to a kind of cultural syncretism displayed when much of this literature merges the Jewish tradition with contemporary "secular" values and cultural patterns, ones that have little or no precedent in the older tradition.[2] Haredi popular literature presents these as part and parcel of Torah or a Torah way of life. At the same time, the literature works to protect the community from what it perceives as the dangers of contemporary culture by filtering that general culture. In filtering, some aspects of general culture enter the enclave by way of the popular literature while others are left out. Sometimes authors and publishers filter deliberately and self-consciously, while at other times the complex social and economic factors that influence popular literature prevent authors and publishers from controlling boundaries neatly. Finally, the literature helps to patrol the community's border by monopolizing, or attempting to monopolize, the Haredi public's reading. By providing an alternative to non-Haredi popular literature, the Haredi version encourages readers to consume exclusively Haredi literature and discourages them from consuming the potentially dangerous outside literature.

This chapter will consider examples of these three aspects of the relationship between Haredi culture and the general culture that surrounds it by focusing on Haredi diet guides, self-help books, and guides for a proper Torah-centered family life. Further, the chapter will point to ways in which the elements of coalescence, filtering, and monopolizing are interconnected. The attempt to distinguish them is a heuristic device, but they are intertwined to such an extent that they cannot be fully separated from one another.

Coalescence

The first function of Haredi popular literature involves the "coalescence" of the Jewish and the non-Jewish. In defining coalescence, Sylvia Barack Fishman distinguishes it from two other common ways of describing relationships between Judaism and general culture. First, "compartmentalization" involves a situation in which the Jewish tradition holds sway in its own spheres, such as the synagogue or Shabbat table, while non-Jewish culture dominates in other areas of life, such as the workplace or the theater. Despite its conceptual clarity, Fishman claims that "compartmentalization" does not accurately describe actual American Jewish practice, since contemporary American Jews are too Americanized and America is too welcoming of Judaism for such neat divisions to have much explanatory power. Second, "adaptation" involves a situation in which the Jewish and the non-Jewish exist side by side. Tension between the two remains, and the individual or community "privileges one or the other as the situation seems to demand."[3] Adaptation, she explains, "implies a continuing awareness of difference" between Jewish and general values and an attempt to negotiate these differences.

Yet, claims Fishman, many American Jews have lost an awareness of differences between Jewish and American values.

> During the process of coalescence... the 'texts' of two cultures, American and Jewish, are accessed simultane-

ously.... These values seem to coalesce or merge, and the
resulting merged message or text are perceived not as
being American and Jewish values side by side, but as
being a unified text, which is identified as authoritative
Judaism.... Many American Jews – including some who
are very knowledgeable and actively involved in Jewish
life – no longer separate or are even conscious of the
separation between the origins of these two texts.[4]

Haredi popular literature, like much of Haredi popular culture, seamlessly merges aspects of the Jewish tradition with contemporary American
cultural norms and styles. In coalescence, normative Judaism becomes a
hybrid or syncretic combination of the Jewish and the American, the traditional and the modern, the past and the present. For example, Haredi
music takes its lyrics from traditional Jewish texts, but its musical style
imitates contemporary pop music.[5] Haredi self-help books, as we shall
discuss, present contemporary values of individualism, personal happiness, self-expression, and (according to some critics) self-absorption as
Jewish values, supposedly in the self-improvement tradition of *musar*.[6]
Haredi novels borrow literary genres and formulas from the general best-
sellers and fill them with Haredi characters and values.[7]

Given Haredi commitment to isolationism and rejection of non-
Haredi culture, Haredi coalescence seems surprising. Still, Haredi Jews
are genuinely acculturated, and the same cultural forces that make a
genre or idea popular among the general public make it popular among
Haredi Jews as well. Community members may prefer a Haredi version
of a literary genre, such that it will more precisely match their values
and concerns. In addition, imitating the most contemporary styles helps
make the tradition seem sophisticated and up to date. This allows Haredi
Judaism to respond to modernity and its perceived anti-Orthodox biases
on modernity's own terms.[8]

Take the example of Yaakov Levinson's book, *The Jewish Guide to Natural Nutrition*. According to Levinson, there are "Jewish roots to natural
nutrition." Holistic health and natural foods are presented as traditional
Jewish values. Levinson works to "combine a system for healthy living
and eating with a strong connection to our important Jewish heritage."
He rhetorically grounds his work in traditional Judaism, explaining that
"Rambam's [Maimonides'] medical writings contain the Jewish roots of

today's system of natural nutrition. Our modern approach is basically an extension of his main principles and teachings."[9]

Yet, the author says little about Maimonides' specific nutritional advice or his medieval biology, and Levinson quotes from Maimonides' medical writings only very rarely. Instead, Levinson focuses on contemporary scientific concepts such as cholesterol, vitamins, and the USDA food pyramid. Maimonides does not serve as an authority on the workings of the body. Rather, he is an authoritative precedent for the borrowing of contemporary medical advice. Levinson is, to a great degree, aware of and articulate about the fact that the medical and nutritional advice he suggests does not come from Torah, but from modern science. He dances a cautious dance between the new and the old, the modern and the traditional. Maimonides' "medical writings were based on Jewish Talmudic sources as well as on secular, non-Jewish teachings."[10] In other words, Levinson argues that it is authentically and traditionally Jewish for today's Haredi Jews to self-consciously adapt contemporary scientific theories, just as Maimonides did in his day. Maimonides is important to Levinson not as a source of information about eating and health, but as a figure whose very name and reputation can help make the book seem authentically Jewish and grounded in the tradition, even if the book's content is not actually derived from his writings.

The dust jacket of *The Jewish Guide to Natural Nutrition* clearly articulates coalescence. The author's biography on the dust jacket celebrates his extensive Torah studies as well as his accomplishments in the field of medicine. Photographs visually reinforce this. The front cover shows a professional studio photograph of a bearded man – presumably the author – carrying a large, attractive basket of fresh green apples and dressed in a clean white lab coat. The apples signify the value of natural and healthy eating, while the lab coat symbolizes the scientific validity and authority of the book's nutritional suggestions. The back cover includes a parallel photo of the same man dressed in Hasidic garb carrying a stack of Maimonides' halakhic writings. Science and Jewish religion, including both its mystical-Hasidic and its rationalistic-legal-Maimonidean strands, are not only compatible with one another, but mutually enforcing. The authority of science is backed, symbolically and visually, by Torah, and Torah leads to an appreciation of contemporary nutritional science. Not accidentally, the book opens with three almost identical approbations: two by well-known yeshiva deans and one by a professor at a Jerusalem medical school. The approbation from the medical doctor praises coalescence, in that the book "melds an expert's view of nutrition and disease with its special implication and application to religious Jewish tradition."[11]

Levinson's coalescence goes further. He not only provides standard American nutritional advice for Haredi readers, but also claims that following that advice is fundamentally a spiritual experience and religious obligation. Here Levinson goes beyond his Maimonidean precedent. For Maimonides, maintaining one's health is a means to an end, a requirement so that illness or weakness would not distract the individual from the higher values of study and religious self-development. "It is impossible to understand or know anything of the knowledge of the Creator when one is ill. Therefore a person must distance himself from things which damage the body, and a person should become accustomed to things which make one healthy." For Levinson, in contrast, health is not merely a means toward a higher end; rather, there is an inherent "spirituality in eating."[12] Combining kabbalistic language and basic biology of the digestive system, Levinson explains that healthy eating exemplifies a central religious goal of separating the "good" from the "evil" in creation. The "nutrients" are good and therefore associated with the holy "sparks" of the Kabbalah, while the "waste" is the evil, associated with the evil kabbalistic "husks." "The separation of nutrients from waste in the act of eating has its spiritual counterpart in the extraction of the sparks of holiness which are contained in food. And is not the physical and spiritual separation of good from evil the very meaning of human existence?"[13]

Levinson also hints that the foods people eat and how they eat them are not value free, but exemplify their cultural identity. "Foods are much more than just a collection of nutrients; they are a wealth of influences and connotations.... The various religions use foods to connote their special approach to life." Levinson's health advice exemplifies this point, perhaps more clearly than he intends. While he intends to underscore the inherent spirituality, according to Judaism, in eating, he also implies that eating like an American means having absorbed American mores and sensibilities. He advocates a "healthier, lighter style of eating," which became a virtual American infatuation in the nutrition discourse of the late twentieth and early twenty-first centuries (even as Americans grew fatter).[14] Levinson's concern with calorie counting, weight-loss, and balanced consumption of nutrients reflects the biological knowledge and cultural aesthetics of contemporary America, a community of plenty with an almost infinite variety of foods to choose from, with a deep concern with the long-term health impact of overeating, and an aesthetic that celebrates thinness. For almost all of human history, the central culinary dilemma facing humans involved procuring enough food to fend off starvation or at least chronic hunger. In contrast, Levinson and his American Haredi readership share with other middle-class Americans a challenge of negotiating an almost unlimited quantity and variety of food.[15] The late twentieth-century American infatuation with light, healthy eating, which Levinson exemplifies, supports values that Haredim and the general population share and which are reflected in their culinary culture and popular literature. Levinson's book suggests that religious people, even those profoundly committed to a given canon, read and interpret their scripture and tradition not only in their own terms, but "in order to make sense of their lived experiences."[16]

That Haredi Jews share a culinary culture with their neighbors, and that they follow the best medical and health advice available, are relatively unproblematic notions from a Haredi perspective. After all, the Jewish tradition for the most part supports the idea that Jews should seek quality medical treatment,[17] and Maimonides indeed advocated learning from the best available science. However, other examples of coalescence raise significant ideological and religious challenges.

For example, Haredi popular literature, like its devout Christian counterparts, adopts the modern notion of the "companionate marriage." Here the coalescence appears in a matter of profound ideological and religious significance, since, as Helen Hardcare explains about Protestant Fundamentalists, the family is a "primary unit for ritual observance as well as an influential site of religious education and the transmission of religious knowledge from one generation to the next."[18] Or, as one Haredi author puts it, "The Jewish family [is] a vital force in insuring our people's continued existence."[19] Popular Haredi works identify the Torah's "timeless formula for marriage," and contrast that with the "non-Jewish system" that is "floundering in its own confusion" and therefore "has nothing to offer the Jew."[20] Yet, a brief historical comparison reveals how acculturated Haredi families have become, and how the Haredi popular literature coalesces by presenting the modern, monogamous, suburban nuclear family as part and parcel of the tradition.

Both the contemporary Haredi family and the pre-modern Ashkanazic one share a commitment to strict monogamy, as opposed to the polygamy of ancient Judaism and at least some of historical Sephardic culture. Yet, in pre-modern Ashkenaz, parents contracted marriages for their children, often with the help of professional matchmakers. When choosing a partner for their child, parents paid less attention to emotional or romantic compatibility and more to finding a spouse who could offer the greatest socio-economic advantage. Often, marriages were arranged, if not always consummated, when the children were in their mid-teens. This marriage was more of an economic agreement than a romantic one, certainly at the outset. The couple might continue to live with the bride's family for some time, until they became financially and socially independent. In this constellation, "personal compatibility not to speak of romantic attachment [between the couple] were not taken into account at all." [21] On occasion, feelings of love and mutual attraction would push a young couple to choose one another as marriage partners, but rabbis and community members saw this as a rebellion against communal values rather than a fulfillment of them.[22]

Today, Haredi couples, usually in their early 20s, care deeply about emotional compatibility and therefore search for marriage partners through dating. This period of courtship allows the young couple to determine if they are emotionally compatible and romantically suited. Under these circumstances, when courtship and emotional compatibility have become central to Haredi images of marriage, Haredi authors write dating guidebooks for such young people, providing "guidelines for dating and courtship," so that the dating couple can most effectively determine if they share the same values, if they have the same expectations from married life, and if their "personalities" will enable "the couple to get along with each other."[23]

Furthermore, for medieval Ashkenazic Jews the home was a center of economic life, because merchandise and services were produced in the home for the use of its residents as well as for trade with others. Women, though also mothers, played central roles in the medieval Jewish marketplace, at a time and place when parenthood was not considered a full-time endeavor and where raising children was perceived as requiring less moment-to-moment vigilance than it does today.

For contemporary Haredi rhetoric, in contrast, the "Jewish home" rather than being a locus of economic production, serves as a "haven in a heartless world," a domestic shelter from the dangers of the marketplace and the outside culture.[24] It is a modern, middle-class, child-centered, nuclear family. In these families, rearing offspring, who require full-time attention and continuous nurturing, requires parents primarily and educators secondarily to be sensitive, vigilant, and loving toward children more or less on a constant basis. Women are, therefore, encouraged by Haredi literature to dedicate themselves first and foremost to being mothers and wives, and to go to work only if the family's financial situation requires it.[25]

As numerous historians of both the Jewish and non-Jewish family have noted, these modern family patterns, in broad terms, developed with the rise of the middle class, under conditions of urbanization and industrialization.[26] In their popular literature, acculturated contemporary Haredim describe, analyze, and celebrate this modern family. In particular, Haredi popular literature celebrates one particular aspect of this modern family: what historians and sociologists have come to refer to as the "companionate marriage." In this modern family, marriage ought to lead to self-fulfillment, happiness, and the satisfaction of the psychological need for friendship and emotional closeness.

> The ideal of companionate marriage came to dominate discussions of marriage in twentieth-century America.... It elevated anticipation of achieving emotional, sexual, and interpersonal fulfillment in marriage. The goal of marriage was no longer financial security or a nice home but emotional and sexual fulfillment and compatibility. Though marriages were not expected to be conflict and tension free, it was hoped that disagreements could be overcome if husbands and wives talked about their feelings, recognized the existence of conflicts, and worked out their problems through close "communication."[27]

The norm of the companionate marriage has penetrated Haredi circles, and Haredi books which guide couples to achieving that kind of relationship serve as prime examples of coalescence. For medieval Ashkenazic Jews, there was "an absence of any philosophy promising happiness in marriage."[28] Today's Haredi books on marriage view happiness and self-fulfillment as the central goals of married life. These works focus particularly on communication skills between couples, in order to assure that the couple will remain emotionally responsive to one another. "A healthy relationship is built on clear and honest communication. Listening, understanding and conversing all contribute to the empathy so vital to a marriage."[29] Furthermore, "Marriage... creates the possibility of the closest emotional relationship that can exist between living beings, the love between husband and wife." "Happiness in marriage" can be achieved by "building trust... maintaining affection... [and] creating intimacy." Ultimately, "Marriage is a primary catalyst for the development of each partner's individual potential to the utmost."[30]

The adoption of the model of the companionate marriage relates closely to another very popular genre of Haredi popular literature, namely the parenting guide. Here, too, coalescence prevails, with these parenting guides presenting images of child rearing as part and parcel of the Jewish tradition. And here too the coalescence appears in discussions of central religious values: how to raise children to become Torah-observant and God-fearing Jews. Hence, one might expect a greater reliance on traditional sources and a more suspicious stance toward contemporary norms. Still, Haredi parenting guides, even those that claim to reject so-called "modern" approaches to parenting, adopt the strategy of coalescence and share much of their style and content with their non-Haredi counterparts.

Lawrence Kelemen's parenting guide, *To Kindle a Soul*, for example, claims in the subtitle to contain "ancient wisdom." "At the foot of a mountain in the Sinai desert, the Creator of the universe directly revealed His profound wisdom to approximately three million people.... Those present received... a comprehensive guide for raising great human beings." The book attempts to describe "this ancient, Torah approach to education" which is "more comprehensive and effective... than any of the schools of child psychology I studied at university." Kelemen describes the "significant" differences between these supposedly "ancient traditions" and the practices of contemporary parents.[31]

Yet Kelemen's parenting approach fits neatly within late twentieth-century American parenting discourse, and it differs significantly from that of pre-modern Jewish sources. Kelemen combines an American religious-right critique of supposedly decadent American family life with a child-centered parenting approach advocated by endless American mass-market parenting guides in the 1990s. Criticism of American materialism and permissiveness; advocacy of limiting the mother's time at work; polemics against spanking; emphasis on good nutrition, proper sleep time, and bedtime routine; concerns about the adverse impact of television viewing; claims to provide a "system" for raising moral children; and advocacy of "quality-time" for empathy and close communication between parents and children, all characterized American experts' suggestions to worried middle-class parents at the end of the twentieth century. Even Kelemen's claim that his approach derives from the Bible follows the pattern of American religious parenting guides. Indeed, the book's unstated assumptions – that parenting is a full-time endeavor, and that parents should actively monitor their children's moment-by-moment lives – typify experts' advice and popular assumptions in America during the so-called "century of the child." [32]

Not only does Kelemen's approach match that of contemporary parenting experts, but it differs from traditional Jewish sources on the topic. While a complete history of Jewish approaches to children and family has yet to be written, it is enough in this context to note that traditional Jewish literature speaks of childhood and parenting in spotty and unsystematic ways, scattered in works focused on other topics. [33] This reflects a historical past in which families were considerably less child-centered than they are today, and parents learned how to parent more by imitation, instinct, face-to-face conversation, and osmosis than from the written word of experts. Pre-modern Jews did not write parenting manuals since they assumed that knowing how to parent was an intuitive or natural thing. [34]

Take the example of Kelemen's approach to corporal punishment and spanking. This is a particularly important example because traditional sources do say quite a bit on the topic, and what they do say clashes rather dramatically with the approach of contemporary Haredi parenting literature. Kelemen polemicizes against corporal punishment of children, and even harsh verbal reprimands. Instead – reflecting both contemporary notions of individual autonomy and the voluntary nature of modern religious commitments, which make it difficult to coerce people into religious conformity – he insists that parents should calmly explain to their children what is proper and improper. Parents should then serve as living role models of the proper, hoping thereby to help children come to their own appreciation of and identification with the parents' values. While Kelemen advocates setting clear and consistent boundaries on children's behavior, he claims that enforcing those boundaries with violence and verbal harshness undermines the child's respect for the parents and prevents children from being receptive to higher values. "Yelling and hitting usually flips [sic] children out of the learning mode... which is characterized by a relaxed and happy state that facilitates accepting the educator's values... and into the obedience mode... which is character-ized by a nervous, distrusting or rebellious state." Spanking is part of an "authoritarian" approach typical of "dictatorships," which leads to unin-spired obedience in which youth do not come to identify with the values of the parents. Ultimately, "harshness" leads to "rebellion." Kelemen also argues for the importance of parental affection. "Affection is more than just attention. Attention just requires being responsive to a child's needs. Affection is the next step. It is warm and it is the most powerful medium we possess for communicating love." Kelemen teaches that, "If we want to produce people with integrity, internally driven by a specific value system, we must utilize gentle means."[35]

This advice stands in stark contrast to traditional Jewish sources on child rearing, which explain that spanking does not promote rebellion but prevents it. In a typical passage, the ancient Jewish text, *Midrash Rabbah*, quoting the book of Proverbs, relates that, "'He who spares his rod hates his child.' This teaches that preventing physical punishment (*mardut*) leads [the child] to bad culture."[36] R. David Altschuler, the seventeenth century Galician author of the Biblical commentary *Metzudat David*, goes further in commenting on the same verse: "Do not refrain from making [your son] suffer even if you see that this is not effective, because there is hope that much reproof will be effective."[37] Sources, particularly from early-modern Ashkenazi culture but from other contexts as well, openly polemicize against fatherly affection. For example, R. Alexander Ziskind of Grodno, the eighteenth century mystic, explains that, "Even though I had many sons, I never kissed even one of them, and never held them in my arms, and never spoke with them of frivolous things, God forbid."[38] The seventeenth-century rabbi, Yeshayahu Horowitz (the Shlah), states: "If the father rebukes his son early in his life with the staff... and uses fear while he is young... then he will be accustomed to fear his father always.... If in childhood the father displays great affection... then later when he matures he will not listen.... Mothers are... not to spare the rod but to strike their sons even if they scream.... Women who are compas-sionate with their children... murder them."[39]

In the next chapter we will examine the complex ways in which

Kelemen defends the idea that his approach derives from the ancient tradition. Here it is enough to note the way in which his book reflects the strategy of coalescence: identifying contemporary American values as being authentically Jewish. *To Kindle a Soul*, like other contemporary Haredi books on parenting, shares more with contemporary American mass-market parenting guides than it does with pre-modern Jewish sources on parenting. However, a close examination of other aspects of these works on families reveals that coalescence is not the whole story. Haredi works may borrow the companionate marriage and child-centered parenting from contemporary culture, but they borrow selectively. This leads to a second function of Haredi popular literature in mediating the tension between isolation and acculturation: filtering.

Filtering

With all their acculturation, Haredi guides to a happy marriage differ from and reject certain aspects of modern American visions of family and sexuality. In addition to coalescing, Haredi marriage guides also *exclude* some rejected notions of gender relations and filter out aspects of general culture that the community and/or its leadership consider problematic. Standing at the borders between the Haredi community and general culture, popular literature struggles with the challenges of boundary maintenance, working to determine which aspects of general culture enter the community to be coalesced with the tradition, and which are excluded and rejected.

The metaphor of filtering suggests that there is a mass of general culture, and that popular literature plays a role in determining which aspects of general culture enter the enclave and which do not. The Haredi community welcomes with open arms the aspects of general culture which it desires, coalescing them with Torah, while excluding unwanted aspects of general culture, deeming them incompatible with the perceived tradition. Yet, the filter does not always operate in a neat and controlled manner. Often what enters the community by way of the popular literature has less to do with ideology and more to do with the market, with what consumers are interested in and are willing to buy.

Let us return to the example of dating and marriage. Twentieth-century American culture has often viewed dating without intention to marry as a teen-age pastime, even an initiation ritual necessary for proper teen socialization and psycho-emotional development. As early as 1933, a government pamphlet, for example, defined teenage dating as "wholesome."[40] Contemporary Haredi rhetoric, in contrast, values dating only as a means to marriage and frowns upon or prohibits all inter-gender socialization prior to dating-for-marriage. A young person should only "start dating" when his or her "expectations of marriage" are "realistic."[41] Haredi norms absolutely reject intercourse prior to marriage, taken for granted in so much of American culture. Indeed, Haredi Jewry prohibits any physical contact between unmarried couples.[42] Family, community, and matchmakers play important roles in "setting up" potential marriage partners, echoing but shrinking the pre-modern tradition of having parents and matchmakers contract the marriage.[43] Haredi literature and culture reject serial monogamy – a lifelong series of short- or long-term monogamous relationships, whether in or out of marriage – a pattern that has become a, perhaps the, normative structure for American sexual relationships. Haredi culture advocates a single lifelong monogamous marriage. According to one author, the serial monogamy of contemporary society exemplifies the fact that "we live in a throwaway society." Instead, Haredi women should understand that "God is involved in the predestination of each unique pair," and therefore "problems in marriage are signals, not to divorce, but to identify the problem more clearly and get to work on its resolution."[44] Haredi literature certainly rejects alternative postmodern families, single-sex marriages, single parenthood, and the like, which have increasing resonance in at least some circles of American discourse. Haredi acculturation into aspects of the modern family also involves the filtering out of other aspects of modern culture.[45]

These examples from Haredi popular literature, which both borrow from and reject components of contemporary images of marriage and courtship, problematize the Haredi rhetoric that declares strict opposition between contemporary American values and those of Judaism. Haredim accept, indeed celebrate, many contemporary values, and they follow many contemporary cultural patterns, even as they reject many others. Haredi popular literature coalesces Jewish and non-Jewish values, even as it filters those non-Jewish values.

The filter functions in both formal and informal ways, and it is probably impossible to construct a precise schematic model of its function. Still, an author typically submits a proposal or manuscript to a Haredi publisher. The author, generally committed to Orthodox or Haredi norms, may or may not be aware of aspects of his or her own acculturation, and may well be interested in expanding the community's horizons by introducing the community to knowledge, information, theories, genres, or ideas that originate outside of Torah. The publisher must determine not only whether the book is likely to sell, but whether the book matches the publisher's religious and ideological commitments and whether it will maintain the publisher's reputation as a purveyor of adequately kosher books. In situations of doubt, the publisher may turn not only to its marketing department, but also to rabbis or a more formal rabbinic advisory board to comment on the acceptability of certain ideas or language. Or, put more precisely, the marketing department and the rabbinic advisors work together to ensure that books match the company's attempt to brand itself as properly pious. A publisher may either reject a manuscript or demand revisions to make the book more in line with the company's branding and public image. The publishers must walk a fine line. The more narrow their ideological boundaries and the fewer things they are willing to talk about, the smaller their potential market. Yet, if they push the envelope too far, they may alienate more isolationist readers and undermine their own reputations. At the same time, the publishers and rabbis not only filter out potentially damaging material, but they might actively encourage the filtering *in* of various non-canonical ideas, if they think that such ideas will sell and/or can help the community in some way. The publishers and their rabbinic advisors help determine for the community what the latter can and should be reading. However individual publishers negotiate those tensions, the Haredi publishers and their rabbis serve as formal and institutionalized gatekeepers, determining what material qualifies as adequately Haredi and what material is too acculturated.

Once a book is published, the publisher can then market it on websites, in Jewish and Haredi periodicals, and in local bookshops. For the most part, books published by Haredi publishers meet hegemonic Haredi standards of acceptability. (Indeed, these publishers in their editorial decision might help *create* those standards.)[46] Hence, whether a book sells widely or not, it creates no waves. Once the book is published, however, other gatekeepers still play a role, and that role can be more informal, ill-defined, and even chaotic. Educators, booksellers, rabbis, parents, and laypeople – in short, anybody in a position to recommend a book or not recommend it, purchase it for themselves, for their family, or as a gift – also act as gatekeepers, determining which books are read and which are not. A mother might determine that this particular children's book is not "frum" [devout] enough for her child; an educator might choose not to recommend a certain book to his students; and a rabbi or yeshiva dean might, as we shall see, even come out publically against a book for violating Haredi norms, as he sees them. Alternatively, the same individuals might actively encourage the consumption of another book that *does* introduce new ideas to the community. As consumers and community members make their decisions about what they consider acceptable and desirable, they may well also influence the publishers and their rabbinic advisors, who need to be very sensitive to the community's wants and desires, at least if they are going to continue selling books to the community. The community of consumers not only learns from the publishers and leaders what they should be reading, but also helps teach the publishers and their rabbinic advisors and leadership what standards should be set.

That is to say, then, that in some ways the filter functions deliberately and in a relatively controlled manner, and at other times it functions more informally and chaotically. To get at these dynamics, I will examine the deliberate and self-conscious strategy of expurgating and filtering out sexuality from Haredi popular literature, the deliberate and self-conscious strategy of allowing various pop-psychological theories through the filter and into the community, and the more chaotic and inchoate attempts to reject and ban controversial books that had already been published.

The strategy of expurgating sexuality from Haredi popular literature reflects a deliberate, collective understanding, on the part of publishers, their rabbinical advisors, and much of the community, that the dictates of *tzniut* [modesty] do not allow Haredi culture to imitate contemporary Western culture's relatively free and public expression of sexuality. One Haredi author of fiction, explaining her writing to a non-Haredi audience, explains that, "Everyone in the field agrees that expletives and sex are objectionable."[47]

Haredi culture invests heavily in the creation of large families, in part as a means of self-preservation for a tightly knit minority that perceives itself as threatened. Wives should sacrifice high-powered and ambitious careers for the sake of motherhood, and the community invests significant resources in preserving a nuclear family with clearly defined gender roles. Less restricted discussion of sexuality, particularly in the context of America's sexually open society, might expose the community to more fluid and less regulated family and sexual norms.

In some cases, Haredi books leave out sex in contexts that seem to call for such a discussion. One novel, a surprisingly sympathetic portrayal of delinquent drop-out Orthodox teen boys, does not hesitate to discuss their rejection of Orthodox practice, drug abuse, and even criminal activity. It says nothing about their young-adult libidos (though in a private correspondence, the author suggested that she would have included such a discussion if publishers would have allowed it).[48] Even guides to marital relationships speak about sex reluctantly if at all. Secular and Christian self-help books on happy marriages often include chapters such as "Married Sex." The general market offers sex guides aimed specifically at monogamous couples, married or otherwise. Haredi guides are less explicit.[49] Haredi popular literature includes extensive discussion of the intricate details of what this literature refers to as the laws of "family purity" – what until the twentieth century was referred to in halakhic literature as the laws of *niddah* – which determine which times during and after a woman's monthly cycle husband and wife are prohibited from physical contact.[50] There is nothing, at least that I have seen, on ways of improving sexual pleasure or communication. Many Haredi marriage-guides avoid using the term "sex" entirely, preferring euphemisms such as the husband's obligation "to be with his wife in the actual intimate act." In another book, a family therapist acknowledges that sexual incompatibility might cause stress in a marriage. He implicitly apologizes for failing to address the issue, creatively hinting to readers that they must find private forums in which to address such matters. "Problems related to the intimate aspects of marriage [sex]... have been deliberately omitted here in deference to the tenets of *tznius*."[51] Other guides to a happy marriage do not say even this much, ignoring the subject entirely.[52]

The expurgation of sexuality from Haredi popular literature differs dramatically from what occurs in the parallel evangelical Christian literature, even though both share a commitment to pre-marital abstinence. Yet, as Heather Hendershot has argued, in pushing for abstinence, evangelical popular culture and literature talk quite intensely about and explore pre- and post-marital sexuality. Teen magazines, youth-group events, and even ritualized commitment ceremonies to abstinence keep discussions of sexuality in the forefront of Christian discourse by and about youth, encouraging teens to explore and think about their own sexuality even as they work to control it.[53] And, unlike Haredi versions, evangelical literature for married couples advocates explicitly for good sex and describes it in some detail. Haredi literature, with its greater investment in gender separation, prefers silence. (The co-ed out-of-state teen bus trip with a three-inch separation rule between sexes that Hendershot describes would be unheard of in Haredi circles.)[54]

If popular literature deliberately filters out sexuality, it also deliberately filters in other things. Authors can serve as cultural agents, to a degree taking responsibility for which outside ideas enter the communal discourse and which remain excluded. These cultural agents, in cooperation with publishers, take aspects of general culture with which the community might not be familiar and deliberately and self-consciously introduce them into the Haredi enclave, where they merge or coalesce with Torah. Yet, at the same time, they also choose which aspects of that general culture to exclude. The Haredi encounter with modern psychology is a case in point. Despite fears that modern psychology raises central questions of philosophical anthropology and answers them in unacceptable ways, Haredi Jews remain fascinated by and extensive consumers of Haredi pop-psychological literature, which allows aspects of modern psychological theory to make their way through the communal filter.[55] In particular, Haredi mental health professionals who have gained extensive general education play the role of cultural agents. As authors, they help determine which aspects of psychology should enter the community by way of their writings. Prolific author R. Dr. Abraham Twerski has dedicated much of his career to spreading the idea that the Orthodox community must gain a richer understanding of psychology and psychiatry in order to treat dysfunctional or abusive behavior. For example, in his book on depression, *Getting Up When You're Down*, he emphasizes that, "Modern medical science now knows that depression and many related emotional conditions are not... symptoms of weakness. Such judgments [within the Orthodox community] betray an abysmal lack of understanding that most such moods are physical problems that can be remedied with the proper understanding and treatment."[56]

Best-selling author Miriam Adahan also uses her secular psychological training to introduce the community to new ideas. Author of over a dozen self-help books, she borrows many of her ideas from non-Jewish theories of personality types, modifying them for her Orthodox audience and arguing that the self-awareness which these theories provide can help make people more calm, considerate, and happy in their relationships with themselves, with God, and with others.[57] She acknowledges, as we will see more extensively in Chapter 3, that her theory "is *not* Torah, not 'Absolute Truth.'... It is simply another way of understanding people and becoming attuned to our Godly essence."[58] Still, she claims, "It would be unfortunate for the Orthodox world not to have access to this valuable information."[59]

For cultural agents such as Twerski and Adahan, the ability to filter in depends on the ability to filter out. When introducing new ideas into a community that claims to fear outside influences, authors must tread cautiously when choosing what to include or exclude. For example, Adahan's book, *Awareness*, is based on a popular theory of personality typing and self-help called "The Enneagram." This theory divides people into nine personality types, and it provides self-tests to help individuals determine which personality type they match. According to Enneagram proponents, that self-understanding serves as a "guide to psychological and spiritual growth.... The Enneagram shows how you can overcome your inner barriers, realize your unique gifts and strengths, and discover your deepest directions in life."[60]

Most literature on the Enneagram associates it with new-age spirituality, multiculturalism, the occult, and Eastern religions, and the theory claims to derive from an eclectic combination of ancient Babylonian wisdom, Greek Neoplatonistm, Sufi mysticism, as well as Christianity, Kabbalah, and Buddhism, among many other things. The Enneagram belongs firmly within late twentieth-century American religion's regular attempts to merge tradition with new-age spirituality and self-help.[61] This multicultural eclecticism and religious syncretism seem entirely incompatible with Haredi Judaism and its exclusivist truth claims. Indeed, the Enneagram has been attacked rather viciously by Catholic writers for being incompatible with religious values.[62]

Adahan prefers to downplay the new-age and multi-religious rhetoric. She secularizes the Enneagram, stripping it of this baggage, no doubt in order to avoid potential critiques by traditionalists who might dislike this borrowing. Instead of elaborating on the self-proclaimed sources of the theory, she briefly explains that, "Though the precise origin of this personality system is not known, it is believed to be quite ancient."[63] Filtering out certain aspects of the Enneagram allows Adahan to filter in those aspects that she deems valuable.

If the introduction of pop-psychological theories and the exclusion

of sex are largely self-conscious and deliberate, often the factors determining what is filtered in and what is filtered out are more complex and
ambiguous. In some cases, tradition and modernity do not merge quite
as seamlessly as Fishman's model of coalescence suggests. Contemporary
non-Jewish concepts or ideas may enter the community despite attempts
to exclude them. The complex interplay of ideological, personal, and market forces can create tension between authors, publishers, consumers,
rabbis, and educators. Each of these players shares an interest in making
available popular works on a variety of subjects that will support Haredi
values. At the same time, each player has slightly different motives and
interests, which can create conflict. Authors and publishers want to
sell books, but authors may have a more intense desire than publishers for self-expression, or they may advocate a unique and idiosyncratic
ideological-religious agenda. They may write books that seem threatening or problematic to readers or rabbinic leaders. Publishing such a book
could undermine the publisher's reputation as a purveyor of "kosher"
works. Yet, if consumers will buy "problematic" writings, finding them
entertaining or edifying, then authors may continue to write and publishers might continue to produce them, despite the opposition. Pushing
the boundaries of legitimacy may even create controversy, which could
increase sales. Rabbis and educators who disapprove of a book can also
benefit from controversy, which can enhance their reputations as leaders
in the effort to protect Haredi Judaism from outsiders or from its own
weaknesses.[64]

When such tensions arise, no single factor or actor can deliberately
control what the literary filter lets in and what it keeps out. An example
which received a great deal of attention in recent years involves the
works of a young rabbi, Nosson Slifkin, who has an interest in zoology,
biology, and the sciences. He wrote several books which were published
by the Haredi publisher Targum Press. In these books, Slifkin raises apparent contradictions between Torah and contemporary science, and
he accepts science as an independent source of truth. If scientists reach
consensus on a certain matter and the evidence is strong, Slifkin accepts
the scientific position. In the end, he reaches harmonistic conclusions,
in which science and Torah do not contradict one another. But in the
process he raises and unapologetically accepts evidence that the universe
is a great deal older than the approximately 6000 years suggested by
some traditionalists, that many contemporary animal species share com-

mon ancestry, and that the Sages of the Talmud did not have an accurate understanding of the scientific workings of the cosmos. Slifkin asserts that, "The scientific evidence for an old universe [11-19 billion years] is... vast and overwhelming."[65] He then works to reinterpret Torah to make it compatible with scientific ideas. Slifkin wanted to coalesce, to construct a combination of traditional Torah and contemporary science that would satisfy the standards of both disciplines. However, Slifkin used rhetoric that could offend some pietistic sensibilities when he argued that certain traditionalist understandings are simply wrong and indefensible. The plain reading of the book of Genesis, which seems to indicate that God created all the animal species in a very short time span, is not scientifically defensible. "Certain people are still unaware [of the evidence]... and contend that there was indeed only one act of creation in which all species were created.... In light of the paleontological and geological evidence, however, this is untenable."[66]

This angered rabbinic leaders and communal gatekeepers, who claimed that certain scientific information should be filtered out and should not be allowed to undermine Haredi sensibilities. Slifkin began receiving phone calls in late 2004 demanding that he recall his books, and in January of 2005 placards appeared in Jerusalem streets and advertisements appeared in Haredi newspapers, signed by leading rabbis, declaring the books to be heresy and forbidding Jews to read or own them.[67] While there is a great deal more to the ban and its development than fits here – it deserves a full length study of its own – suffice it to say that for these rabbis, Slifkin's filter did not work properly: it allowed in what should have been left out.

The original ban decries Slifkin for the sin of coalescence, for "making the words of the Talmudic sages match the opinions of the scientists."[68] Scientific information that seems to contradict texts of the tradition should be rejected, not advertised. In a lecture at the 82nd Annual Convention of Agudath Israel of America, R. Uren Reich, a New Jersey *rosh yeshiva* [yeshiva dean], made this quite explicit. "Anything we see with our eyes is less of a reality than something we see in the Gemara [Talmud].... Every word of *Chazal hakedoshim* [our saintly Sages] is *emes* [truth]."[69] Another *rosh yeshiva* explained that the sages could not possibly err in matters of science because "the source of *all* the knowledge of the Sages is either from Sinaitic tradition (received at the giving of the Torah) or from Divine inspiration."[70] Ironically, however, this opposition demonstrates

Haredi acculturation, since it focuses on issues typical of the religion-science conflict in America: the age of the universe and evolution. As it does for American Christian evangelicals and Fundamentalists, a literal reading of the opening chapters of Genesis, and the consequent rejection of the scientific theory of evolution, reaches the level of dogma for some contemporary Haredi Jews.[71]

While there is adequate consensus about the need to filter out sexuality or filter in certain pop-psychology ideas, in the case of the Slifkin ban there was no consensus about how the Haredi literary filter ought to operate. Attempts by gatekeepers – educators, rabbis, yeshiva deans, activists (askanim), and laypeople who agreed with the ban – to filter out ideas can backfire, creating publicity that increases awareness of the controversial notions. Since there were many people both in and out of the Haredi community for whom Slifkin's writings were perfectly acceptable, or at least interesting, the controversy and publicity that surrounded the ban only increased sales, with copies of the books being sold on eBay for up to four times their original value.[72] Furthermore, while some Haredi Jews may not read the books due to the ban, distribution and publication continued when Yashar Books, an Orthodox but not Haredi publisher, continued to market the books to anybody who would buy them, Haredi or otherwise. According to one insider in the American Orthodox book trade, some booksellers in Haredi neighborhoods, out of deference to the ban, did not display the books, but continued to sell them "behind the counter," whether out of pure profit motives or because they sided with Slifkin in the debate.[73] And, in any case, the "problematic" books remained available for purchase online. Under the market conditions of modern American freedom of religion, the filter of Haredi popular literature works, at best, in spotty and unpredictable ways.[74]

At one level, controversy can help sustain the public reputation of rabbis, educators, and activists who stand at the borders protecting the community. In this case, however, a failed attempt to ban a book can also simultaneously diminish the strength and cultural impact of the gatekeepers who tried to censor it. Rabbis and laypeople alike opposed the ban, claiming that Slifkin had said nothing radical or problematic. Prominent rabbis Aryeh Carmel, Berel Wein, Chaim Zev Malinowitz, Yehudah Levi, Yitzchok Adlerstein, and Zeff Leff issued public defenses of Slifkin and his works. In an open letter as the controversy was erupting, Carmel explained that "after giving the matter further careful consideration... we stand by the approbation given to the author."[75] The internet also provided a venue for backlash, with Orthodox laypeople, Haredi or otherwise, questioning the wisdom of the rabbis who banned the books, critiquing them for obscurantism, ignorance, and backwardness. "Shame on the Gedolim [great rabbis]" railed one writer on the internet. "Such little men with such big hats," summarized another sarcastically.[76]

That is to say, the filter helps maintain boundaries, but it does so imperfectly. When Haredi consumers want a certain product, and when authors create such a product, the dissatisfaction of would-be communal gatekeepers may not prevent it. Haredi culture itself can become contaminated with materials that, at least according to some voices, it should reject.

Monopolizing Culture

Even when the filter succeeds in keeping undesirable content out of the Haredi popular literature, Haredim can still gain access to that content from other sources. Haredi novels may be devoid of sex, but Haredim can and do read less puritan, non-Haredi novels, and Haredim can and do participate in internet forums where hegemonic Haredi standards of appropriate sexual behavior and discourse are breached.[77] Acculturated Haredim have access to virtually any aspect of general culture that they desire. Recent Haredi discussions about the dangers of the internet focus particularly on this problem, since the computer grants a Haredi Jew access to any aspect of non-Haredi culture, or to un-policed and anonymous Haredi culture, with the click of the mouse. "A user of the Internet can travel worldwide by several clicks on a mouse and visit the most immoral of sites and the most amoral of people."[78] The Haredi community struggles to enforce its boundaries by limiting members' consumption of materials and ideas that the hegemonic communal leaders reject. If the Haredi filter is to work as effectively as it could, communal attempts at boundary maintenance must also account for the ways in which Haredi laypeople can circumvent that filter.

One partial solution to this dilemma is, of course, educational. Rabbis and educators can preach and teach about the dangers of secular literature, movies, the internet, professional sports, popular music, etc. Some community members will certainly internalize those values. When enough do, that collective sense of propriety can create informal social pressure that, for example, might make it uncomfortable for a Haredi

Jew to be seen on line to buy tickets at a movie theater. Still, not every Haredi individual will internalize the educational message, and they may disagree with educators about what makes for proper Haredi behavior. Such individuals can find more private outlets for their cultural tastes and interests, outlets that may be less subject to public scrutiny. Haredi gatekeepers and the watchful eye of the Haredi social network have limited influence over what is contained in a yeshiva student's iPod or internet history. Furthermore, when a significant percentage of community members ignore or do not internalize the educators' values, or if they act contrary to the norms that educators and rabbis advocate, then no social pressure may exist against the particular practice. Educational efforts to oppose such things may have little effect.

Jeffrey Gurock has traced such an example by following American yeshivas' relationship with organized sports. Traditional Judaism has placed little value on athletic competition, and Orthodox and Haredi educators earlier in the twentieth century opposed such activities, even in America. Today, however, Haredi Jews participate in American sports, whether in youth leagues, pick-up games, or as fans of professional teams. This has become so common that there is little need to defend or apologize for interest in sports, particularly among young men. And, if early twentieth-century elements within Palestine's Haredi Old Yishuv could vilify Rabbi Abraham Isaac Kook for his religious praise of exercise, today *The Jewish Observer* can dedicate an issue to "a healthy and productive life as a Torah Jew" in which the magazine emphasizes the critical importance of exercise.[79] Press reports suggest that in at least one important Haredi community, rabbis and educators have prohibited the community's youth from attending local minor-league baseball games, at threat of expulsion from school, but educators can do little to prevent students from taking an interest in sports.[80] No matter what pious educators might think about their students playing athletic games or following professional sports, there exists little widespread Haredi social pressure to refrain from involvement.[81]

Even if Haredi educators and would-be gatekeepers cannot force Haredim to avoid the dangers of contemporary culture, they can help to make that culture less attractive and necessary by providing a Haredi alternative. Haredi music stars, like Mordechai Ben David or Yaakov Schweky, with their own CDs and concerts, can help limit a yeshiva student's consumption of secular hits. Easy access to Haredi thriller novels might push a Haredi housewife to read them rather than the latest secular bestseller. To maximize Haredi consumption of Haredi culture and minimize Haredi consumption of general culture, the Haredi enclave has an interest in making available Haredi versions of whatever resources exist in general culture. The Haredi reader can consume the Haredi version and let down some of his or her guard, since the Haredi version will more likely conform to deeply held Haredi values than the non-Haredi version. Were such an enterprise to succeed fully, it would result in a Haredi cultural monopoly, in which Haredi Jews would consume only Haredi culture. Under current conditions, such an extreme cannot materialize, but the desire to push in that direction exists.

The goal of monopolizing dovetails with other aspects of Haredi ideology, namely viewing Judaism as an all-encompassing religion, one that regulates, governs, and incorporates every aspect of life. If there is, as the title of one work of popular theology explains, a *Jewish Theory of Everything*, then it follows that "Judaism is not just an aspect of the Jew's life; it is the totality of it."[82] As part of their attempts to separate themselves from the surrounding culture, enclave communities throughout the world do everything that they can to monopolize the time, effort, and concerns of members.[83]

A "material Judaism" – all of those distinctively Haredi objects that help construct the Haredi enclave – helps envelop all activities and locations in religion. Haredi decorative arts, for example, transform the home into a sacred space. Haredi board games transform play into something holy, at least partially replacing the secular games that children might play, and placemats with religious themes make mealtimes into a Jewish experience.

Haredi popular literature also helps the enclave community reach for a cultural monopoly. We have already touched on Haredi nutrition guides, parenting guides, and self-help books. Their coalescence diminishes the need of community members to leave the enclave in order to find medical, domestic, or psychological advice. Furthermore, placing such works on the bookshelf at home transforms the living room or study into a sacred space, even when the topics seem, on the surface, irreligious.[84] If secular versions of these resources were the only ones available, the individual might be tempted to emerge from the enclave to consume them. Ultimately, this could undermine the sense of complete identification with and sense of belonging to the community.[85]

As an example of monopolizing, take *The B'nei Torah Edition of the Lebovitz System: The Revolutionary Breakthrough for Smokers*.[86] Some yeshiva students and other Haredim, primarily men, smoke, some rather heavily. Many of them would like to stop or cut down. While endless guides, books, systems, workshops, and medicines are available to help such people, a "B'nei Torah" [Torah-studying, upstanding Haredi men] edition of such a guide makes a special contribution. The first 245 pages of the book say nary a word about Torah or Judaism. Little or nothing in this section of the book distinguishes it from any other self-help book for smokers. Yet, Haredi smokers and their loved ones may be better off gaining help from within the community than from without it. Hence, the final eighty pages contain detailed, small-print, Hebrew-language notes and texts "based on extensive Biblical, Talmudic, and Midrashic sources." According to its authors, the book focuses on "*musar* and the improvement of character traits, in practical terms." It is not just "an intellectual and academic book from the world of wisdom," but rather a work of "*musar* which draws and drinks from the Torah of our rabbis, from the words of the Sages, and from [Torah] wisdom."[87]

Another example of an essentially secular book marketed to Haredi purchasers by a Haredi press is Tammy Poltsek's guide to carving fruit for decorative purposes, *Aristocratic Fruits*. The book makes no claim to contain any Torah, though it does deal with decorating at Shabbat meals, Jewish life-cycle events, and the like. The heavily marketed *Kosher by Design* series of cookbooks plays a similar monopolizing role. One need not look to secular gourmets for instructions on preparing "steak and green beans with wasabi [ersatz] cream sauce," and "asparagus tivoli," or advice on how to make a table setting look appealing and aesthetic. Readers of this book can discover that entertaining and table decorating can also be encompassed in the warm embrace of the religious enclave.[88] Monopolizing supports the goal of filtering, in that Haredi cookbooks keep out not only non-kosher recipes but also potentially subversive gender images. Hyman Goldberg made a bit of a splash in the 1960s when he dropped his pseudonym, Prudence Penny, to publish his cookbook, *Our Man in the Kitchen*, the title of which deliberately challenged the association of women with the domestic sphere. Today, cookbooks like Christopher Kimball's *The America's Test Kitchen Family Cookbook* no longer feel the need to wear their egalitarianism on their sleeve, with both men and women appearing as cooks in the photographs on its pages as a matter of course.[89] Haredi housewives should not be influenced by the gender images in these secular cookbooks, so Haredi cookbooks provide an alternative that makes clear the religious significance of feminine domesticity and the aesthetics of the home. The cookbooks focus on the housewife and mother, who ought to prepare the food and assure that the home's décor and ambiance support the proper Shabbat or holiday atmosphere. Recipes and advice for creating the proper domestic atmosphere for each Jewish holiday appear alongside short religious messages about the meaning of the yearly cycle. "It is not only what you serve, but how you serve it." The goal is to "elevate the mundane to the magnificent."[90]

The Interplay Between Coalescence, Filtering, and Monopolizing
As we have noted, the three functions of coalescing, filtering, and monopolizing reinforce one another. For example, reader-friendly Haredi guides to pregnancy and childbirth coalesce medical and scientific information with aspects of Jewish law and tradition. These works monopolize by limiting the need of expecting Haredi parents to read non-Haredi guides. This, in turn, enables filtering, by limiting the Haredi reader's contact with subversive images of family, femininity, motherhood, and sexuality contained in the non-Haredi books. The Haredi book *Nine Wonderful Months: B'Sha'ah Tovah*, for example, contains much of the same kind of medical and biological information available in best-selling secular guides like *What to Expect When You're Expecting*.[91] The jacket cover declares the book to be "The Jewish Woman's Clinical and Halachic Guide to Pregnancy and Childbirth," intimating that the Haredi enclave already contains what the Jewish mother needs to know about fetal development and neo-natal nutrition. The Haredi version merges that general medical information with uniquely Jewish material derived from the tradition, such as the laws of *niddah* as they relate to pregnancy and childbirth, appropriate prayers for pregnant women, as well as details about planning a *brit* [circumcision] or naming a child according to the Jewish tradition. At the same time, the Haredi book also filters, leaving out those aspects of the secular version that provide potentially inappropriate notions of motherhood and femininity.

The very title, *Nine Wonderful Months*, reinforces an idea that the book repeats throughout: motherhood and childbirth are almost unambiguously positive, leading directly to a sense of wholeness and fulfillment for the mother. "The desire to bring new life into the world is the manifestation of the essence of the Jewish woman." A pregnant woman need not suffer from negative body-image because, "Pregnancy is a *zechus* [privilege].... Our body changes are badges of pride and honor that we want to show our joyful participation in building the future of Am Yisrael [the Jewish People]." Furthermore, in this book, pregnancy occurs exclusively in the context of a monogamous, loving, and happy marriage, according to the normative Haredi vision. The book declares that, "At the moment of childbirth, the spiritual bond between *husband and wife* reaches its pinnacle."[92] The book excludes childbirth outside the context of marriage, and it does not explicitly address the fears and frustrations of expectant Haredi parents who might not experience things in quite such an idyllic fashion. In contrast, *What to Expect* deals extensively with the stress, misery, and anger that may accompany childbirth, particularly for single mothers, and the book explicitly acknowledges that the parents may not be married, or even in contact with one another.[93] The secular version also addresses issues that the Haredi version ignores: sex during pregnancy, unwanted pregnancies, abortion, single motherhood, and drug use during pregnancy. In the example of *Nine Wonderful Months*, coalescence facilitates monopolizing, and monopolizing facilitates filtering. A Haredi version of a resource, one that includes both general and Jewish information, makes the secular version redundant for the Haredi reader. This allows the Haredi title to exclude from the enclave those aspects of the non-Haredi version that are out of line with hegemonic norms.

Between Ideological and Market Forces

In all these examples, Haredi popular literature plays an important but paradoxical role. This literature stands at the gates of the community, at times finding ways of merging and coalescing the Jewish tradition with general culture, at times struggling (successfully or less so) to keep out aspects of general culture, in part by encouraging Haredi Jews to consume only Haredi versions of a particular genre. Paradoxically, this literature constructs and maintains collective boundaries, but also blurs them. In some ways the distinction between in and out remains sharp. Haredi popular literature rejects and excludes aspects of contemporary culture, like discussions of sexuality, and these works declare radical difference between Haredi and contemporary American values. Yet, in other ways, Haredi boundaries remain hazy if not incoherent, as in the case of Haredi parenting guides that claim to be pure Torah but are largely indistinguishable from parallel secular and Christian books.

Haredi books not only exemplify these tensions and paradoxes, but also reflect on them, trying to explain them to readers. Haredi authors do not use the terms coalescence, filtering, and monopolizing, but they are often aware that the medium and message of their books are not identical with the traditions of the past. The notion that the pure and unadulterated Torah of Haredi culture should coalesce with contemporary values creates problems from a Haredi perspective, since coalescence implies that the tradition is not self-contained and perfect, that modernity and its values are not entirely mistaken or dangerous. This leads to a great deal of debate, as Haredi authors struggle to shore up the boundaries that coalescence implicitly calls into question. By focusing on Haredi parenting guides and self-help books, the next chapter will examine how various authors explain their coalescence to their audiences. How do they defend their borrowing from non-Torah sources? How do authors maintain the claim that their ideas are identical to or compatible with Torah, even when they are derived from the outside? In Chapter 3, I will examine three different strategies that authors use to explain and defend the coalescence of Jewish and general ideas. Some deny the influence of outside culture on their writing; others acknowledge and defend it while still trying to maintain a proclaimed continuity with Torah sources; still others suggest that under some circumstances secular ideas may be superior to Jewish ones.

But this internal Haredi discussion of the ideal relationship between outside values and internal Jewish ones is fundamentally an ideological discussion. Descriptions of how various voices within the community think that boundaries *ought* to be maintained are not the same as descriptions of the more complicated social, economic, and literary forces that confound these ideological attempts at boundary maintenance. Unwanted elements enter the Haredi enclave, even when ideologues oppose them. Authors and publishers may ignore the limits that Haredi ideologues try to place on Haredi publishing, and acculturated Haredi Jews in an open and media-saturated American culture continue to consume non-Haredi popular literature, thus further undermining the attempts at monopolization.

Hence the next chapter will also examine Haredi fiction as a case in point. Ideologues and educators want uniquely Haredi fiction in order to surround Haredi readers with a complete envelope of Haredi values and to keep the perceived dangers of general fiction out of the community's boundaries. But once Haredi fiction began to appear, it took on a life of its own, refusing to bow to the strictures of the ideologues and educators. Haredi fiction became a tool for acculturation, for internal communal criticism, and for the penetration of potentially subversive ideas. The filter may not work in the ways that communal gatekeepers desire, and the monopoly may itself become contaminated by what some Haredim consider problematic elements.

Chapter III
"Not Absolute Truth": Haredi Writers Debate Their Own Acculturation

In the previous chapter, we noted the role that Haredi popular literature plays in coalescence, filtering, and monopolizing. These functions assist in communal boundary maintenance, as Haredi Jewry struggles with the tension between isolation and acculturation. The community's own rhetoric about sharp boundaries between Haredim and others oversimplifies the very real porousness of those boundaries, and it hides some of the ways in which this literature borrows from general culture. The inclusion of values, ideals, and cultural patterns taken not from the tradition, but from general culture, raises a series of challenges for Haredi authors and spokespeople. If Torah directs and encompasses all of life, then why the need to look elsewhere and incorporate contemporary American values? How do Haredi authors explain to themselves and their readership the borrowing from outside sources, the merging of Torah with secular wisdom? How can a community ostensibly committed to the notion that Torah is the sole arbiter of values and norms, committed to isolation and rejection of what it perceives as American values, explain the absorption of those self-same values into the community? How does Haredi popular rhetoric face up to the difficult awareness that the tradition often says something quite different than what this literature says that it says?

Various Haredi writers articulate differing approaches to these questions. They suggest alternative visions of the relationship between Torah and the cultural values that they have absorbed from the outside, and authors use different strategies to present their ideas as identical with or compatible with Torah. Let us return to the examples of Haredi parenting guides and self-help books. In this chapter, I would like to examine three strategies that authors use for addressing these issues: 1) *Denial* that there is any influence of secular ideas. This approach has the advantage of maintaining the dogma of a complete and totalizing Torah, but its lack of historical self-awareness leads to internal contradictions. 2) *Acknowledgement* of such an influence and defense of its legitimacy. Authors in this position have the advantage of a more accurate self-understanding, but they must then try to explain what makes their educational advice authentically Jewish. 3) On occasion, authors reflect on the possibility that certain contemporary Western approaches might be *superior* to traditional ones. The potentially subversive nature of this strategy requires authors and publishers to express things cautiously, and therefore such an approach is often implied rather than stated explicitly.

Denial

In discussing Lawrence Kelemen's parenting guide, *To Kindle a Soul*, we noted several elements in the substance and style of his book. He claims that his theories are ancient and more effective than the "modern" parenting approaches that he claims to reject. At the same time, his ideas about parenting in general and discipline in particular are, in fact, quite modern, and they are at odds with traditional sources. That is to say, Kelemen denies the modernity of his approach. He claims that his ideas about parenting come from "a 3,300 year old Jewish tradition" that was "carried through history by a tiny, Hebrew speaking community" of observant Jews.[1] The book's ideas represent, according to this author, pure and unadulterated Torah. This approach has a certain rhetorical advantage, in that it maintains the Haredi doctrine that Torah provides a complete and timeless guide to living. Yet the approach also raises problems. How does Kelemen deal with the fact that traditional Jewish sources say very different things than he does about parenting?

Kelemen makes a particularly fascinating case study of denial, since he attempts to answer this question in complex, if not contradictory, ways. In a community as text- and canon-based as Haredi society, he must relate in one way or another to the canon that, according to Haredi ideology, defines the authentic Jewish tradition. *To Kindle a Soul* quotes from traditional Jewish sources only rarely, and simply avoids many of those sources that reject the book's contemporary attitudes toward children.[2] For example, given his previously noted rejection of spanking, Kelemen does not mention most of the traditional sources that advocate corporal punishment for children. When he does cite sources, he often decontextualizes them, such as when he cites the Gaon of Vilna [eighteenth century] in *Even Shelemah* in *support* of the idea that one should not spank. Kelemen explains the Gaon's position as follows: "The Talmudic prescriptions for spanking apply only to those who can spank entirely without anger," a standard which most parents cannot meet. In fact, however, while the Gaon did prefer spanking without anger, he, like so much of the rabbinic tradition, clearly and unambiguously advocated regular, consistent, and at times quite violent corporal punishment. "If one loves his son, it is not enough to make him suffer for what he deserves, but he should examine him closely in case he has done a minor misdeed, and should make him suffer for that.... [One is commanded to hit one's son] even when he [the son] has not done any minor misdeed."[3]

In other circumstances, Kelemen reads traditional sources homiletically in order to make them more compatible with his concerns. For example, he realizes that the verse, "He who spares his rod (shivto) hates his child" (Proverbs 13:24, also see 19:18), seems to undermine his opposition to corporal punishment and spanking. He borrows from his teacher, R. Shlomo Wolbe, a clever reading of that verse by juxtaposing it with another verse (Zachariah 11:7), which refers to "rods" (makelot), one of which God calls "pleasantness." Kelemen concludes that the rod referred to in the verse in Proverbs can refer to positive reinforcement. "When we offer encouragement, this is also a rod."[4] To the best of my knowledge, traditional Jewish sources do not juxtapose these verses in this particular way, not only because the verses use different words for what Kelemen translates as "rod." Rather, the Sages assumed that the rod in question was a physical one, which caused suffering and which was an indispensable educational tool.[5]

Even if Kelemen convinces his readers that his ideas derive from tradition, he is left with an additional question. Why do his ancient ideas correspond so neatly with what contemporary non-Jewish parenting experts are telling their own readers? Noach Orlowek, who shares with Kelemen the modern American notions of affectionate child-centered parenting, solves this problem by not citing, or being unaware of, the similarities between his stance and that of non-Haredi parenting guides. He can convince his readers that he has provided them with ancient wisdom only if they lack that historical self-awareness. "Except for one footnote, psychological sources are neither quoted, nor indeed, consulted. Our Torah is a powerful guide to all areas of life, and certainly to the all-important area of parenting."[6] In no uncertain terms, Orlowek denies that he has been influenced by contemporary parenting styles and attitudes.

Kelemen has an even more complex relationship with modern educational literature. He cites several hundred contemporary academic and scientific studies to support his supposedly ancient theories. Aware that his parenting advice shares so much with that of his non-Jewish counterparts, Kelemen must try to explain his claim that his position contains only Torah. He explains that the most innovative contemporary pedagogues and scientists have re-discovered what Jews have always known. "Pedagogic science has swung full circle, and today the data supports the ancient theory described herein as well as (if not better than) it supports most modern theories."[7]

This passage does not clarify the difficult distinction between contemporary "pedagogic science," of which Kelemen approves, and "modern theories" of education, of which he disapproves. Reflecting a love-hate relationship with science that characterizes many fundamentalist groups,[8] Kelemen wants to claim that his theory is ancient Torah, and he equally wants to be perceived as an expert by the standards of contemporary science. Quoting these scientific studies helps with marketing. Science contributes to Kelemen's image as an expert. Scientific authority was central to self-proclaimed parenting experts throughout twentieth century America.[9] Anxiety-ridden parents will pay for the advice of a scientific expert, but have little reason to pay for the speculations of non-scientists. Haredi authors and readers are embedded deeply enough in Western scientific culture that at least some of them consider science to be a standard by which to measure expertise. Further, quoting scientific studies supports Haredi self-confidence. Minority groups that perceive themselves as threatened gain self-confidence when the elites of the dominant culture support their values, or are perceived to support their values. Scientific support for what the community considers Torah can increase the value which readers attach to Torah.[10]

Quoting scientific studies is also part of Kelemen's ambiguous attempt to market his book outside the Haredi community. The book was published by Leviathan Press, an imprint that does not imply any overt religious affiliation. The dust jacket includes praise for the book by a CNN anchor, two syndicated radio columnists, and a professor of pediatrics. The praise from Abraham Twerski – himself an Orthodox rabbi and author of many Haredi self-help books – refers to him as a professor of psychiatry and not as a rabbi. Furthermore, Kelemen presents himself as an academic, despite his own lack of academic credentials and experience. Kelemen has not earned a graduate degree and works professionally as a rabbi, teacher, and religious outreach worker. He has not taught in a university or published academic works. Still, the biography on the book jacket refers to him as a "professor of education" in a "college... where he also lectures in modern and medieval philosophy,"[11] and it claims that he "traveled to the Middle East to conduct 12 years of postgraduate field research." He speaks of his "research" as "anthropological," and refers to the professors at Harvard and Stanford whom he quotes as his "colleagues."[12] His website explains that "Professor Kelemen brings to his lectures and writings his impressive academic background."[13] *To Kindle a Soul* does not include *haskamot*, rabbinic approbations, de rigueur in most Haredi parenting guides, presumably because they would identify the book's Haredi nature. Instead, a small Hebrew note on the bottom of the copyright page identifies a website where these *haskamot* can be found.[14]

By presenting himself as an academic, Kelemen hopes to market his book outside the Haredi enclave, thereby increasing influence and sales. (I do not know what percentage of readers come from outside the Haredi community.) Still, marketing the book for a general audience also influences Haredi readers, who can discover that the general population also has much to learn from Torah. Torah is not the strange legacy of an obscure and eccentric minority, but meets or exceeds the standards of the hegemonic majority. Writing for a mass-market audience and grounding the authority of Haredi Judaism in secular science can help improve the collective self-confidence of a Haredi readership as well.

Kelemen presents his ideas as pure, ancient Torah, unadulterated by the influence of what he considers problematic modern trends. At the same time, he wants to take advantage of what modern scientific authority can provide for him as an author and for his audience. Once again, the popular literature both blurs and strengthens Haredi symbolic boundaries and sense of uniqueness.

Acknowledgement

Kelemen's complex, if not contradictory, denial of the influence of non-Jewish sources is not the only response in Haredi parenting and self-help literature to the tension between tradition and innovation. Indeed, it is not the most common response. The majority of authors acknowledge that they coalesce the Jewish and gentile, and they celebrate their ability to borrow from outside the tradition. Abraham Twerski, for example, draws on his "credentials as a rabbi and as a psychiatrist" to help his readership address life's complications and stresses, and he advocates a self-proclaimed "psychological-Torah approach to parenting" to help Haredim raise their offspring.[15] Like Twerski, the majority of Haredi authors of parenting guides do not hide the influence of contemporary psychology, even as they work to present their books as Torah oriented. Miriam Adahan openly displays her psychological expertise, which derives from her Western higher education, on the dust jacket of her *Raising Children to Care*. "She has a B.A. in psychology, with honors, from the University of Michigan. She also holds a Masters in counseling psychology from Wayne State University, and did three years of post-Masters work at the Humanistic Psychology Institute in San Francisco." She speaks proudly of her "training as a counselor," and openly proclaims what she has learned from her "academic training."[16]

More than many other authors, her works self-consciously adapt specific non-Jewish books and theories for an observant audience. Her self-help book, *Appreciating People (Including Yourself)*, is based on Isabel Briggs Myers and Peter Myers' popular theories of personality types; her parenting guide, *Raising Children to Care*, is grounded in David Keirsey and Marilyn Bates' book, *Please Understand Me*; and her *Awareness*, as noted, derives almost entirely from a popular theory called the Enneagram.[17] Works of general pop-psychology appear in her bibliographies alongside Torah sources.[18] Unlike Kelemen, she does not claim that these works have rediscovered what Torah always knew; she acknowledges them as non-Jewish.

Furthermore, Adahan admits that she has quoted selectively from the Jewish tradition. Others could quote "their own [Torah] sources which seem to say the very opposite" of what her books suggest about childrearing.[19] She responds to "those who object on grounds that it [the book] is not based solely on Torah." Disagreeing with those writers who claim that Torah includes all valuable knowledge, Adahan adopts a position remarkably close to that of Modern Orthodox advocates of *Torah UMadda* [Torah combined with general education], who claim that a humanities education can help students of Torah become more sensitive to the contours of the human condition. "Anything which helps us to be more aware and understanding *is* in the spirit of Torah." Her psychological theory "is *not* Torah, not 'Absolute Truth.'... It is simply another way of understanding people and becoming attuned to our Godly essence."[20]

Not accidentally, all the female authors of parenting guides and self-help books that I have examined adopt the strategy of acknowledgement, while I have not (yet) found an example of a female author who denies the influence of general psychology. Haredi women, who for the most part do not receive the same degree of education as men in the most sacred and authoritative texts of tradition and who for centuries have received a less restricted secular education, can less plausibly claim to speak in the name of pure Torah, and they have less invested in denial.[21] Haredi women are more likely to be aware of the influence of their non-Torah educations, and they can more easily gain a voice of authority by emphasizing that secular education.

This strategy of acknowledgement avoids the self-contradictions of denial by admitting the influence of ideas that come from outside the tradition, but the strategy raises another challenge. Given the similarities between these Haredi works and their secular and Christian counterparts, what makes them uniquely Jewish or Torah-oriented? Like their secular and Christian counterparts, Adahan's books share in the therapeutic religion that, according to Christian Smith and others, has become a commonplace in American culture, shared by members of a plurality of religious groups and denominations.[22] Haredi, Christian, and secular works focus on the individual's achievement of validation, self-esteem, and psychic equilibrium as tools for finding personal contentment and for transmitting values and a positive self-image to children. Self-help books across the board adopt an optimistic, encouraging, and friendly style, urging people to reach happiness. Absent are the pietistic preaching and austere moralism, the pessimistic anthropology and the emphatic hortatory style, of the classical Jewish *musar* literature. As Haym Soloveitchik notes, "Through a millennium of [Jewish] ethical writings runs a ceaseless warfare between will and instinct, as does the pessimistic feeling that the 'crooked timber of humanity' will never be made quite straight. Little of all this is to be found in the [Orthodox] moral literature of the past half century."[23] Self-restraint as the key to sanctity has been replaced with self-acceptance as the key to happiness. If these works have such little precedent in the tradition, and so much in common with contemporary non-Jewish approaches, why should a

Haredi reader not see them as a threat of contaminating pure Torah with dangerous outside influences?

Adahan's rhetoric helps to minimize this problem by creating an aura of Torah and distinctiveness around the book. First, she refers to her ideas as Torah. She entitles one of her self-help books *EMETT* [truth], an acronym for Emotional Maturity Established Through Torah. "Torah principles" are "the foundation of EMETT."[24] Indeed, one of her self-help books strives to "integrate the lofty ideals of Torah into the most minute aspects of our daily lives."[25] She subtitles one of her parenting guides "A Jewish Approach to Childrearing," where the term Jewish is generally used in this literature as a synonym for Haredi. Her books contain *haskamot*, one of which explains that Adahan provides "an admirable Torah guide for our troubled times." On occasion, like Kelemen, she contrasts her parenting suggestions with the "unsound advice" of "modern parents," which she claims is the "opposite... from the Torah view."[26]

Adahan also plays up the Jewish nature of her books by using examples, names, experiences, and language drawn from the realia of contemporary Haredi life. In one example, a young mother overcomes her desire to "call my husband to come right home from the kollel" when a minor emergency strikes. Encouraging the use of controlled and constructive speech, rather than angry outbursts, she suggests that a parent say to the child, "I know that your *yetzer tov* [positive drive] does want to cooperate and would be so happy to be able to do a mitzvah [commandment], especially *kibud ame* [honoring one's mother]."[27]

Furthermore, references to traditional Jewish sources lend Jewish form and content to her books. In her parenting guide, *Raising Children to Care*, she generally quotes sources not directly related to parenting, both because of the scarcity of such sources and because so many of them are decidedly out of line with contemporary concerns. Instead, she quotes sources that deal with general ethics and character, drafting them as prooftexts for contemporary therapeutic ideas. For example, the Biblical expression, "God is my salvation; I will trust and not be afraid," demonstrates the "need to recognize temper and combat it with secure thoughts."[28]

Adahan's approach of acknowledging that she merges the Jewish and the contemporary reflects not a minority voice in American Haredi self-help, pop psychology, and parenting literature, but the majority. For authors like Adahan, Twerski, or many others, there need be no tension between traditional Torah values and contemporary educational or psychological theory, much as for Levinson there is no tension between contemporary nutritional advice and the tradition.

Times Have Changed: Between Denial and Acknowledgement

One approach, adopted by several authors, combines aspects of both the denial and acknowledgement strategies. A historical self-awareness that times have changed allows authors to deviate from traditional sources while simultaneously maintaining a claim of continuity with the tradition. Authors understand that traditional sources do not advocate the particular parenting strategies that the authors suggest. Yet, these authors do not claim that they merely replaced traditional Jewish attitudes with non-Jewish ones. Instead, traditional sources remain valid and binding, but contemporary conditions require applying those sources differently than what they seem to say on the surface. Noach Orlowek, whose other works often adopt the denial approach, rejects authoritarian parenting and corporal punishment, replacing them with affection and warmth. In an article in *The Jewish Observer* he admits that the traditional texts advocate what he rejects. "What worked in previous generations will not work today.... While the age-old principles of Torah remain totally relevant [today], their application needs to be in tune with current realities.... We need to be such good students of our teachers... that we are able to assess what they would have said today, and to project how they would have reacted to the challenges of our generation."[29] Continuity does not necessarily mean doing the same things as one's predecessors, because eternal principles apply differently in changing conditions. Genuine continuity involves speculating – perhaps knowing – what the great rabbis of the past would have said under current conditions.

In a variation on the theme, Twerski, who often adopts the approach of acknowledgement, sometimes uses language that fits with the times-have-changed strategy. "The challenges and stresses of modern-day parenting are both qualitatively and quantitatively greater than those confronting previous generations." Hence, "We cannot have recourse to practices of the past."[30] A modern approach is a better one. R. Shlomo Wolbe, one of the most renowned musarists of the second half of the twentieth century, suggests something similar, in the process reinforcing the Haredi notion of the dangers of contemporary culture and its inferiority to that of the Jewish past. "In previous generations the situation was different. Children had more tolerance, and therefore they could tolerate spanking. Children also had stronger character. It didn't damage them to receive a few blows. However, today the whole environment is one of rebellion.... If someone tries to crush a child by spanking him, he can hurt the child and his relationship with the child, and when the child grows up he might close himself off from his parents."[31]

Unlike Orlowek, Rabbis Wolbe and Twerski do not claim that their non-violent parenting derives from the tradition or its sources; instead, they claim that times have changed. But this approach raises problems since it seems to call into question the timelessness and perfection of Torah. An exchange of letters in *The Jewish Observer* regarding matters of education raises precisely that challenge. Dr. Benzion Sorotzkin cites R. Wolbe as saying that educational competitiveness and perfectionism currently undermine the Haredi educational system by putting too much pressure on youngsters to excel in their studies at the expense of all else. Yet, Sorotzkin points out that at least some sources seem to encourage educational competitiveness, such as the Mishnah's aphorism, "It is better to be the tail of a lion than the head of a fox" (*Avot* 4:15) or sources that speak of "*kinas soferim* [jealousy among scholars]" (BT, *Bava Batra* 21a). He explains that a source that encourages competitiveness "no longer applies, because such an approach would break the spirit of most people.... In times past, this process [of competitiveness] didn't undermine the motivation of those who didn't make it to the top."[32] Today, schools should eliminate competitiveness.

Yet, in the following issue of the magazine, another reader took issue with this attitude toward the sources, which seems to undermine the dogma of a timeless and all-encompassing Torah. "Neither the author [Sorotzkin] nor the authorities quoted [R. Wolbe] could have intended to claim that the timeless words of the Mishnah can actually become obsolete."[33] That might lead to wholesale abandonment of the binding tradition. The times-have-changed approach subverts the authority of Torah. The great rabbi could not possibly have meant what was quoted in his name.

Sorotzkin, however, did not back down. Due to "*yeridas hadoros* [decline of the generations]," Jews today cannot implement the wise advise of the Sages. Granted, the claim that the older sources no longer apply might lead others (the Conservative and Reform, perhaps the Modern Orthodox) to undermine the authority of the Sages as a whole. But, "not acknowledging these [historical] changes and using educational methods that are no longer effective pose an equal, or perhaps even greater danger." Caught between respecting the binding nature of the sources and an awareness that the educational advice of those sources will not be effective today, Sorotzkin concludes that "only our *gedolim* [great rabbis] can decide when or if established educational practices should be adjusted because of changing circumstances.... This is the only possible protection from 'casual dismissal' of *divrei Chazal* [the words of the Sages]."[34] This debate indicates that the creativity of the times-have-changed approach finds only an uncomfortable middle ground between the denial and acknowledgement approaches.

Superiority of Secular Approaches

On rare occasions, the educational literature acknowledges the superiority of some general theories over traditional ones. An example comes from the *The Jewish Observer*, where a special-education expert, Leah Steinberg, discusses the mainstreaming of special-education students into regular classrooms. "Significant changes have been taking place in the general educational scene in terms of meeting the needs of special education children... and many of the benefits of these changes are being realized in the yeshiva system as well.... If this revolution of inclusion [mainstreaming] exists in the public-school system – and it does – how much more so should it exist in our yeshivos."[35]

On the surface, this statement about the importance of helping weaker students seems innocent enough. However, under the surface lies a surprising statement about the relationship between traditional education and modern non-Jewish ideals, accompanied by a significant internal criticism of Haredi educational culture. Steinberg goes out on a limb by suggesting that a public-school education – generally viewed in Haredi literature as little more than a "bucket of dross"[36] – might offer better education than some Haredi institutions. Further, Steinberg refers to "yeshivos" in her criticism, a term particularly symbolic of traditional education. Indeed, there was no accommodation for what we would call today "special education" in yeshivas of the past, which focused almost exclusively on the intellectual-spiritual elite. Steinberg could easily have used less threatening terms, like "schools" or "classrooms." She not only suggests a modification in Orthodox educational policy, but also hints that the very conservatism of Haredi education causes part of the problem. The willingness of the public educational system to sacrifice elitism for more democratic education has certain advantages, but the Haredi educational system has yet to internalize them. Steinberg's rhetoric contrasts sharply with that of Kelemen, for whom the tradition already contains all the wisdom of the general approaches, or with the rhetoric of another influential Israeli rabbi, who says that "none of the atmosphere of the street should penetrate it [the yeshivah] at all, [and the yeshivah should be] hermetically sealed [with]... special insulation."[37]

A few factors allow for Steinberg's seemingly subversive rhetoric. First, she published her essay in *The Jewish Observer*, a Haredi periodical which prides itself on its willingness to speak relatively openly about controversial issues (see Chapter 6, below). Second, Steinberg is a woman, who therefore cannot ground her authority in Torah scholarship but rather in her expertise in special education. Coming from outside the hegemonic centers of traditional authority, she has a perspective more distanced from conventional communal ideology. Third, the special-education context makes her critique less subversive, since it focuses on the margins rather than the centers of traditional Torah education.

These three approaches – denial, acknowledgement, and superiority – reflect three differing ways that Haredi authors can describe, but also deny, their own acculturation, in the process reflecting on their own ambivalent relationships with the surrounding culture. Yet, acculturation raises other questions for Haredi culture and its boundary maintenance. Advocates of denial, acknowledgment, and superiority argue about ideology, about how Haredi Jewish authors would like to filter general culture. But in practice, ideologues may have less control than they imagine regarding what enters the enclave of the isolationist religious group and what does not. In the next section, we will examine the internal Haredi debate regarding Haredi fiction. While ideologues raise a range of positions on the legitimacy and value of fiction, Haredi fiction demonstrates that market forces wield power along with ideological forces in determining how ideas and cultural patterns enter the Haredi enclave.

Debating Wanted and Unwanted Acculturation: The Case of Fiction

Even if one acknowledges acculturation, why and when should Haredi literature borrow from the outside culture, and when should that borrowing stop? Haredi Jews legitimately borrow from general culture, as the dominant "acknowledgement" strategy indicates, but how much should be borrowed and at what point does borrowing lose its legitimacy? These questions challenge Haredi leaders to identify how they would like the filter to function, what they would like to see enter the community, and what they would like to exclude.

But this abstract discussion of how Haredi popular literature *ought* to function does not tell us precisely how the literature *actually* functions. Even when dealing with literature written and published by community members, the literature does not always do and say what the ideologues would like it to, since literature appears not only for ideological or educational reasons, but for creative and economic ones as well. Ideologues may discuss at length how Haredi popular literature can help protect the community from dangerous ideas, but the same literary tools that the ideologues advocate may turn on those ideologues, serving as a means for unwanted ideas to enter the community's discourse.

Fiction is a good example. Authors like Marcus Lehmann and R. Yudl Rosenberg had written (and, in the case of Rosenberg, plagiarized) Orthodox fiction in the late nineteenth and early twentieth centuries, but the trend did not take off in America until the 1970s. Over the course of that decade, Haredi authors began widespread production of children's fiction to satisfy the voracious appetites of young readers whose parents wanted literature that would reinforce Haredi ideas and practice. After teen fiction gradually began appearing, the first works of adult fiction appeared in the mid-1990s. As these works began to sell, publishers and authors became bolder, producing the first works of crime and adventure fiction in the late 1990s.[38]

Some opposed the development of Haredi fiction, and debate appeared on the pages of *The Jewish Observer,* among other places. Some polemicized against the innovations of the new fiction, for reasons directly related to coalescence. They claimed that Haredi Jews should not borrow a literary genre from general culture. The Jewish people "has produced hundreds and thousands of *seforim*.... We *never* had any tradition of fiction! Stories of *Gedolim*, yes; fiction, no."[39] Similarly, "In the vast literature of the Jew, there is no tradition of fiction." In fact, "the Haskala, the enlightenment, brought darkness into Jewish life, [and] did bring forth a body of fiction."[40] Another Haredi woman, writing for a non-Haredi audience, who in the end emerges as a staunch advocate of Haredi fiction, still identifies serious religious flaws in the enterprise, particularly because fiction involves made-up stories. "Fiction has something unappealing: the bitterness of lies. The religious mind feels more comfortable with truth."[41] Another author suggests that fiction's falsehood can damage children in particular. "Fairy tales and other make-believe stories" can "confuse... their [children's] perceptions of truth. Boundaries between truth and falsehood became hazy."[42]

Novels for adults raised even more severe challenges. Ambitious authors had written Haredi adult novels, but publishers were reluctant to produce them. Children may need satisfying distractions, but adults should spend their spare time on Torah study and religious growth, not fiction. As one character in a novel says – subtly undermining both the novel in which he appears and its readership – "Man was born to toil [paraphrasing Job 5:7]. A person is not born into this world in order to indulge himself in good and luxurious sleep. He was born in order to work – hard. Wasn't this world only the entrance to the next?"[43] By these strict standards, who can justify relaxing in the reading of a novel, no matter how Orthodox? Perhaps, thought publishers, religious leaders and readers might view Haredi adult novels as distractions from Torah study and character development. According to author Malka Schaps (who writes under the penname Rachel Pomerantz), her first novels sat unpublished for more than a decade as she searched for a publisher willing to push the envelope and risk this innovation.[44] The ideological problems with adult fiction were eased by the fact that most of the literature was written by and for women, who have lesser obligations to study Torah and who, for centuries, were given a much broader general education than men, even in the most Orthodox of circles.

Adventure and thriller novels were even more ideologically problematic, though they began to appear in the 1990s. Rabbis, educators, and some readers explicitly and vocally criticized these novels, since the critics had trouble identifying the religious value in these genres. Borrowing the formula from non-Jewish culture, with its "drug dealers... shooting incidents, and samples of rough language along the way,"[45] seem to celebrate violence and support the values of militaristic heroism, contrary to Haredi quietist leanings.[46] Furthermore, as we shall see, many of these novels quite openly criticize aspects of Haredi education and culture.

Haredi authors and ideologues defend the enterprise of fiction, particularly in classrooms, to replace the secular literature curriculum and its perceived problems. These ideologues defend fiction due to its ability to monopolize and filter, keeping non-Haredi influences out while assuring that readers would be surrounded more exclusively by Haredi materials. "Secular literature... is a most intimate form of exposure [to general culture]; it is the mirror of the Gentile mind. It is impossible to expose our youth to such a potent anti-Torah force and expect them to remain pure in thought and in deed."[47] We need, claims this author, to replace this decadence with a more holy alternative. Similarly, a "ba'alat teshuvah – or any religious woman who has drunk deeply from secular, Western literature – may find that she turned away from that literature because of its ethical vacancy," and has turned instead to Haredi fiction.[48]

Other defenders look less at the problems with Western fiction and more at the potential positive value of coalescing the Jewish and gentile in uniquely Haredi fiction. Publishing quality Orthodoxy fiction "is taking a craft developed by the non-Jewish world and enlisting it in the cause of Torah, much the same as the invention of printing... was utilized for the spread of Torah."[49] Fiction is not an inherently value-laden medium, but a technological tool, one easily adaptable for Haredi purposes. For still others, the critics of general literature had gone too far in insisting on the decadence of general culture. According to Shalva Mintz, Western literature is not all bad. It is "either compatible with, derivative of, or hostile to Torah values."[50] Even with the advantages of Haredi fiction, some general fiction should also find its way through the filter and into the enclave.

Thus, Haredi educators and writers debate the relative value of general and distinctively Haredi fiction for various audiences. But notice one area of significant consensus among these ideologues. Even the most extreme voices in rejecting secular literature for Haredi readers take Haredi acculturation for granted by advocating significant general education for Haredi youth. Despite rejecting secular fiction almost entirely as a "bombardment of non-Torah ideas into children's minds," educator Faiga Diskind states quite clearly that, "We are not, by any means, proposing the elimination of secular studies – they are crucial."[51] Indeed, some Haredi educational activists struggle to make sure that each student "will take his secular studies more seriously."[52]

Nor does anybody in this debate conclude that the Haredi community should ban fiction, as such, from Haredi bookshelves, despite potentially good reasons to do so. After all, the adaptation of the novel for the Haredi community represents a significant acculturation. According to many literary historians, the novel as a literary form developed in the modern period because its this-worldly realism, its focus on the individual personality over time, and its middle-class readership exemplify modernity itself. Production and consumption of Haredi novels signifies that Haredim, too, share a modern sense of self-as-an-individual, rooted in a particular time and place, whose personal and subjective experiences of self-over-time matter a great deal.[53] Within the Jewish world, Robert Alter has argued that the realism and individualism of the nineteenth century Hebrew novel was itself part and parcel of the maskilic critique of a traditional Jewish sense of self.[54] At that time, an Eastern European yeshiva student found reading a newly minted Jewish novel had surely been caught by the bug of Haskalah, considered the arch enemy of Jewish tradition by today's Haredi world. Yet today, despite this history, even those Haredim who argue that Judaism has no tradition of fiction do not suggest doing away with it entirely. The positions range from those who prefer the gradual replacement of secular literature with Haredi literature in Haredi schools and homes to those who advocate limited and careful exposure to some non-Haredi literature as well. Indeed, the *Jewish Observer* never stopped advertising and reviewing Haredi novels.

Under these circumstances, internal Haredi discussion about fiction revolves more around how to write proper Haredi fiction, rather than if to do so at all. Some authors of Haredi fiction defend it as a didactic tool. Yet, defending Haredi fiction on didactic grounds raises serious problems for the selfsame authors, who can find didactic writing stifling. According to popular author Yaffa Ganz, Haredi juvenile fiction is "important" because it is a "potent means of educating, of forming opinions, of bonding loyalties. A good story can often accomplish what hours – maybe even weeks or months – of direct education cannot do."[55] Yet, working too hard to promote certain values can make the stories thin and shallow. Ganz realizes that she must sacrifice compelling or attractive writing for the sake of ethical and religious edification.

> How didactic should the book be? Most people, includ-
> ing children, don't particularly like being lectured at.
> But if you rule out didactics, how can you be sure your
> message will come across clearly?... How do we keep the
> heroes in religious books from being "goody goody"?
> Because if they are *not* basically good, we don't really
> want them as heroes, do we? But if they are *too* good, we
> don't particularly like them, either!... When dealing with
> teen novels, how much of the adult, contemporary world
> and its attendant problems do we want to bring into the
> pages of our books? Should marriage, divorce, sickness,
> death and other difficult subjects be given an airing?[56]

The educational and ideological message must control the book's content, but that can prevent it from being entertaining or compelling.
Ganz leaves her questions open, implying a measure of hesitancy in the
face of this dilemma. Another Haredi educator answers this question
clearly and unambiguously. Haredi novels or stories should depict only
positive behavior. "A story which is not consistent with behavior which
can be emulated should not be told.... Stories should be told in such a
way that their moral is clear."[57]

Other authors reject this last approach as unsound on both educational and literary levels. "Too much of what passes for '*frum* fiction' is
trite, shallow, and kitschy – little more than a commercial for, by, and
about impeccably right-thinking and acting *Yidden* [Jews]." This kind of
literature is so "bland" that it is neither enjoyable to read nor educationally effective. Didactic goals contradict what this writer sees as the real
goal of fiction, to reflect on "the struggles of men and women with life,
for meaning, for redemption."[58]

Between Ideology and Practice in Haredi Fiction

Thus far we have seen ideological discussions about what Haredi fiction
should look like. Yet, ideology remains only part of the story. Haredi
fiction, like other types of fiction, does not merely follow the dictates of
ideologues, supporting some pre-existing religious-pedagogic agenda.
Fiction has always been a potentially subversive voice, with its ability to

challenge social norms, question conventional morality, and suggest alternatives to existing institutions. Fiction, in a word, can be dangerous, particularly because the filter is not entirely under the control of those who would like to control it. Once Haredi fiction became popular, it (inevitably?) began to play the role of a subversive social critic, the very role that advocates of a more didactic Haredi fiction wanted to avoid.[59]

To begin with, Haredi fiction, along with parenting and self-help books, give extensive voice to female authors within a community that envisions the normative Jewish woman as a mother, housekeeper, and wife, but not as a public intellectual. Women's fiction may not have the same pride of place in the hegemonic hierarchy as men's halakhic or Talmudic writing.[60] Still, the very act of writing and publishing – by now without any need for apology or self-justification – not only reflects existing empowerment of women, but helps to extend that empowerment by giving voice to women's concerns, by enabling a sense of personal satisfaction, and by producing income. And Haredi women can be some of the most critical and sharp, at times subversive, voices in Haredi publishing.

In some cases, female authors would like to break out of the constricting confines set by publishers and by the sense of communal propriety. Indeed, a group of female writers which met regularly complained bitterly of the "restrictiveness of the Orthodox publishers' standards of what could or could not be discussed."[61] Furthermore, Yael Shenkar points to subtle and creative techniques that female Haredi authors of fiction use to give voice to their concerns and to circumvent the formal and informal censors. They are not permitted to speak poorly or criticize normative Haredi men or to subvert the image of harmonious Haredi family life, yet they want to address the domestic tensions and concerns that affect their lives. Hence, claims Shenkar, they use non-Orthodox characters and newly Orthodox Jews to present alternative images of ideal families and ideal masculinity. She points, for example, to a novel by Malka Schaps in which a newly observant woman chooses a husband who prefers to pursue a career in academia rather than advancing as a Torah scholar.[62] Similarly, female Haredi authors address questions of marital strife by describing the lives of marginal and not-yet-Haredi families, since authors may not paint Haredi family life as flawed. As one female Haredi author put it, "There are things that a religious character cannot do in my texts, so I sometimes use a secular character."[63] Yet, of late, female authors have become less discreet. For example, two novels written by women about teen-age Haredi dropouts depict insensitive and overly critical fathers who, in their zealousness to see them emerge as Torah scholars, push their sons out of the community.[64]

However, male authors also use their fiction to expand the boundaries of Haredi internal discourse and to raise potentially subversive criticism of the Haredi community. I would like to focus more closely on the works of one author, Yair Weinstock (pen name, M. Arbel), in large part because of his role as a pioneer of Haredi adventure fiction, because his novels are self-consciously critical to the point of being subversive, because that subversiveness led to controversy, and because they reflect on the tension between Haredi isolation and openness. That is to say, his novels not only serve the didactic ends suggested by the various ideologues who defended Haredi fiction, but they also broke out of the limitations. In the end, controversy ensued when educators, ideologues, and would-be-gatekeepers decided that Weinstock had not written the Haredi novels he "should" have. Weinstock writes ideological and message-driven fiction, but he does not send the precise message that the ideologues wanted.

One of the first to write Haredi thriller fiction, Weinstock's novels first appeared in Hebrew, serialized in the magazine *Mishpacha*, and ArtScroll later translated them into English.[65] His thriller novel, *Calculated Risk*, reflects on the tension between isolation and involvement in general culture by incorporating an ongoing debate about the value of Haredim working in high-tech jobs. Computers, according to some characters, threaten to undermine Haredi life. They open the door to the dangers of the internet, television, and movies. They are addictive. They transform people into unfeeling robots and drag Haredi Jews out of the safety of the Haredi enclave and into spiritually hazardous secular offices.[66] The novel's Hebrew title, *Sikkun Mehushav*, was translated as "Calculated Risk," but it is also a play on words that hints at "computerized danger."[67] In this novel – as in many popular technological thrillers – technology makes the entire world vulnerable. Master hackers have no trouble shutting down subway service, major airports, and America's nuclear arsenal. The terrorists want "to penetrate the systems that Americans used daily and show them how vulnerable the American public was to disaster."[68]

Yet the dangers of technology do not justify an utterly isolationist or rejectionist attitude, and the novel ultimately advocates computers as a profession for Haredi Jews. Akiva, one of the anti-heroes in another of Weinstock's novels, *Eye of the Storm*, exemplifies the dangers of extreme rejectionism. As a result of his father's death in an electrical accident, young Akiva developed an irrational hatred of electricity, science, and technology. He became a social outcast and was eventually drafted into the treacherous and militant group, "Friends of the Mikdash [Temple]." Akiva represents the outright rejection of change, development, or technological progress. Yet, according to the novel, his approach is both unrealizable and, more importantly, ideologically misguided. One night, as Akiva makes his way toward the heroes' yeshiva, he "was helped... by, ironically, electric light." In an ensuing conversation, one of the yeshiva students explains to Akiva that, "Electricity also brings life into the world. If everyone got rid of electricity... people would die on operating tables. Sick people who are attached to respirators would stop breathing.... True, it's artificial, but it's also a gift from Hashem [God], Who put the potential for electrical power into water, into coal, into the atom, and gave men the wisdom to figure out how to use it."[69] This overtly positive attitude toward technological development contrasts with the reported position of another American Haredi leader, R. Ya'akov Perlow (the Noviminsker Rebbe), who explains on the pages of *The Jewish Observer* that "electricity, the telephone, and all sorts of other technological marvels [are]... the great *bedi'eved* [acceptable only after the fact]."[70]

The continuing dialogue between Akiva and the yeshiva students places Akiva's rejectionist stance in broader historical and cultural perspective. Akiva tells the yeshiva students that life was simpler and more holy in the pre-technological past, and the students agree. Yet they explain that, "The world has changed a little, my friend. Have you ever heard about the guy who yelled, 'Stop the world, I want to get off'?"[71] An ideology of *"hadash asur min ha-Torah"* [novelty is prohibited by the Torah] is not only impossible to implement, but incorrect ideologically. Haredi Judaism is not and should not be an utter rejection of change or novelty as such.[72] Proper Judaism, according to the yeshiva students, filters modernity, accepting the valuable while rejecting the unacceptable. Indeed, as we have seen, that is just what much of Haredi popular literature does; it allows positive (and some less positive) aspects of modernity to filter into Haredi culture without inordinate exposure to the dangers of the outside.

Instead of rejecting change, Haredi Jews should openly deliberate on the value and dangers of different aspects of contemporary culture. In the ongoing discussion of computers in *Calculated Risk*, one wise school-teacher conducts a school-wide debate over the issue. Students on both sides of the question address the school and its staff, airing their opinions in a rational and polite manner. The debate allows students to clarify the issues, and its success derives in part from the fact that the spokesperson against computers is herself the daughter of a successful programmer.[73] This novel advocates a relatively open educational program (by Haredi standards), which allows people, including female students, to debate the educational and ideological issues at the center of the Haredi agenda. This education forces students to challenge their natural assumptions, to think for themselves, and to move beyond what they are told by their parents or surroundings.

Furthermore, Weinstock's novels reflect extensively on the ways in which Haredi taboos stifle internal Haredi discourse and prevent the kind of open airing of ideas and problems that could, in the long run, prove constructive. His novels reject those forces that push Haredim "not to speak about real issues, to sweep everything under the rug."[74] An honest approach, one that evaluates both the positive and the negative, will serve the Haredi community better than one that tries to highlight only the positive and ignore the negative. In *Blackout* (Hebew, *Bilti Hafikh*), Gili – a *ba'al teshuvah*, a journalist, and the hero of the book – is assigned to write an exposé of various Hasidic groups for the secular press. Along with praise, the articles include negative aspects of Hasidic life: "alliances and enmities in the [Hasidic] court... behind the scenes... [and] weak links." While the article is "free of any hint of slander... it doesn't merely pat them [Haredim] on the back, in 'with us everything is perfect' style." While "not everything that is true has to be aired in public," ignoring real problems is neither believable nor productive.[75] Slander for the sake of voyeurism or self-promotion causes problems. But Weinstock's own works, like Gili's newspaper articles, offer constructive criticism for the sake of Haredi self-evaluation and eventual improvement.

The articles' constructive criticism and open airing of problems contrast with the dangers of secrecy, another theme of *Blackout*. Haredi Jewry makes itself vulnerable to enemies because of secret conflicts which fester under the surface of Haredi public life. The Israeli secret service (GSS) plants a mole in the Haredi community to uncover the underlying fights, so that anti-Haredi GSS leaders can publicize the problems and fan the flames of internal Haredi strife. These anti-Haredi forces expect the Haredi community to tear itself apart from the inside. The comparison to Gili's articles is critical. If Haredi Jewry tries to hide its faults and does not address them constructively, then Haredi enemies will air them destructively.

Weinstock's openness raised the ire of his critics, who felt that his novels did not further the proper Haredi agenda. *Blackout*, as well as Moshe Garylak's adventure novel, *The Runaway* (*Ketonet Pasim* in Hebrew, published in both Hebrew and English under the pseudonym Chaim Eliav), were attacked vehemently when they appeared in Israel since they were, in the eyes of many readers and educators, too critical of Haredi educational and rabbinic leadership.[76] Numerous schools in Israel pulled the books from their libraries, and there was pressure to remove them from stores (though an official ban was never pronounced). At the end of the day, the English publisher chose to modify the English version of *Blackout* to remove the elements that drew the sharpest criticism.[77] An American critic, writing in *The Jewish Observer*, suggested pulling one particularly egregious adventure novel from stores. Though he did not specify which book he had in mind, in order not to provide it greater publicity, he may well have been referring to one of Weinstock's works. He attacked "one of the latest, best-selling, techno-thrillers" for its "lengthy accounts of the behavior of 'turned off' youths, momentarily disenchanted with all we cherish."[78]

Yet, despite success in modifying the book's English edition, the attack on the book in many ways failed. As in the case of Slifkin's coalescence of science and Torah, gatekeepers were unable to stifle Weinstock's advocacy of openness, his critique of contemporary Haredi culture, nor his coalescence of a Haredi agenda with the secular form of the adventure novel. Publishers kept the books in stores in Israel and the United States – whether because they disagreed ideologically with the naysayers, or in order to earn a profit, or some combination of the two.[79] In the case of *Ketonet Pasim/The Runaway*, the fact that the author was also the editor of *Mishpacha*, the Israeli Haredi weekly in which the novel was originally serialized, gave him more power to ignore his critics. The author told me that *Gordian Knot* and *Blackout* each sold some 13,000 copies in Hebrew and a parallel number in English, a staggeringly high quantity by the standards of Haredi publishing.[80]

Sometimes it is not the particular content of a novel that undermines the didactic values that ideologues advocate, but the form itself. Adventure novels, for example, almost by definition encode the value of heroism and strength, seemingly undermining Haredi quietist sensibilities. The plot of one of Weinstock's adventure novels, *Calculated Risk*, points to this tension. Israel's security forces need a Haredi agent to go on a sensitive and dangerous mission to save a kidnapped rabbi. There are no qualified agents. "You would need a religious intelligence man. There is no such thing."[81] The hero of the novel had been an Israeli intelligence agent before leaving the profession when he became Orthodox. Adventure and crime-solving, it seems, should not occupy a Haredi Jew. The novel explores the tension between attraction to and rejection of adventure through a series of role-reversals, in which religious and secular Jews switch their respective positions. A secular backpacker and thrill-seeker, dressing up as a quiet yeshiva student, becomes the best replacement for the non-existent religious agent. The novel's climax reveals that the kidnapped rabbi is also a secular agent who was surgically modified to look like the rabbi. Similarly, the now-Orthodox retired agent returns temporarily to a life of action and danger in order to help solve the crime, during which time he struggles to maintain his habitual level of prayer, Torah study, and observance. These role reversals echo what these novels can do for the Haredi reader, who can vicariously live a life of adventure despite the fact that the novel itself had presented this as a secular value. A Haredi novel attracts readers to values that the novel itself defines as non-Haredi, blurring Haredi cultural boundaries in ways that authors may not have intended. This may be no different than the attraction of these genres for the general public. Much mass-market adventure fiction allows readers to imagine doing what, in reality, they would neither do nor want to do.[82]

Still, the way in which Haredi thriller fiction undermines that which it simultaneously works to uphold points to a wider tension between Haredi popular culture and official religious values.[83] According to Haredi didactic theory, people should not read adventure fiction. Why not stick to fiction that is more supportive of Haredi values? The answer points to cultural and economic paradoxes that are built into monopolizing. Producers of Haredi popular culture are not guided exclusively by didactic or religious values, but also, perhaps primarily, by the forces of the market. Publishers want not only to educate the public, but to sell products and earn money. The acculturated community will purchase works, and therefore publishers will produce them, even if ideologues find this difficult to defend.[84]

Furthermore, the drive for monopolization pushes Haredi culture to imitate general culture, even if the particular form that that culture takes seems problematic from the perspective of Haredi collective values. In order to monopolize effectively, producers must copy styles and genres that exist in general culture in order to limit Haredi consumption of the even-worse general culture. If general culture produces popular music or movies, the Haredi community has a cultural and economic interest in producing its own versions of those genres. Yet, one cannot imitate an existing genre without following its codes and unwritten rules, which may well reflect values foreign to ideal Haredi norms. General culture is hegemonic, and it leads the way. To a great degree, general popular culture dictates to the Haredi enclave what it must produce, even when that undermines things that Haredi Judaism holds dear.[85]

If the community members were not so deeply acculturated this might not be such a problem, both because there would be less push to consume the secular versions and because the Haredi culture could more freely construct itself along religiously desirable lines. However, given the acculturation of so many Haredim, the Haredi market imitates those genres and styles that the secular culture already produces, at times despite the values and messages encoded in that genre or style. Hence, like other aspects of Haredi popular culture, thriller fiction may run the risk of profaning the sacred rather than sanctifying the profane. One Haredi writer, critiquing the perceived abuses of Haredi popular literature, explains that, "We must clearly distinguish... what is *kodesh* (sacred) and what is *chol* (secular)." The Haredi community may be better off reading secular adventure fiction, so as not to blur that distinction. "The use of Judaica literature will totally dissolve this *havdalah* [distinction] and is therefore not acceptable."[86]

In the context of American Protestantism, Carol Flake has referred to this paradox as "Redemptorama." The notions of redemption and sanctity have become so pervasive and hackneyed that they can become reduced to second-rate entertainment, cheapened to appeal to the least common denominator.[87] In a Haredi context, this paradox has received particular attention regarding music, where Haredi musicians imitate the styles of general pop music, even as they use words derived from the sacred texts of the tradition. Musicians, treated like celebrities and stars by the Haredi public, perform their music at concerts that imitate those of their secular counterparts. All this has led to consternation on the part of at least certain ideologues and gatekeepers, who see this as an unwanted intrusion of secular styles into the Haredi enclave. Haredi musicians "dancing around the stage like non-Jewish performers... gyrating, as if they were imitating the rock stars of the 60s.... Is this not the opposite of what should be happening?" The youth should be learning to idolize "*talmidei chachamim* [Torah scholars] and *osei chessed* [doers of kindness], not entertainers." This critic understands that the push for such music comes, in part, to create a cultural monopoly. He hopes that this music might "stop someone from listening to secular music," but still insists that its problems make it unacceptable for Haredi consumers. "*It is not for us!*"[88] Others go further. In the summer of 2007 and again in the winter of 2008, several rabbis and community activists attempted to ban at least some Haredi music concerts, which led to the eventual cancellation of several concerts.[89]

At the end of the day, market forces may be more important in the Haredi book market than ideology, whether to publishers, authors, or readers. Writers and publishers will produce what the public will buy, often whether or not the ideologues can justify its existence.[90] Another factor allows authors of fiction to write and sell potentially questionable works: lack of formal rabbinic review. Authors of fiction do not need *haskamot* the way authors of theological or halakhic works do. Indeed, the leading Haredi rabbis have kept strangely silent about the value of this fiction, reflecting at least tacit acceptance of the phenomenon. Ideologues desire popular literature in order to keep out ideas and images that are considered dangerous. To some degree they succeed in creating such a literature – I have yet to find a Haredi novel that describes sexuality, despite authors who told me that they would like to be able to include it. But Haredi writers, publishers, and consumers have minds of their own, and they produce and consume Haredi literature that ideologues consider problematic.

Diverse Voices
If Chapter Two examined the broad functions of Haredi popular literature, this Chapter has looked more closely at the diverse voices and disputes within that literature. Popular stereotypes notwithstanding,

Haredi Jews are not a monolithic group, in complete agreement with their rabbinic leadership about the need to separate entirely from general culture. Voices from different groups and subgroups within the Haredi community meet in Haredi popular literature. When heard together, these different voices reflect a diverse community that is struggling mightily to explain to itself the value and limits of its own acculturation. Not all Haredim agree about how and when to coalesce, how and when to filter, and how and when to monopolize. Furthermore, irrespective of theoretical agreements and disagreements, Haredi Judaism's popular literature is constructed not only by ideological conviction, but by market forces, which can sometimes work at cross purposes with religious ideology. Publishers and authors have religious motivations and financial ones, and we cannot separate these motivations from one another. Ideologues want one kind of writing; the public may be willing to buy very different things; and publishers need to figure out how to find the right balance, as they wend their way between articulating the kind of religion in which they believe, protecting their reputations, and making a buck. As onlookers, we cannot separate these motivations.

In the coming chapter, I would like to turn to Haredi works of history and biography and suggest another role that Haredi popular literature plays in creating a subjective sense of Haredi distinctiveness. Namely, Haredi works of history construct a historical narrative that explains to Haredi readers where they come from, how they got here, and how they should behave. For a devout religious group, social boundary-maintenance requires not only literary tools, but historical ones as well.

Chapter IV:
"There Was Only One Man in the *Shtetl*...": Haredi Judaism's Founding Myth

The past, as Edward Shils reminds us, is a plastic thing, something to be shaped and reshaped.[1] What happened may be less important than what stories we tell one another about what happened. Telling these stories is inevitably an act of construction. Individuals and communities pick and choose what to report, interpret and contextualize. They invent occurrences that never happened or suffer from "collective amnesia"[2] about ones that did. They weave that information into a story, a narrative. All groups and communities tell such stories about their pasts and their origins. These stories help create and reinforce group identity by teaching members what it means to be part of the group. They help the group define itself, organize its stance toward the world, and imagine its future, since a shared image of the past inevitably implies a shared vision of the present and the future.[3]

Haredim work particularly hard to define and distinguish themselves in the context of contemporary culture. They reject a great deal of what they see around them as spiritually damaging and dangerous. They isolate themselves from others and work to maintain allegiance to the religious traditions of the past. As a demographic and cognitive minority, they must do a great deal of work to explain to themselves who they are, where they came from, and why they insist on being so distinctive. Orthodox and Haredi historiographies have been, throughout the modern era, important elements in these devout Jews' attempts to negotiate their self-definition. With their conservative, tradition-bound culture, Haredi Jews find the past to be a matter of particular importance. By telling stories of their historical origins, these Jews can help explain their distinctiveness to themselves and to others, and can help transmit to listeners and readers the community's most deeply held values. In this chapter, I would like to examine the way in which contemporary American Haredi Jewry describes its roots in the Jewish immigration from Eastern Europe to the United States that began in the end of the nineteenth century and continued in various waves until after the Second World War. This Haredi Jewry perceives itself as a spiritual descendant of a certain segment of Eastern European Jewry, and its identity is bound up with the story of the transition of those Jews and their Judaism to the United States.

Haredi popular literature includes voluminous historical writings, some of the most important of which center on Eastern Europe, immigration, and the history of American Orthodoxy. As noted by several scholars, Orthodox historiography serves an important ideological and apologetic function in Orthodoxy's ongoing and complex attempt to navigate its way between those aspects of modernity it finds attractive and those of which it is frightened. Borrowing from and indebted to the methods, conclusions, and literary styles of modern academic historiography, but wary of many of its teachings and perceived biases, Orthodox Jews in the modern period write a "counter-history."[4] Or, in Haredi Judaism's own terms, "Every historian has to choose from the infinite number of historical facts... and our distinct approach is that we present those facts that the Torah tradition marks as significant."[5]

Modern "scientific" Jewish historiography developed, at least in part, as a response to the loss of the taken-for-granted collective memory which had helped ground pre-modern traditional Judaism.[6] Haredi Jews share this challenge of identity formation with their non-Haredi coreligionists, and Haredi historians help to construct the community's collective memory. These goals can lead to error, distortion, and falsification.[7] Still, to make sense of the roles that popular literature plays in constructing Haredi identity, scholars must look not only at what Orthodox historiography gets wrong, but also at the narrative that it struggles to construct.

The narrative of the "yeshiva world" of Eastern Europe and its destruction, the emptiness of early twentieth century American Judaism, and the renaissance of European-style Orthodoxy on American shores thanks to the yeoman efforts of a handful of immigrants, qualifies as one of the central "founding myths" of contemporary American Haredi Orthodoxy.[8] This myth describes the origins of the group in an idealized, even ahistorical,[9] past, grounding contemporary Haredi life in a romanticized picture of Eastern Europe and helping Haredi Judaism negotiate its complex and tension-filled relationship with the United States.

This historiography is only a part of a wider attempt by Haredi Jews to inculcate a sense of continuity with Eastern European Orthodoxy. American Hasidic men dress in clothing closely related to that of their Eastern European predecessors, and yeshiva students wear fedora hats, popular among European yeshiva students (and others) in the 1920s, together with American suits that match the latest fashion.[10] Haredim speak a "Yeshivish" jargon that combines the Yiddish of Eastern Europe with the English vernacular. Haredi higher educational institutions hearken back to Eastern European precedents for some aspects of their structure and identity, and some, like Beis Ya'akov, the Telz Yeshiva, or the Mir Yeshiva, are named for Eastern European institutions or towns.[11] Haredi culinary culture includes foods such as kugel, chulent, and herring, which echo the foods eaten by Eastern European Jews, even as they are updated to match contemporary taste. "Gedolim stories" [stories of great rabbis], which circulate in the Haredi community and which are related to the Haredi historiography, play a similar function. These practices and the popular historical literature reinforce one another, helping to develop a collective memory that is grounded in a particular image of Eastern Europe.[12]

I focus on three aspects of this historiography's description of the transition of Eastern European Jews and Judaism to the United States. 1) *Nostalgia* that involves envisioning the destroyed world of Eastern European Jewry as a model worthy of emulation, particularly in contrast to the proclaimed religious destructiveness of American culture. 2) *Inspiration* to be derived from the handful of overachieving immigrants who overcame the threats of American culture. 3) *Ambivalence* regarding a process of Americanization which this Orthodoxy underwent in its transition from Eastern Europe to the United States. Together, these themes tell a story that creates and reinforces Haredi symbolic boundaries and the community's sense of distinctiveness.

Nostalgia

Like many conservative groups that feel pressured and challenged by rapid and unpredictable change, particularly groups with immigrant roots, Haredim recall history nostalgically. Homogenizing the past and smoothing out its rough edges, nostalgia helps to construct a usable past by creating and then recalling images of a simpler, more perfect yesterday to contrast with and provide meaning for the challenges of today. Nostalgia idealizes the recalled time and place, ignoring its less pleasant aspects and suggesting identity with and longing for the good that the past is thought to represent. Fundamentally conservative in nature, nostalgia is implicitly pessimistic about the present, comparing it unfavorably to the past. Yet, nostalgia also hints at optimism, implying that the future could be improved should it be constructed in light of the perceived past. Furthermore, nostalgic memory can create social cohesion among those who share the connection to that perceived past and, by implication, share similar ideals.[13]

American Haredi historiography pays a great deal of attention to Eastern European Jewry. Indeed, Feldheim recently republished a biography of a nineteenth-century Hungarian rabbi entitled *The Light from the West*, suggesting that the center is located to the east, in Poland, Lithuania, and Russia.[14] Haredi Jews expend a great deal of energy on nostalgic reflection on aspects of the Eastern European Jewish past. The series of high-school text and workbooks entitled *The World that Was* is an extreme example of the trend. The series consists of several volumes that focus on "the world of the Orthodox Jew of Eastern Europe before World War II."[15] That a school produces a multi-volume series of textbooks focusing on a particular segment of late-modern Eastern European Jewry highlights the central role that that memory plays in contemporary Haredi self-understanding and how important the community considers it to transmit that image to the next generation.[16] In defining the scope of the project, the introduction focuses on the ideal character of the communities described in the book and the role that the study of those communities plays in constructing contemporary Haredi values and identity, particularly in an educational context. "European Jewry took on many forms which reflected several diverse approaches to the Torah way of life. Each [subgroup of European Jewry] represented a microcosm of pure Jewish values which combined to create a heritage and legacy unparalleled in Jewish history.... It is our moral obligation and spiritual legacy to preserve and transmit these memories."[17] The books present an Eastern European Jewry that lived up to the highest aspirations of the contemporary Haredi Jews who produced the book, and its authors hope to transmit those aspirations to the next generation.

The description of Eastern European Jewry in *The World that Was* and similar books focuses on two themes. First, the population of Jews who studied and taught in yeshivas (and to a lesser degree, their wives).[18]

Yeshivas were bastions of uninterrupted Torah study and character development. "In Europe, the groundwork for *Harbotzas Torah* (Torah dissemination) was there. The concept and ideal of studying *Torah 'Lishmoh,' Toras Hashem* [God's Torah] for its own sake, because of its inherent value as the word of Hashem, was ingrained in European Bnei Yeshiva [yeshiva students].... Love of Torah and a deep desire for true greatness in Torah were in the air and in the blood; they were the themes of mothers' lullabies."[19] Second, the piety and unique spiritual atmosphere of the *shtetl*.[20] "The residents [of the *shtetl*] were simple *Yiddin* [Jews], great *Yiddin*, living together, and most importantly learning together, using their lives to serve *Hashem*."[21] Eastern European Jews had little money, but even the simplest townsfolks possessed an honest piety and extraordinary level of observance. "The legacy of the Jews of Poland and Eastern Europe... [is] their spiritual heroism, their pure faith and trust in Hashem.... Many people in the small towns and villages felt that life without Torah was not really living.... In a Jewish town... Torah was the sole justification for life."[22]

A minority group that feels threatened is even less likely than others to want to publicize unflattering information about itself, and, accordingly, these works pay little attention to the less ideal aspects of yeshiva life. Staff and students did not always see eye to eye on matters of ideology, religion, and discipline. Choosing staff and replacing those who left, retired, or died could often become a source of serious dispute both within the yeshiva and outside it. In some cases, these tensions would erupt into open hostility and even violence.[23] In addition, the concentration of idealistic, intelligent, and committed young men in one place made yeshivas particularly susceptible to underground consumption of Haskalah literature and to a measure of ideological ferment. A young, sheltered, Orthodox boy might come to a yeshiva, only there to have his first in-depth meeting with non-Orthodox ideas.[24] Haredi historiography downplays these sides of yeshiva life, as they would call into question the idealized image of these institutions.

Furthermore, this literature describes the social and ideological makeup of the Eastern European Jewish population in a way that reinforces important Haredi ideas. First, these works present the overwhelming majority of the population not only as observant, but devout. The sporadically observant and skeptical Jews of Eastern European communities disappear. Second, Haredi historiography depicts

Eastern European Jews as either heroic or wicked, with little room for ambiguity or middle ground. Sharp boundaries separated the ideal Jews from their contemporaries, much as contemporary Haredi Orthodoxy struggles to maintain clear boundaries in the face of a modernity it deems threatening.

Haredi writing also downplays non-observant Jews and their ideologies, which had an increasing attraction to a great many Eastern European Jews into the twentieth century. According to one Haredi report, the interwar town of Mir [at the time, Poland, today, Belarus], famous for its yeshiva, included only observant Jews.

> There was only one man in the *shtetl* who was known to be *mechalel Shabbos* [violate the Sabbath] publicly. The city was filled with *bachurim* [students], *kollel* students and *rebbeim* [rabbi-teachers], all connected with the *yeshiva*. But others, too, had lives centered on Torah. The doctors, lawyers, grocers, shoemakers, and proprietors of any businesses were *frum* Jews. Most of them would work only half the day, enough to support their families, and devote the remainder of the day to learning Torah.[25]

This image of the town's residents matches an ideal of the contemporary American yeshiva world, but disregards the secularization that spread rapidly among Polish Jews during the interwar years. By the outbreak of World War Two, it seems likely that no more than half of Polish Jews were observant. (The number was probably higher in small towns, but lower among the young.)[26] At that time, the town of Mir housed an active group of secular-socialist Bundists, a secular Yiddishist school, a Hebrew-language Haskalah-oriented Tarbut school, and a socialist Zionist HaShomer HaTza'ir youth movement, as well as other secular Zionist groups.[27] Certainly the troubled economic situation and the fact that so many Jews lived from hand to mouth meant that only a small number of people were able to divide their time equally between work and study.[28]

When American Haredi historiography mentions *maskilim*, it generally vilifies them. "*Haskalah* was not successful in creating the new Jewish culture and people it desired, [but] it was quite successful in destroying the ancient values of Judaism."[29] Historically, Haskalah has never exerted significant influence on American Jewish culture and, hence, on the writers of Haredi histories. Nonetheless, one reads: "The Jewish community of Brisk maintained their Torah educational system, while the *maskilim* continued to plot against it at their meetings." In this story, the heroes emerged victorious. "Today we speak of Brisker Torah with awe, while the *maskilim* of Brisk have long been forgotten."[30] Yet, this claim disregards Alan Brill's observation that, "Every American Hasid or sectarian Orthodox Jew knows more secular studies than the Haskalah was originally asking to be taught (because he knows arithmetic, geography, and can functionally read the vernacular of the country)."[31]

When this historiography mentions non-Orthodox Jews, it often presents them as a foil for highlighting the greatness of the Orthodox rabbinic leadership. Equating Haskalah with assimilation, and implying that these lead directly to conversion, *The World that Was* declares that:

> The *Haskalah* (Enlightenment) movement came to War-saw.... Assimilationists assumed active roles in the leadership and cultural life of the city, with a notable number of wealthy Jews converting to Catholicism. Fortunately, Warsaw was blessed with an assemblage of great *Talmidei Chachomim* [pious scholars] and *Chasidic Rebbes* and their followers, whose spiritual strength and influence kept the Orthodox community strong and vibrant. These accomplished Orthodox *Rabbonim* [rabbis] managed to overcome the potential dangers of the *Haskalah*."[32]

Haredi popular historiography tends to ignore observant Jews, such as moderate *maskilim* or religious-Zionists, who do not fit into contemporary Haredi Jewry's neat categories of pious and wicked. Discussing individuals and groups from the past who could bridge the gap "between the yeshiva world and modern Orthodoxy" would blur the clear boundaries that contemporary Haredi Judaism struggles to construct.[33] A significant number of Eastern European rabbis advocated educational reform, increased acculturation, Zionism, or academic Jewish studies, and maintained at times cordial and at times polemical relations with other, less traditional *maskilim*. Eastern European rabbis such as Yehiel Mikhel Pines, Shmuel Mohliever, Ya'akov Barit, Yehiel Ya'akov Weinberg, or Yitzhak Ya'akov Reines have no place in the contemporary

Haredi discussion.[34] When the Haredi community canonizes a given rabbi as a hero, the biographies overlook or ignore his secular education or Zionist orientation. Thus, when a well-known Haredi school circulated a book entitled *My Uncle the Netziv* that indicated that R. Naftali Tzvi Yehuda Berlin (The Netziv, 1817-1893), the famous head of the Volozhin yeshiva, had acquired some general education and maintained cordial relations with a number of *maskilim*, the school quickly recalled the book and publicly apologized for presenting material that "does not correctly portray the *Netziv*, his *hashkofos* [worldviews], *kedusha* [holiness], and *yiras shamayim* [fear of heaven]."[35]

Rabbi Noson Kamenetsky's hefty 2002 collection of stories of great Eastern European rabbis, *The Making of a Godol*, suffered a similar fate. Kamenetsky's opponents attacked the book bitterly and eventually banned it, because they were upset by, among other things, the suggestion that these heroes acquired some general education and thought that such acquisition was a good idea.[36] The book, its opponents claimed, supported, "an admixture of other (secular) studies in the study of our holy Torah and its purity."[37] By presenting East European rabbis as more open to general education, Kamenetsky's book, according to critics, threatens to undermine the sharp boundaries between Haskalah and true Judaism.

Indeed, rhetoric about Haskalah became central in the debate over *The Making of a Godol*, with opponents accusing Kamenetsky of following in the path of the *maskilim* of the nineteenth century. Kamenetsky and his writings are as dangerous as those of the well-known *maskil* "*Yalag* [Yehudah Leib Gordon] in" the Eastern European Haskalah-oriented journals, "*haMelitz, haKarmel* and *haMaggid*."[38] The rhetoric points precisely, if unintentionally, to the different self-understandings of contemporary Haredim and the *maskilim* of the past. The *maskilim* of old, like Kamenetsky today, did not see themselves as destroyers of tradition, but as righting that tradition, saving it from obscurantists. They tried to ground their innovations in history and tradition, and hence wrote extensive historiography that supported their agenda. Critics see Kamenetsky's own attempt to deviate from the Haredi nostalgic historical image as a maskilic attempt to rewrite history for the sake of contemporary dangerous innovations. Just as *maskilim* were "really" dangerous destroyers of tradition, Kamenetsky is also such a danger. Just as the great rabbis of Eastern Europe supposedly rejected Haskalah completely, today's Haredi Jews must battle Kamenetsky and his maskilic-style historiography, which blurs boundaries.

Haredi historiography contrasts the idealized image of Eastern Europe with the image of America as spiritually destructive. Haredi Jewry paints American culture negatively, setting it up as an "other" against which to define itself. Haredi historiography grounds these perceived dangers of American culture in history. America destroyed the religious commitments of immigrants from Eastern Europe. "America in those days [the 1930s] was a 'spiritual desert.' Only a handful of yeshivos dotted its map and few American Jews had any contact with Torah ideas and personalities.... Not many Jews observed *mitzvos*."[39]

The image of American culture as destructive highlights, by contrast, the beauty of Eastern Europe and sets the groundwork for the claim that American Orthodoxy succeeded only because it imitated Eastern European Orthodoxy. This literature regularly juxtaposes the positive image of the *shtetl* with the negative image of America. "It was not long ago that many of our grandparents lived in a *shtetl*, protected by a double lock, that of the home and that of the community.... Your children [in contemporary America] will be exposed to more *tuma* (defilement) going to the corner to buy a soda than your grandfather did his whole life in the *shtetl*."[40] One book reflects on:

> the contrast between the *shtetel* and a city in America.... Various communal/social institutions... together with a strong family unit[41] helped preserve *Yiddishkeit* [Judaism] in the *shtetel*.... Not only that, but each community had a *rav* [rabbi] who was a *talmid chacham* who had profound influence on the community. The *Kehillah* [community] institutions and leadership of community rabbis were sorely lacking in America during that period. Leaving Europe was a great spiritual risk.... It was not uncommon for an immigrant arriving at these shores to be greeted with the following words: "young man... you must forget about your G-d and your religion."... Many immigrants succumbed to leaving G-d on the other side of the ocean.[42]

Another book dedicates three pages to summarizing and quoting

Ridvaz's (R. Ya'akov Dovid Wilowsky of Slutzk, Russia) early twentieth-century vitriolic attack on immigration to America: "Anyone immigrating to America is a sinner.... The very essence of this country precludes adherence to Torah."[43] A biography of a leading twentieth-century rabbi, Elchonon Wasserman, reports that the rabbi refused to help a student emigrate to America, even when that student was faced with being drafted into the Polish army.[44]

Haredi rhetoric maximizes the contrast between Eastern Europe and the United States by implying that the immigrants were deeply observant until they left Europe. "It was not only home that the Jews left behind in Europe.... It was their Torah, their Talmud, their *yeshivos* – in a word, their Yiddishkeit, their entire way of Jewish life."[45] Furthermore, this literature does not hide its evaluation of these historical trends. The decline in observance among immigrants is entirely negative and the fault of American culture. "The unprecedented openness of American society ensured that... the *yezer hara* [evil inclination] to accept its [American] mores and emulate its practices was increasingly strong, even among religious Jews."[46]

To be sure, academic historiography agrees that immigration correlated with decreased religious observance and sometimes intergenerational conflict. However, it frames and evaluates these trends by noting that secularization had already had vast influence on Eastern European Jews at the end of the nineteenth and the beginning of the twentieth centuries and that immigrants often came from the more secularized segments of the population. Further, academic historiography takes a less judgmental stance, viewing these trends more as inevitable responses to the forces of history, and less as lamentable religious catastrophes. For example, Jonathan Sarna, a leading historian of American Judaism, writes: "Anecdotes have been interpreted to show that the process of immigration itself loosed East European Jews from their religious moorings, or alternatively, that the immigrant stream included a disproportionate number of those who had abandoned their faith years earlier. Both propositions are likely correct."[47]

Haredi historiography cannot afford such detachment. Acknowledging widespread secularization among Eastern European Jews would undermine the idealization of that community and weaken the implication that American culture remains dangerous even today. The Haredi rhetoric emphasizes the need for vigilance in maintaining proper religious discipline despite the lure of America. Further, emphasizing the problems in America highlights the valor of this literature's heroes, immigrants who fought against American trends and sought to rebuild an Eastern-European-style Orthodoxy in America.

Inspiration

Like so much Haredi popular writing, Haredi historiography is inspirational literature. Biographies work to motivate readers to learn from and emulate the example of the heroes whose stories these works retell: Jews who immigrated from Eastern Europe and through untiring efforts, boundless dedication, and uncompromising loyalty to Torah rebuilt what the Nazis had destroyed. These history books implicitly exhort readers to be equally uncompromising in their own dedication to preserving Judaism, following the Eastern European example and distancing themselves from the American threat.

Indeed, the late R. Shimon Schwab, one of America's leading Haredi rabbis, argued explicitly that the inspirational message should trump historical truth.

> What ethical purpose is served by preserving a realistic historic picture? Nothing but the satisfaction of curiosity. We should tell ourselves and our children the good memories of the good people, their unshakeable faith, their staunch defense of tradition, their life of truth, their impeccable honesty, their boundless charity and their great reverence for Torah and Torah sages. What is gained by pointing out their inadequacies and their contradictions? We want to be inspired by their example and learn from their experience.[48]

Schwab knows that there are alternatives to inspirational history, but he has consciously chosen to privilege the inspirational version.[49]

Some books tell inspirational stories about great Jewish laypeople, such as a biography of Agudath Israel leader Mike Tress (1909-1967) or Hindy Krohn's memoirs, which recall just how difficult it was to maintain observance in the 1920s and 30s. Krohn's subtitle – *Touching Vignettes about Growing Up Jewish in the Philadelphia of Long Ago* – emphasizes the book's inspirational focus. The book recounts her childhood growing up in one of the few families in the region who kept Shabbat scrupulously and who struggled not to compromise their religious values in the face of seemingly overwhelming challenges raised by employers, public-school teachers, neighbors, and friends who made observance so difficult. Her heroes include her family and friends who managed to maintain observance despite these challenges.[50]

However, laypeople gain less attention in inspirational biographies than do the great rabbis, who overcame the impossible conditions to remake American Judaism.

> Unnoticed by the official leaders of the Jewish establishment in America and by the majority of America's Jews, a number of determined people set about to build a more intensive Jewish life in America. They were European-trained scholars who arrived on this continent before the Holocaust and were determined to dedicate their lives to the building of Torah institutions. Among them were Rabbi Moshe Feinstein, Rabbi Yaakov Yitzchak Ruderman, Rabbi Yaakov Kamenetsky, Rabbi Yitzchak Hutner, [and] the father of Jewish education in America, Reb Shraga Feivel Mendlowitz.... They were undaunted by the failure of their rabbinic predecessors and eschewed compromise or adjustment of Torah practices and values to American lifestyles. They represented the noblest tradition of Eastern European Jewry.... They were... inwardly impelled to accomplish the impossible in America.[51]

According to this narrative, Eastern European rabbis arrived in the United States to discover a spiritual wasteland, where the vast majority of immigrant Jews and their children were indifferent or hostile to "authentic" Judaism. Yet, pursuing the model of Eastern European piety and rejecting the Americanizing of the tradition, these immigrants built new institutions aimed both at protecting those American Jews who remained committed to Orthodoxy and attracting new ones. This narrative sends a clear inspirational message. Just as these immigrants sacrificed themselves for the sake of Orthodoxy's future, just as these immigrants refused to compromise their Eastern European values, just as these immigrants founded new institutions and attracted new follow-ers, contemporary Haredi readers must do the same.

Tens of biographies of both rabbinic and lay leaders – in several literary forms – retell this story. Book-length studies tell the stories of great immigrant rabbis like Moshe Feinstein, Aharon Kotler, and Ya'akov Kaminetzky.[52] ArtScroll's *Noble Lives, Noble Deeds* series or *The World That Was: America* prefer to collect shorter biographical essays on a larger group of figures. Agudath Israel plays a particularly active role in publishing inspirational biographies of Eastern European immigrants. It also released a coffee-table book entitled *Daring to Dream: Profiles in the Growth of the Torah Community*, which focuses on figures who had significant influence on the movement's growth in America. Agudath Israel's now defunct monthly, *The Jewish Observer*, regularly included short biographical essays on influential rabbis and laypeople. Many of these essays appeared in books bearing titles such as *The Torah Personality*, *Torah Leaders*, or *Torah Lives*. Many, though not all, of the figures de-scribed in these works came to the United States from Eastern Europe, and their biographies share a common theme: the story of religious success in America despite overwhelming odds.[53]

Moreover, in order to preserve the "success against the odds" nar-rative, Haredi biographies under-represent the largest immigration of Eastern European Jews to America, that of nearly two-and-a-half million Jews who came to the New World from Eastern Europe between 1881 and 1924, including hundreds of rabbis. Haredi biographers give these rabbis small attention. *The World that Was: America* includes biographies of forty-nine rabbis who immigrated from Eastern Europe to the United States (plus another seven biographies of American-born rabbis or im-migrants from other places), all credited with the "transmitting of the Torah legacy to America" in the years "1900-1945." Yet, only fourteen of them arrived in the United States prior to 1924.

The biographies of immigrant rabbis from the earlier period, the stories left untold, offer less inspirational material. A great number of these rabbis struggled in obscurity—scattered as they were through-out the United States—to influence an American Jewish immigrant population that was little interested in the rabbis' religious and halakhic concerns.[54] The life stories of rabbis with a somewhat higher profile of-ten reflect similar lack of influence. For example, Rabbi Jacob Joseph [1840-1902] was hired in 1888 as New York's "Chief Rabbi," in order to bring unity and consistency to the city's Orthodox community and to kashrut supervision. Hounded by constant conflict, endless politics, an uncooperative Jewish community, and an indifferent laity, Joseph ultimately succumbed to a stroke that left him powerless for the last five years of his life. Despite tens of thousands attending his funeral, the ultimate indignity ensued when an anti-Semitic riot disrupted the procession and left a number of Jews beaten and wounded. R. Joseph is mentioned in *The World that Was: America*, but the essay describing his life is by far the shortest of the book's biographies, and it ignores the riot at the funeral.[55]

Paying little heed to the ineffectiveness of these rabbis, Haredi historical literature prefers to celebrate those who created yeshiva day schools, Beis Ya'akov schools, advanced yeshivas, and Hasidic courts on the shores of the New World – the institutions that contemporary Haredim see (justifiably) as responsible for the resurgence of devout Orthodoxy in the second half of the twentieth century. These institutions developed and grew, for the most part, closer to mid-century, thanks to the efforts of many refugees from Europe. Emphasizing inspirational examples has been more important to Haredi historians than inclusivity. A biography of a heroic figure provides an excellent path to inspiration.

The desire for inspiration helps explain why most English-language Haredi historical writing takes the form of biography or personal memoir. Attempts at a synthetic historical account of longer periods are few and far between, the popular series authored by R. Berel Wein being the most important exception.[56] Feldheim's 2005 Chanukah catalog, for example, advertises some twenty-three titles on "history and biography." Only two attempt synthetic history, with the overwhelming majority offering either biographies or personal memoirs.[57] This pattern derives, at least in part, from the fact that those not trained as historians will likely find synthetic history harder to write than biography, particularly when dealing with individuals who lived within living memory. Publishers may also prefer these genres for financial reasons, since biographies, memoirs, and collected anecdotes are easier to read than synthetic history, which makes them more entertaining and more likely to sell.

Biography and memoir provide the reader a real hero to emulate. As one collection of short biographies puts it, "There is a lesson to be derived from the power of the *yachid*, individual. The people included in this volume were individuals who refused to accept negativity, did not succumb to apathy, and overcame challenges with resolution and fortitude."[58] Yet, by focusing on the power of the individual, Haredi literature ignores another aspect of the revival of American Orthodoxy that is central to academic discourse: the changing nature of America's religious culture.[59] During the 1950s, mainstream American culture celebrated the value of institutional religion. The 1960s witnessed an increased emphasis on distinctiveness, a development that made it more comfortable for devout religious groups to stand out. In later decades, the same forces that helped the evangelical and Fundamentalist Christian movements grow also propelled the Orthodox Jewish right. Ironically, in America's developing multicultural atmosphere, distinctiveness became increasingly normal. Freedom of religion and America's growing celebration of diversity bear much of the credit for the successes of Haredi Judaism, as do the benefits provided by the welfare state to yeshiva students and their families.

However, Haredi literature shies away from these aspects of the story. In part, this is because non-professional historians are less likely to see history in terms of long-term cultural trends. More to the point, such a story would diminish the importance of the individual heroes. It would imply a similarity between Haredi Judaism and other religious groups in America and depict American culture as inviting rather than threatening. Educationally and didactically, explaining Haredi Judaism's successes in social and cultural terms would prove counterproductive.

Other typical features of Haredi biographies reinforce the inspirational message. Haredi biographies spend less energy on contextualizing their hero within his contemporary historical and cultural environment. Instead, they recall inspiring anecdotes and inspirational stories about the hero. Moreover, they tend to rely heavily on interviews and steer away from archival materials and other similar documentation that scholarly history considers its bedrock. Haredi biographers tend to interview those who remained upstanding members of the Haredi or Orthodox camp, and who think highly of the book's hero. The interviewees view the past in light of their own current identity within Orthodoxy. Interviews with those who left or were never part of the Orthodox community, or with those who had less pleasant interactions with a book's heroes, might recall the past differently, in ways less compatible with the Haredi worldview presented by this literature.[60]

Devorah Rubin's book, *Daughters of Destiny*, recounts the early years of Polish Beis Ya'akov schools based on interviews with elderly graduates of that school system, all of whom remained observant and part of the "yeshiva world." Claims noted above about the entirely observant community of Mir, for example, derived from an interview with a daughter of a member of the Mir Yeshiva staff. Her recollections grew in the social milieu of a family whose life revolved around the yeshiva. It is hard to imagine that the setting did not skew her picture of the interwar Polish Jewish population in ways that dovetail nicely with contemporary Haredi nostalgia.

Haredi biographies retell anecdotes and stories meant to inspire readers to model their own lives on the spiritual legacy attributed to the subjects. "This book [of biographies] is not mere history; it is filled with timeless wisdom as opposed to information."[61] The stories tell of heroes who dedicated their lives to Torah study and Torah teaching; refused to compromise religious commitments; sacrificed time, money, health and personal well-being for the sake of teaching the truth; and relied unfailingly on the wisdom of great rabbis. A book about R. Aharon Kotler [1891-1962], for example, weaves biography, inspirational stories, short *divrei Torah* [homilies], student recollections, and excerpts from Kotler's writings. The book tries not to be "a biography in the conventional sense," but a "living biography," designed to express ideals about how one should live today. The book's "wealth of stories and anecdotes... combine to demonstrate how he lived as he taught.... We trust that the *glimpse* afforded here... into the Rosh Yeshiva's beautiful, inspiring inner-world... will give the readers a renewed appreciation of the Torah of Hashem." The book sometimes makes the moral of the story quite explicit. "You had to be like Reb Aharon [Kotler] and to say, 'I am ready to risk everything that I cherish for the sake of Emes [truth].'"[62]

These biographies generally present their heroes as flawless, or nearly so. The introduction to a collection of biographical sketches of great rabbis asks a rhetorical question, and provides an answer: "One may wonder how a mere mortal can succeed in so absorbing Torah thoughts and values to the point of forming a unified entity with the Torah. The answer to this can be found in the life story of every *gadol*."[63] Naturally, then, the biographies collected in the book lack criticism, descriptions of flaws, or analysis of errors in judgment. Indeed, even a Haredi critic who attacked "*gedolim* biographies" for being too formulaic and for "the stereotyping of their subjects," admits that the goal of these biographies is and should be inspiration derived from the extraordinary personalities of leading rabbis. "A *gadol* is the ultimate model against which his generation measures itself. Without living examples, we are not inspired to use our full potential."[64]

This presentation of virtually flawless heroes provides historical support for a central dogma of contemporary Haredi Judaism: the doctrine of *da'as Torah*. This doctrine declares that leading rabbis posses a supernatural means of understanding reality and developing policy, and are therefore the final arbiters of all personal, communal, and political questions. Indeed, R. Eliyahu E. Dessler's extensive discussion of *da'as Torah* – a cornerstone of contemporary Haredi discussion of the doctrine – appears specifically in a historiographical context, as a response to a student who suggests that the great rabbis of the pre-Holocaust generation may have "made a terrible mistake" in not encouraging emigration from Europe. Dessler responds that, "It is forbidden even to listen to words like these, let alone to say them,"[65] because the great rabbis of Eastern Europe were so much more intellectually and spiritually astute than today's Jews. Hence, contemporary Jews must not question their judgment.

The centrality of the inspirational image of nearly flawless rabbis underlies the fury – including bans and book burnings – that followed the publication and republication of Kamenetsky's *The Making of a Godol*. Though he focused almost exclusively on yeshivas and rabbis, Kamenetsky earned the wrath of much of the worldwide Haredi community by presenting his subjects as flawed humans with a range of ideological and religious positions, rather than as uniform and mythical heroes. The original letter pronouncing the ban claims that the work is "full of severe degradation, debasement, humiliation and defamation of some of our great, holy teachers, luminaries of Israel... whose great stature and the glory of whose honor and holiness are rooted in the heart of every G-d fearing Jew."[66] These Haredi gatekeepers reject biography not focused strictly on inspiration and on the greatness of heroic rabbis.

Ambivalence

Haredi literature regularly emphasizes the continuity between Eastern Europe and today's American Orthodoxy, no doubt due to the Haredi identification with Eastern European Jewry, the fear of non-Haredi American culture, and the inspirational narrative of immigrants who helped bring about the restoration of Orthodoxy. "'The world that is' [American Haredi Judaism] [is] as similar as possible to 'the world that was [Eastern European Jewry].'"[67] Some books present contemporary American Haredi life as a natural continuation of what is said to have existed in Eastern Europe. "The Torah that we enjoy in America is European Torah, rescued, transplanted, nurtured, and flourishing. But, in every sense of the word – it is European."[68] Similarly, the contemporary Haredi enclave in Brooklyn replicates "the majesty of Jewish life in pre-World War II Eastern Europe.... One need walk only a couple of blocks... behold the selection of *shtieblech* [small synagogues], of *botei midroshos* [study halls] and *mosdos* [institutions] of Torah learning... marvel at the myriads of children going to and from their *yeshivos*... note the visual smorgasbord of *chasidishe* attire... to be struck by a fleeting sense of being transported to another world. *Der alter heim* [the old home, i.e. Eastern Europe], alive and well in America!"[69]

When examining Haredi Orthodoxy's successes in America, Haredi history books highlight the problems with American culture, such as the proclaimed insipidness of existing Jewish life in America, the value of American Haredi separation from the Jewish establishment, and the overall superiority of Haredi Orthodoxy to other forms of American Judaism. Haredi historian R. Berel Wein describes an American Jewish community with skewed priorities and vapid Jewish commitments. The "agenda of Jewish public life" focused on support for "the State of Israel and the memorialization of the Holocaust," which together became "a substitute Judaism for a large number of Jews."[70] The United Jewish Appeal and Israel Bonds "valiantly raised enormous sums of money... [but] they also had a passively negative effect on the development of American Jewry" because they "ignored other Jewish issues in America, and Judaism now became synonymous not with a Jewish way of life or belief, but rather exclusively with support of the State of Israel. This short-sighted policy led to an acceleration of assimilation."[71] American Jews traded their faith and heritage for an opportunity to climb America's socio-economic ladder.

Under these circumstances, the heroic immigrant rabbis focused their energies on isolating Haredi Jewry from the existing Jewish establishment, particularly from the non-Orthodox denominations. Haredi historiography emphasizes a 1956 ban on Orthodox participation with non-Orthodox denominations – signed by eleven leading Orthodox rabbis – as a watershed event. "A new consciousness about the necessary autonomy of Orthodox Jewry exploded into the minds of thousands.... A new spirit of struggle against 'Torah counterfeiting' was awakened among Orthodox Jews."[72] This points to and reinforces the contrast between Haredi self-perception as authentic Judaism and the deviance of the non-Haredi movements. Indeed, Haredi historiography never tires of contrasting the Haredi leadership with that of the non-Haredi Jewish majority in the United States. Orthodoxy in the second half of the century was developing a "new-found self image" and was becoming "less tolerant" as "the fabric of [non-Orthodox] American Jewish life was fraying."[73]

Many of these works contrast the American Jewish leadership's supposedly inadequate commitment to saving Jews from the Holocaust to that of the Orthodox rabbis and organizations, which, these works claim, left no stone unturned in their diligence at rescue. "We must never lose sight of the vast gulf between the response of Orthodox Jews, raised on the imperative of *pikuach nefesh* [saving human life], to the news of the annihilation of their fellow Jews in Europe, to that of the secular Jewish leadership."[74] By emphasizing the continuity between American Haredi Judaism and its East European predecessors, and by highlighting the contrast between American Haredim and the existing American Jewish establishment, this historical narrative helps reinforce the Haredi sense of difference and superiority.

Still, contemporary Haredi Jewry remains deeply Americanized. Indeed, Haredi historiography makes its claims of continuity with Eastern Europe in the English language, a sure sign of linguistic acculturation. Haredi historical writing struggles to explain the tension between the proclaimed continuity with Eastern Europe and contemporary Haredi Americanization. In doing so, it reflects profound ambivalence about the process of Americanization which Haredi Jewry underwent. The English Haredi biography of R. Shraga Feivel Mendlowitz (1886-1948), an immigrant leader of Orthodox education in the United States, is a case in point, as it tries to explain a clash between what Haredi literature attributes to Eastern Europe and Mendlowitz's activities in Americanizing Jewish education. The book acknowledges Americanization, but articulates its profound ambivalence about that project.

Upon arrival in the United States in 1913, Mendlowitz dedicated himself to founding a network of Orthodox elementary schools, yeshiva high schools, summer camps, and advanced yeshivas that required or at least allowed secular studies and college attendance, all in order to enable Orthodox young people to find their way in American culture and its workplace. Yet, this seems to contradict a central theme running through Haredi descriptions of the past, namely the absolute refusal of Eastern European rabbis to allow secular studies in yeshivas. One of the perceived flaws in the recalled edition of *My Uncle the Netziv* was the book's acknowledgement that some small measure of general education was taught in the Volozhin yeshiva.[75] Similarly, one of the bans of Kamenetsky's *Making of a Godol* criticized the stories that depict Eastern European rabbis who were "blending external studies with the pure study of our Holy Torah."[76] Mendlowitz grew up in that Eastern European milieu, had studied in those great yeshivas before immigrating to the United States, and, according to the biography, viewed Eastern European rabbis as his authorities and guides. How could Mendlowitz deviate so dramatically from the authoritative Eastern European tradition? The biography makes this question more challenging by presenting Mendlowitz as one who "would not compromise on matters of principle and religion."[77] Mendlowitz rejected "the prevalent attitude" that one could "save" some of American Judaism "through a series of strategic retreats and compromises. Reb Shraga Feivel not only rejected such compromises on principle, he was sure that they would not work in practice."[78]

To be sure, the current state of research does not allow a conclusive explanation of why and with what enthusiasm Mendlowitz included general studies in American Jewish education.[79] Still, a comparison between two Orthodox biographies and their presentations of this issue will prove instructive. In 1969, prior to the growth of Haredi popular literature and before anti-America rhetoric became widespread in some Orthodox circles, Rabbi Dr. Leo Jung, a leading Modern Orthodox figure, edited a collection of inspirational biographies of great Jewish figures and included an essay on Mendlowitz. This biography celebrates Mendlowitz's Americanization of Torah education. Mendlowitz's Jewish day-school movement "would combine secular education with religious education, harmonize the best of our two great cultures, and create out of our youth proud American Jews aware of both their heritages."[80]

For the later Haredi biography, this celebratory approach accommodates too much Americanization and loses the desired continuity with

Eastern Europe. Instead, the more recent Haredi biography problema-tizes Mendlowitz's innovation, quoting (without citation) a contempo-rary Eastern European rabbi as saying that, "*Yeshivos* in America [which] combine *limudei kodesh* [sacred studies] with secular learning... [are] not in accordance with the tradition we have received from our ancestors."[81] Further, the book claims that Mendlowitz only acquiesced to secular ed-ucation after gaining the reluctant approval of other Eastern European rabbis.[82] Eastern European Jewish values remain the ideal point of ref-erence, the model to be emulated whenever possible. The biography also explains that Mendlowitz would have preferred not to include extensive secular education. He "had no European models to guide him... [and] was forced to provide a secular education equivalent to that provided in pub-lic high schools to have any hope of surviving."[83] However Americanized these new educational institutions were, the model from which they had deviated is that of Eastern Europe. Similarly, Mendlowitz permitted col-lege attendance because he "feared that if he told a *talmid* [student] that college was forbidden and he nevertheless went... that student would come to view himself as a rebel against Orthodoxy and no longer bound by its rules. Reb Shraga Feivel's approach to college was typical of his lifelong method of balancing the optimal with the possible."[84] Deviation from the no-college model represents an unfortunate, if unavoidable, detour from the proper Eastern European ideal.

In another place the biography goes further. It argues that despite its great deficiencies, one should not separate from American culture entirely. Eastern Europe may be a utopian past, but in the present one must suffer the American reality. The biography analyzes Mendlowitz's difficult relationship with an extremist group of students, known as "The *Malachim* [angels]," followers of the charismatic Rabbi Chaim Avraham Dov Ber Levine HaCohen. "The lure of American society was so powerful that they felt the need to cut themselves off from it in radical ways.... But their approach of ostentatious separation from all manifestations of American Jewish life was far from Reb Shraga Feivel's.... Their conduct was not the Jewish way."[85]

In one particularly creative passage, the rhetoric redirects the Ameri-canization by framing it largely as Europeanization.

> Reb Shraga Feivel self-consciously set out to create a
> new type of *bochur* in the melting pot of America, one

who would... draw from all that was best of the many
strands of European Jewish life. America... would produce a new Jew, combining within himself the best elements of Europe: the Lithuanian intellectual acuity, the
bren (warmth) of *Chasidus*, the organizational abilities
of German Jewry, and the appreciation of *hiddur mitzvah* (beautification of the mitzvah) of the Hungarians.
Above all, the American Jew would be characterized by
his *temimus* (sincerity), a trait that was much more a
part of American culture than of Europe.[86]

Haredi writers acknowledge that Haredi Jewry Americanized in the
transition from Eastern Europe, but the rhetoric reflects deep ambivalence at every step.

On the Functions of Collective Memory

The narrative told by these Haredi works of history follows a pattern that
Eviatar Zerubavel refers to as a "fall and rise narrative, in which a sharp
descent is suddenly reversed, thereby changing to a major ascent."[87] The
story begins with an ideal, an Eastern European Jewry painted in idyllic
and nostalgic colors. The ideal, the highpoint on the historical trajec-
tory, was suddenly shattered by two cataclysmic events, the transition
of Jews and Judaism from Eastern Europe to the United States and the
Holocaust, which resulted in the physical and spiritual destruction of
that ideal Judaism. Yet, out of these ashes, a handful of idealistic immigrants to the United States succeeded in recreating on American soil
a Judaism modeled after the Eastern European ideal. As inspirational
literature, this historiography points to heroes who live up to the values
that Haredi Jewry holds dear, implicitly and at times explicitly calling
on readers to live up to those values.

Haredi historiography is part of a wider attempt by Haredi culture to
construct the collective memory of group members. The story described
here plays several functions in building Haredi collective memory,
and thereby Haredi identity and commitment. First, shared collective
memory can unify and create solidarity within a coalescing social group
and maintain that solidarity within an existing group.[88] Haredi Jews can
come to see themselves as part of a larger group all of whose members
share origins in Eastern European Orthodoxy and share challenges on

the American scene.

Second, this kind of historiography and the memory it constructs serve to identify the significant "others" against which the group defines itself, and they contrast the historical roots of the in-group with the historical roots of various out-groups.[89] We are Haredim, this literature implies, because we are not the destructive *maskilim* of Europe, nor the indifferent, non-observant Jews of America, nor any of their ideological descendents. We are the followers of the great Eastern European rabbis.

Third, Haredi historiography works to combat, implicitly or explicitly, other historical narratives in circulation and it provides a normative memory in the face of other memories that might challenge the group's self-image. As Schwab suggests, Haredim should prefer inspirational stories, even if that requires stretching the truth. Similarly, if Modern Orthodox historiography celebrates the Americanization of the Jewish educational system, Haredi historiography teaches readers to lament it, or at least live with it uncomfortably.[90]

Fourth, Haredi collective memory combats the tendency to view personal experience or proclivities as sources of authority. Haredi Jewry, with its rejection of modern individualism, its ethic of submission, and its claim that authority rests in the Torah as interpreted by the community's rabbis and spiritual leaders, needs to motivate people to accept that authority upon themselves. Readers of Haredi historiography come to understand that they do not stand alone, but are responsible to and bound by the traditions and values of a historical community that can trace its history from the ideal conditions of Eastern Europe to the struggles of contemporary America.

Finally, Haredi historiography and collective memory can offer precedents from the past for solutions to today's dilemmas and problems. Once the Haredi reader has properly understood the past, he or she can and should use judgments about the past to determine current approaches. Attitudes, strategies, and decisions that worked in the past, or are read into the past, can and should guide contemporaries, and approaches that failed in the past should be jettisoned today.[91] Uncompromising Jewish heroes who remained steadfast in their commitment to tradition, for example, are contrasted with the proclaimed failures of Haskalah and acculturation. Rejectionism succeeded in the past; it will continue to do so today.

Yet, this suggestion that Haredi historiography offers models from the past for contemporary dilemmas also points to a seeming contradiction within Haredi ideology. On the one hand, Haredi ideology insists that the models from the past and the attitudes of the great rabbis should obligate Jews even today. To properly follow the guidance of the great rabbis of old, presumably one would want to know what happened in the past, what those great rabbis did, and why they did it. If good Jews always follow the dictates of the *gedolim*, never deviating, then Haredi historians should tell the story of the great rabbis as straightforwardly as possible. On the other hand, R. Schwab insists that Haredi writers present a sanitized, improved version of the past, and his approach holds significant sway. Haredi writers present the past, particularly that of Eastern Europe and its great rabbis, not as it was, but as it ought to have been.

Put more boldly (and critically), Haredi writers of history claim to know better than the great rabbis of the past how the latter should have behaved. Those great rabbis do not serve as models for the present. Instead, the present and its ideology serve as models for the great rabbis. Haredi historiography becomes a tale of what observant Jews, and especially great rabbis, did, but only provided that these actions accord with, or can be made to accord with, current Haredi doctrine. The historians do not try to understand the *gedolim*; they stand over the *gedolim*. Haredi ideology of fealty to the great rabbis works at cross purposes with the sanitized history of those rabbis.[92]

Chapter V:
"Knowledge of the Clearest and Most Objective Kind": Simple Faith and Haredi Popular Theology

Haredi Judaism makes truth claims, and those who make truth claims inevitably seek to defend and explain them. Haredi popular theological literature helps Haredi Jews explain to themselves and to others what they believe, why they believe it, and how that motivates their practice. I would like to focus here on those popular books most explicitly and directly centered on theological questions. Haredi popular literature includes volumes discussing proofs for the existence of God or the truth of Haredi beliefs, such as Shmuel Waldman's *Beyond a Reasonable Doubt*; elucidations of basic Jewish outlook, such as Shimon Hurwitz's *Being Jewish*; discussions of Jewish dogma, such as Yaakov Weinberg's *Fundamentals and Faith*; clarifications of the meaning of life and the nature of the human condition, such as Noah Weinberg's *What the Angel Taught You*; or explications of the ways in which understanding theological truth can lead to a fulfilled existence, such as Akiva Tatz's *Living Inspired*.[1]

Today, sociologists and anthropologists take it for granted that in broad terms a group's worldview and religious ideology will correspond with its social conditions.[2] Following that social-scientific truism, in this chapter I will argue that Haredi popular theology not only demonstrates and defines ideas about God and faith, but also actively works to construct the community's self-understanding as distinctive, different, and superior in the context of a larger society that appears as both threatening and attractive. These works offer symbolic boundaries between Haredim and others at an intellectual-epistemological level. In order to maximize the distinction between Haredim and others, Haredi authors present Haredi Judaism and its truth claims in the best possible light and general culture in the worst possible light. Haredi Judaism teaches truth, while others teach falsehood; Jewish dogmas are good, and other ideas are bad; Haredi Jewish ideas lead to happiness, and non-Haredi ideas cannot provide help. Hence, popular Haredi theological literature tends to downplay aspects of Jewish theology that do not contribute to a Haredi sense of difference.

Further, the theology constructs Haredi identity to be totalizing and complete. Given the ease with which Haredim can and do participate in and consume aspects of non-Haredi culture, this literature tries to reinforce the sense that one should be a Haredi Jew always and in everything, without dividing one's identity between a Haredi and any other identity. Haredi popular theology also struggles with Haredi status as a social and cognitive minority, which implicitly calls Haredi commitments into question by raising the problem: Why do so many others have commitments so much different from my own? Haredi popular theology presents a vision of Judaism that responds to the social tensions and ironies of the Haredi community, one that is designed to appeal to contemporary acculturated readers.

Simple Faith, Unconscious Theology, and Deliberate Theology

For some, the very notion of Haredi theology comes as a surprise. Much of Haredi Jewry prefers a fideistic "simple faith" attitude. As Binyamin Brown has argued, this attitude developed in the nineteenth century among Orthodox Jews in an environment perceived to be threatening. Intellectuals became associated not with the religious elite, as had been the case in the pre-modern period, but with a non-religious elite, with Haskalah, with secular universities, and with non-observant Jewish movements.[3] Questions about faith raise the possibility of arriving at wrong, if not heretical, answers. Indeed, Brown numbers "the ideal of simple faith and the rejection of theological research" as one of the central tenets of contemporary Haredi ideology.[4]

Yet, as Brown himself points out, Haredi Jews still do write theology, since no religious community can do without theology entirely. Religious Jews, in the course of their study and discussion, inevitably speak about God, commandment, and commitment. In doing so, they must stake out some theological territory, at least implicitly. Indeed, a stated preference for simple faith and fideism itself qualifies as a theological statement. Haredi reflection on truth and values appears not in the deliberate, dialectical, and argumentative style of philosophical debate, but in the form of "hashkafah," a loosely connected set of truths and doctrines which are less often argued for and more often integrated into the fabric of religious life. Notions such as emunat hakhamim [the trust one is to put in the wisdom of great rabbis] or *yeridat hadorot* [the inferiority of later Jews to their predecessors by virtue of being further from the revelation at Sinai], are central concepts in a Haredi worldview, but Haredi discussions of these topics quite often focus on what they imply about how to live, rather than on holding them up to systematic theological scrutiny. Put somewhat differently, much of Haredi theology is what Brown describes as "unconscious theology," ideas that appear *en passant* in works on other topics, such as biblical commentary, homilies, or sermons, contexts which offer a theological worldview without stating that they are doing so.[5]

Yet, Haredi popular literature includes many examples of "conscious theology" as well, works that explicitly and directly clarify theological matters. Haredi books attempting to prove the existence of God or the truth of other Jewish dogmas, works explaining Haredi beliefs to newcomers, and essays explaining the meaning of life or the nature of evil, all focus on classical theological questions, and they attempt, by their own standards, to treat these topics systematically and thoroughly.

Still, examples of Haredi conscious theology generally ignore the history of philosophy and theology. Indeed, as I shall show below, Haredi popular literature rejects in principle an ongoing engagement with the history of philosophy. For this reason, critics may not consider it "serious" theology. I have some sympathy for these concerns, but scholars of religion do themselves a disservice if they ignore ideas that have spread widely and which resonate with a community. An idea's popularity, irrespective of its rigor, requires scholars to take it seriously.[6]

Theology in the Haredi Literary Pecking Order

Haredi popular literature considers theology more serious than many other genres. Men write almost all Haredi popular "conscious theology," while women more often author the "less serious" genres, such as self-help, parenting guides, fiction, and cookbooks.[7] Yet the Haredi preference for simple faith also pushes works of explicit theology down on the scale of importance in Haredi literature, at least relative to the most valued subjects of study: Talmud and halakhah. Several indicators point in this direction. First, much Haredi theological literature is written ostensibly for outreach purposes, to describe to the nonobservant what Judaism believes and to demonstrate that Judaism is true.[8] Often, these works project an assumption that normative Haredi Jews should already know the basics of Jewish belief and should not need such proofs. As we have noted, outreach-oriented works may also have readership among the already observant, and authors may be aware of writing to insiders as well as outsiders. Still, these books send an implicit message that Haredim should ignore theology, and at least the men should spend their efforts on an ongoing engagement with the classic texts of Jewish learning – the Talmud and halakhah.

To some degree, Shmuel Waldman's *Beyond a Reasonable Doubt* is an exception that proves the rule. Waldman wrote the first edition of the book not for outreach, but for inreach. Ideally, yeshiva students should study Talmud and Jewish law almost exclusively, ignoring theology. Still, in large part due to the "outside world" which "presents challenges that no previous generation ever had," educators must now shore up their students' faith.[9] When yeshiva students ask questions and do not hear adequate answers, they come to think that no answers exist, when in fact proofs for the truths of Judaism are readily available and apparent. Waldman's theological book aimed at "internal" consumption does so only as a prophylactic against loss of faith, and not because theological study can compete with Talmud for pride of place. As if to emphasize this point, a few years after publication of the first edition of *Beyond a Reasonable Doubt*, a second "general readership edition" was published, addressing not wavering yeshiva students, but the currently non-observant.[10]

Theology appears lower on the hierarchy of valuable study in part because this literature presents the enterprise as uncomplicated and simple. One straightforward truth exists, one obvious answer.[11] "You don't have to search for the answers. *You already have them!*"[12] One does not need special training or an expert's vocabulary to get at the ambiguities and complexities of theological matters, as Maimonides would claim or a contemporary university department of philosophy might demand. Rather, one has to gather relatively accessible information and briefly think in a straight line to arrive at fairly obvious conclusions. One book focused on the proof of God by design is simply entitled *The Obvious Proof*.[13] "We are not afraid of questions because these questions have clear cut compelling answers."[14]

Theology, then, occupies a middle position, situated between the most valued subjects of Talmud or halakhah and the least valued subjects like fiction or parenting. In the rest of this chapter, I will focus on Haredi popular epistemology, examining this literature's treatment of truth and inquiry. I am not interested in the validity or invalidity of particular arguments that these works make for this or that dogma, or the strength of particular evidence that they assemble for belief.[15] Instead, I want to examine the form that the discussion takes and analyze how particular ways of talking about truth address the concerns of a community struggling to build boundaries. This theological discourse is part of broader Haredi attempts to create a totalizing community and to reinforce the community's porous boundaries. Toward the end of the chapter, comparisons to other kinds of Jewish religious discourses – medieval Jewish theology, Modern Orthodox theology, and the self-perception of *ba'alei teshuvah* [newly Orthodox] – will help highlight the particular rhetorical features of this popular theology.

Science and The Discourse of Proof

The conscious theological reflections in Haredi popular literature do not eliminate the preference for fideistic simple faith. "We must accept everything from Hashem with *emunah peshutah* [simple faith]," declares one writer, when faced with the radical evil of the Holocaust.[16] Waldman, in his book of proofs for the truths of Haredi Judaism, explains that he writes primarily for males, since "females seem to manage much better with *emunah peshutah* than males do," and are better off for it.[17] Simple faith can help protect Haredi commitment in an intellectual environment seen as threatening. But the contemporary environment provides two reasons to move beyond simple faith, both related to social mobility and the modern freedoms that make religious commitments voluntary. First, when individuals are free to abandon the religious commitments into which they are born, when a fear of defection becomes a prime concern to Haredi parents and educators, when technology allows for relatively easy access to information, then a religious community requires intellectual and theological tools to make faith intellectually compelling. That is, theology helps to keep the faithful in. Second, under modern conditions, Haredi writers want to convince the non-observant to join the community, and theology provides potentially coherent and convincing reasons to do so. Hence, Lawrence Kelemen authored his books *Permission to Believe* and *Permission to Receive* in order to encourage non-Haredi Jews to believe in core Haredi dogmas.

With this attempt to use popular theology to encourage commitment to Haredi Judaism, many works invest a great deal in a particular discourse about how one determines truth: one searches systematically and carefully for rational and objective proof of the truths of Judaism. Kelemen's *Permission to Believe* or Robinson's *The Obvious Proof* present arguments for belief in God, the most common one being the argument from design, according to which the complexity and interworking details of nature point to a designer. Kelemen's *Permission to Receive* and Dovid Gottlieb's *Living Up... to The Truth* include demonstrations that the Bible was revealed by God to the Jewish people at Sinai.[18] In particular, these books cite what Gottlieb refers to as the "Kuzari principle." This argument claims that it is impossible to fake or invent a mass revelation, because nobody would believe such a lie or deception. Hence, the Torah's self-description as mass revelation by God to the Jewish people must be accurate.[19]

These outreach works have several characteristics. First, they want to prove, or at least demonstrate, the truth of Haredi dogmas, and they want to do so rationally.[20] Second, they couch arguments in the language of science, or what authors take to be science, and they reject philosophical or speculative language. Third, they project tremendous self-confidence. These characteristics relate to the "strong" and totalizing identity and commitment that Haredi culture advocates.[21] People should be fully and unambiguously committed to something that can be demonstrated, be demonstrated scientifically, and is believed self-confidently.

According to much Haredi theology, "What we call *emunah* [faith] has nothing to do with the words 'faith' or 'belief.' Our commitment is based on *knowledge* of the clearest and most objective kind. We assert that the object of our 'faith' can be proved and known."[22] Since Judaism is true, all other religions are false, and therefore only Judaism can prove itself. "Other religions are founded on belief; ours is founded on knowledge."[23] Other authors more modestly ask, "Do we have all the answers? Of course not." This sentiment echoes an apology that appears regularly in works claiming to demonstrate the truth of Judaism: there are no "mathematically incontestable proof[s]," but "intelligent people" do not require such proofs, since the evidence overwhelmingly supports belief.[24] While this rhetoric might help comfort and draw in the skeptical and uncomfortable reader, the extent of the doubt often remains quite limited. "The Jews are a very smart people. We have enough answers to know that we are the ones with the truth."[25]

The books of proofs suggest that theology functions not so much to figure out what is true – we already know *what* Judaism tells us to believe – but instead to determine how one knows *that* it is true. One guide for educators makes this clear. Teaching *emunah* is about proving dogma, not about exploring its contours or meanings.[26] Another author does not ask whether Judaism is compatible with evolution; he already knows that it is not, and therefore asks, "Why don't we believe in the Theory of Evolution?"[27] Waldman's *Beyond a Reasonable Doubt* cites "solid... evidence for the Divine origin of the Torah,"[28] but it does not include a discussion of questions that occupied other Jewish thinkers through the ages: by what mechanisms does God communicate with humans? How does the person become worthy of receiving divine revelation, and how do those individuals experience prophecy? How can God's eternal revelation become fixed in language?[29] Waldman feels confident in the propriety of writing a book on theology for insiders because he does not question what Jewish beliefs are, but only proves them to be true. And he takes that to be a relatively easy task. "Most of those who read this book will become quite convinced of the truths of Judaism."[30]

The emphasis on rational proofs pushes this literature to invoke narratives of a personal and individual search for truth. That is, one achieves truth by carefully, systematically, and cautiously reviewing the alternative positions that one could adopt, eventually choosing the most rational and convincing alternative. Ezriel Tauber's *Choose Life!* tells the story of a fictional young man, David, and his search for meaning and truth, which he eventually finds in Jewish observance and belief.[31] Moshe Speiser offers visual support for this systematic consideration of alternatives. The illustration for his chapter on "The Logic of Belief" shows a marketplace. Christianity, atheism, and Buddhism all offer their wares for sale, as does Judaism. A young man, showing no signs of being observant, glances at the stalls, deciding what to buy. In a later illustration, the stalls selling the other religions have faded into the background, and the young man studies Torah at the Judaism stand.[32]

These writings work hard to present their proofs as systematic, thorough, and rational. Coopersmith, with no apparent sense of irony, compares the search for "evidence for God's existence and Torah Mi'Sinai [Torah from Sinai]" to diagnosing the problem with a malfunctioning car. If "the mechanic tells you that he can 'feel the needs' of your car by placing his hands on its hood while the engine is running," we would "dismiss his recommendation out of hand, because it is not based on solid facts." "Intuition" is not enough when people "consider life's most important questions." Many believe that "religion is the antithesis of science and reason," and, he claims, this is largely true for Christianity. But Judaism has always advocated "logical evidence" for its truth, rather than "'blind faith' or 'tradition' a la *Fiddler on the Roof*."[33]

Intuition does not provide adequate reason to accept Judaism because the evidence for the truths of Judaism must be objective, i.e. independent of the particular condition and location of the observer or questioner. Dovid Gottlieb's "Martian perspective" asks readers to imagine a "Martian visiting Earth." What, Gottlieb asks, would such an observer, unencumbered by the self-interest that might color a subjective observer of human life and history, say about whether a divine hand has guided Jewish history?[34] This notion of an objective outsider's perspective echoes what the philosopher Thomas Nagle calls the "view from nowhere," a completely objective stance that does not depend on being located in a particular existential or temporal location.[35]

Science has a reputation of being the pinnacle of that view-from-nowhere objectivity – a reputation in part earned on the basis of the wonders of modern technology – and so Haredi popular theology often expresses its demonstrations in the language of science and statistics. In this, Haredi popular literature picks up on an American tradition that goes back at least as far as the evangelical Moody Institute of Science, which produced scientifically grounded proofs of the existence of God for a mass audience as early as the 1940s.[36] We have already discussed Kelemen's attempts to present his parenting guide as scientific and to present himself as a scientific authority. This trend continues in his book of evidence for the existence of God, which includes an elaborate discussion of the structure of DNA as part of a proof of God by design and a lengthy discussion of the Big Bang theory as part of a cosmological proof. Kelemen's bibliography includes works entitled *Vertebrate History* and *The Biology of Dragonflies*. Quoting anti-Darwinian "scientists," Kelemen explains that "the probability that humans evolved" can be measured statistically, and that such odds are not good. At best, there is "a probability of 1 in $10^{39,950}$ for the [unguided, random] production of a bacterium"; how much less likely is the development of so complex an organism as the human! He arrives at this number with an elaborate equation. "Giving Y a value of $(10^{20})2,000=10^{40,000}$, the probability of a typical bacterium evolving once in one billion years $= 1 - (10^{40,000}/[1+10^{40,000}])(1.5x10^{53})=10^{39,950}$."[37] Statistics and scientific language support the image of self-confident and objective truth. Others go further, attempting to treat not only evolution in scientific language, but also history in statistical terms. Gottlieb calculates that the statistical likelihood of Jewish history playing out the way he claims that the Torah has predicted as "1/16,000."[38]

Both non-Haredim and Haredim consider science hegemonic, and science celebrates a largely uncontested role as "official definer of reality."[39] Hence, Haredi popular literature often prefers to discuss its religious beliefs on scientific grounds, or at least on grounds that can be plausibly presented to the reader in scientific language. Use of scientific language exemplifies the ways in which Haredi popular literature has absorbed and adopted ways of thinking that are popular in the general community. But this raises a significant problem, because the scientific community's own consensus often denies Haredi dogmas, such as young-earth creationism. Haredi authors (like their Christian counterparts) find themselves using scientific language to defend positions that the mainstream scientific community rejects. Haredi Judaism wants the prestige and authority of scientific discourse, but without accepting the conclusions that scientists themselves reach. Authors want science to be authoritative enough to offer demonstrations and proof, but to be questionable and flawed enough to be rejected. That is, despite Haredi popular literature's use of scientific language, Haredi ideology, in the words of one American yeshiva dean, "rejects the scientists' claims to being the sole guardians or decisors of truth," even regarding scientific matters.[40]

Evolution and young-earth creationism serve as the best examples, not only because of important debates between some devout Christians and the scientific community on these matters, but because both Haredi and Christian writers want to reject evolution and defend young-earth creationism not only on religious grounds but on scientific ones. As Peter Bowler explains, the debate between religious figures and scientists is "a minefield of rival value systems, all of which seek to justify themselves by discrediting the other's use of science."[41] Generally speaking, questions of evolution and the age of the universe occupy considerably less intellectual energy among Jewish apologists than among Fundamentalist Christians, perhaps because Christian concerns with millenarism and the end of the universe make the origin of the universe more central. Further, evolution could undermine not only the notion of God's control over the universe, with which Jews and Christians share a concern, but also Christian ideas of the fall of man from the Garden and his inherent sinfulness, which Jews and Christians do not share to the same extent.[42]

These differences aside, Haredi popular literature has a great deal invested in making evolution look foolish, as part of the attempts to present the Haredi position as clearly, obviously, and unambiguously correct and the non-Haredi position as valueless. For example, *Beyond a Reasonable Doubt* focuses not on rejecting evolution in a point-by-point manner, but on ridiculing it. "The theory has nothing to stand on." For tens of pages, the book quotes extensively from scientists who identify what evolution cannot explain and who express their own doubts about aspects of evolution. The onslaught of quotes, presenting evolution as self-undermining, has the rhetorical effect of making evolutionary science seem implausible and foolish even to its own advocates. Note also the sarcastic and biting tone of the anti-evolution polemic. Schools and natural-history museums present evolution in ways that qualify as "pure falsification based on wishful thinking" and which "weren't backed up with any evidence at all." Without evidence, evolutionary scientists are "getting very desperate" so they "made up a new far-fetched theory." Advocates of evolution are "desperate people indeed."[43]

After presenting evolution as preposterous, Haredi writers must attempt to explain why so many scientists – heirs to the very tradition of objective scientific rationality which Haredi rhetoric celebrates – *do* accept evolution. In the words of Haredi columnist Yonoson Rosenblum, "How can so many highly intelligent men... say so many patently false and stupid things?" Here, Haredi rejection of scientific theories adopts an ad hominem tone. Rosenblum explains, echoing the position of R. Eliyahu Dessler, that scientists get things wrong not due to problematic ideas but problematic character. "Scientists are no less subject to the influence of personal bias than those engaged in more mundane tasks." Following a pattern of citing respected non-Haredi voices that can be used to support Haredi belief, Rosenblum cites Thomas Kuhn's well-known claim that scientific paradigms change only with very great difficulty. Rosenblum explains that the Darwinist paradigm should be discarded, but biased scientists keep it alive due to ulterior motives, including "ideology" and "social and career incentives."[44] *The Obvious Proof* spends some thirty pages on the psychological theory of "cognitive dissonance" – according to which people will alter their firmly held and even well-grounded beliefs when those beliefs run afoul of their other intellectual, moral, or social commitments – to help "expose and examine the psychological mechanisms that trigger the irrational denial" of God's existence by scientists.[45] Others go further, suggesting that at least some scientists know that their arguments are faulty, but cruel scheming motivates them. Leading scientists "Steven Jay Gould... and Carl Sagan" share a "clear intention to mislead the 'ignorant public.'"[46]

The evidence against evolution and for God is so overwhelming that the scientific community must be made up of dishonest people, or at least people who ignore objectivity when dealing with certain sensitive issues. In this case, scientists not only produce bad science, but do so because of ideological biases and lack of objectivity, the very standards which Haredi rhetoric claims to share with the scientific establishment. The debate revolves as much around personality and character as the data and their interpretation. Irony, of course, abounds, since the suggestion that science, as actually practiced, might mislead those with preconceived notions, might also call into question Haredi books that use science to prove the truths of Haredi Judaism. If secular scientists can be led wrong by bias, how can Haredi apologists rely on science for their own demonstrations, and how can they be sure that their own reasoned arguments might not be similarly colored by self-interest? I have not seen any reflection on this question in Haredi popular theological literature.

Be that as it may, the suggestion that Haredi popular theology rejects the reliability of some scientific conclusions (even as this theology revels in a scientific-style language) may help shed light on the scandal that ensued upon the publication of Nosson Slifkin's books on the relationship between Torah and science. He was not the first in Orthodox literature, even in Haredi literature, to suggest that Judaism may be compatible with evolution and with an ancient universe. But Slifkin goes further. He accuses some Haredi works on Torah and science of using "faulty science," because they assume that "in debates between atheist scientists and religious thinkers, one must side fully with the latter," even when those religious thinkers do not understand science well.[47] Furthermore, while much Haredi reflection on evolution ridicules it, Slifkin spends much of his intellectual energy explaining it: defining terms, summarizing evolution's explanatory power, and describing the evidence that scientists bring for the theory.[48] Much Haredi popular literature either uses science to support pre-accepted beliefs or rejects science and scientists as dishonest; Slifkin uses science to rethink various accepted beliefs, suggesting that traditional rabbinic statements on matters of biology may be mistaken or incomplete.[49] The respect which he holds for science as an independent and valid source of knowledge, rather than as a tool for apologetics, earned him the ire of much of the rabbinical leadership, who condemned the books precisely because they "distort and forge the words of our Sages to make them compatible with the words of the scientists."[50] His books were banned, his original Haredi publisher dropped him, and he found himself increasingly unwelcome in at least some segments of the Haredi community.

Scientific Proof and the Rejection of Philosophy

Despite rejecting certain scientific conclusions, Haredi popular theology still celebrates the notion that scientific objectivity offers the royal road to truth. Emphasizing this scientific discourse allows Haredi popular theology to deemphasize a discourse revolving around philosophy. *Beyond a Reasonable Doubt*, for example, declares that its proofs mean that, "We Jews have no need to philosophize."[51] Haredi popular theology presents the philosophical enterprise as skeptical and relativist. "Certitude is eminently attainable," but not by using the tools of philosophy. "Philosophical debate actually poses for responsible behavior. It's a charade, a tragic one, as we continue to pretend that truth is too elusive to capture.... The philosopher is unsure, but Judaism says we can know."[52] "Mere philosophy," in contrast to science, provides but "a set of opinions."[53]

As a discipline, philosophy does not so much reach final conclusions as it considers possibilities and plays with the implications of ideas. As such, claim Haredi writers, philosophy fails as a guide to life. "2500 years of philosophical ethics has produced nothing conclusive on the question [of ethical values]. We are still floundering around much as we were before Plato and Aristotle started the current tradition. So, instead of arguing about the question philosophically, I am going to argue to you as people.... The method of searching for truth... [must be] the scientific method. It is the only method we have."[54] If modern science can claim, in broad terms, to have made real and convincing progress in understanding the world, the history of theological speculation, Jewish or otherwise, can make no such claim. Theologians still struggle with many of the same age-old questions of truth, revelation, God, evil, commandment, reward and punishment, etc.

That is to say, Haredi popular theology largely ignores the history of Jewish and general philosophy. It does so not necessarily because of ignorance, but because Haredi popular theology rejects in principle serious engagement with philosophy, which it perceives to be loose, speculative, and ill defined. "Philosophy," after all, "is riddled with disagreement."[55] A discourse using scientific language projects knowledge, truth, and finality, while a philosophical discourse suggests speculation, possibility, and temporality.

An Israeli author, translated into English and published by Feldheim, speaks more broadly of a distinction between science and humanities, insisting that Torah works harmoniously with good science but rejects the humanities. "When dealing with the humanities, we have no absolute standards.... Man can only conjecture, guess – and dream. And after conjecturing, guessing and dreaming, he cannot verify that he has indeed arrived at the truth. This human limitation necessitates divine revelation in the field of humanities.... Science, however, is different. We have been granted physical senses which enable us to test assumptions and theories in the light of reality."[56]

Of course, using scientific language to prove Haredi dogmas must encroach, at least implicitly, on philosophical territory, and cannot remain purely scientific. For example, a proof of God by design must move from the sphere of natural science to metaphysics. That is, it must claim that information about natural and physical beings or events can teach us something about non-physical beings or events. Philosophy has spent a great deal of energy questioning the legitimacy of such a move and, at least since Kant, has viewed it as decidedly problematic. Haredi authors take that step without stating that they are doing so. They take stands within philosophical conundrums without acknowledging that they do so, seemingly because they prefer a scientific discourse and are more interested in reaching final conclusions than exploring puzzles.

In fact, even when Haredi popular literature cannot treat theological matters in scientific language – when it discusses religious matters in theological and religious language – it avoids situating the discussion within the history of philosophy. Take the example of Kelemen's first argument for the existence of God, the "Moral Approach to God's Existence." Kelemen begins with the (plausible) claim that, "Many people believe in a universal ethics." He continues, asking why such universal moral principles are binding, or in his terms, "Who or what *made* murder wrong?"[57] He rejects the notion that abstract reason, society, or nature could account for universal moral principles, and draws the conclusion that only God can serve as a valid ground for universal morality. Hence, he claims, anybody who wants to maintain that there is a universal ethics must posit as well the existence of God.

Now, the history of philosophy has had much to say about the source of ethics and the role of God in grounding ethics. But an encounter with that tradition would require authors to address philosophically grounded opposition to the argument for God from morality, and it would require distinctions between different subcategories of arguments. For example, within the Western philosophical tradition, it is difficult to deal with the question of God's relationship to morality without addressing Kant's famous distinction between the *content* of ethics – which can be known rationally since, according to Kant, the categorical imperative is binding by definition – and the role of God as the guarantor of the eventual triumph of morality in creating human happiness. Furthermore, an encounter with the philosophical conversation about God as the grounds of ethics would inevitably raise another question that Haredi authors prefer to ignore: namely, why obey God?

Kelemen also does not contextualize his argument within the tradition of Jewish philosophy, since that might not only complicate, but even undermine his claim. The long tradition in Jewish thought – stated most clearly by R. Sa'adia Gaon when he develops the category of rational commandments, but at least implicit in many sources before and after him[58] – according to which human reason could arrive at many moral laws without divine command, would seem to negate the necessity of positing God as a ground for morality. The best arguments of Jewish philosophy, like those of general philosophy, usually "are unable to establish unequivocal conclusions."[59] While current Haredi theological discussions fit into the history of Jewish and general philosophy, Haredi writers do not acknowledge the context of their arguments in the history of philosophy, apparently because doing so would admit the complexity of matters which contemporary Haredi popular theology prefers to present as simple.

The Challenge of Being a Cognitive Minority

The discourse of rational proof and the rejection not only of evolution but of the scientists who defend it help Haredi popular literature respond to one of the key challenges that pluralistic America creates: if the truth of Haredi Judaism is so clear, why have so many others, both Jews and gentiles, drawn alternative conclusions? How can one maintain that only one's group possesses truth when that group is a cognitive minority? Indeed, Waldman opens *Beyond a Reasonable Doubt* by identifying what he takes to be "the most probable source of doubt": the fact that "there are major powerful 'competing' religions and [that] we are the minority."[60]

Haredi popular theology has developed several creative ways of addressing this question. To begin with, Haredi writers turn minority status into an epistemological advantage, since counter-culture members of a minority can question and challenge the taken-for-granted assumptions that have led the masses astray. The masses of non-Haredi people follow the herd because they are merely products of their environment. Moreover, since the truths of Haredi dogmas are, according to this rhetoric, clear, non-believers must have ulterior motives derived from emotion, intuition, socialization – the very opposite of the scientific rationality that this literature prefers. "The human mind can rationalize almost anything when it so desires. One of the most basic factors that influences our thinking is our desires.... This prevents [a person] from making objective observations."[61] More explicitly, "Someone who is happy with a non-religious lifestyle, and who feels threatened by the possibility of God's existence, will be unmoved" by arguments for the existence of God.[62]

This paints Haredi Jews as reasonable and wise, and others as irrational, at best, or stubborn hedonists who let their base desires think for them, at worst. In either case, this further bolsters the proclaimed separation between Judaism and other belief systems. We have already seen *The Obvious Proof*'s discussion of cognitive dissonance as an explanation of why otherwise intelligent atheists would deny God's existence. "Evidence for the notion of G-d's existence can upset people emotionally because people tend to perceive the evidence as being in direct conflict with their personal and emotional desires."[63] Another book suggests that, "The thought processes of most people revolve around their prejudices. By the time they have decided to tackle a particular problem with logic, they have already arrived at a foregone conclusion on the basis of pre-formed mental habits. These thought patterns have already predetermined their ultimate stance on the issue at hand and have provided them with the rationalization that will justify that conclusion."[64] Since committed atheists "rebel [against religion] for emotional reasons (not intellectual ones), they are not deterred by any demonstration that their position is irrational. Their desire to condemn religion or religious people closes their minds."[65] The rhetoric shifts the argument from the philosophical-scientific matters themselves to the personality of the individual, particularly the objectivity of the Haredi Jewish minority and the flawed personalities of non believers – reinforcing the perceived gap between Haredi Jews and others. Those who arrive at conclusions that are outside Haredi collective norms are not, like the proper Haredi Jew or *ba'al teshuvah*, serious about their intellectual quest, and they are not using an "objective" intellectual approach.

It is worth dwelling here briefly on an author who has less invested than his compatriots in supposedly rational proofs for the truths of Judaism, but who works to present the Haredi minority status as an epistemological advantage. Jeremy Kagan, a *ba'al teshuvah* who teaches in a Jerusalem program for English-speaking female *ba'alot teshuvah*, appreciates postmodern claims about the conditional nature of all knowledge. Attempts to understand the world are colored by "the historicity of experience," and "our vision of the world" is dependent on our subjective "experience of self." Knowledge is therefore "largely extrapolation." To put it differently, "Our understanding of the world is determined by our worldview, our ideology."[66]

On the surface, this would seem to undermine any kind of Orthodoxy, certainly one as grounded in absolute and objective metaphysical truth as this literature's vision of Jewish religion. After all, this subjectivist position would seem to relativize commitment to Torah as well. Kagan, therefore, works to set up Torah as beyond the subjectivity of experience. He does not so much argue for this, as simply state that Torah transcends subjectivity. Kagan borrows an idea expressed in Midrash Rabbah[67] and in Kabbalistic texts, that the Torah itself is a blueprint of creation, to back his claim that Torah qualifies as the only antidote to the inherent subjectivity of the human experience. "The Torah embodies a more essential level of reality than the world we experience.... Torah is not *a* vision of reality; it is determinant of reality."[68] For Kagan, then, even the postmodern discourse about the subjectivity of experience folds back into a claim that only Torah offers true objectivity.

This allows Kagan to relativize what he presents as the dominant secularist ideology of contemporary culture. Modern secularization stems not from increased rationality or knowledge, nor from human progress. Rather, secularization and the worldview that comes with it are socially constructed, and therefore transient phenomena. Modernity has not led mankind to more truth, but has given expression to the contingent historical condition of a decreasingly spiritual and increasingly hedonistic culture. "The decline in religiosity which has characterized the modern age... is not the result of increased intellectual powers, sharper analytical skills, freedom from prejudice, or greater perspective (indeed, careful observation might reveal a deterioration in these areas). Rather, it is an expression of the increasingly physical nature of our sense of self."[69]

This stance brings Kagan back to themes which he shares with other Haredi theological writers: namely, they present the counter-culture nature of Haredi commitments and the outreach focus of the theological discourse as signs of intellectual strength. Haredi "otherness," its minority and outsider status, serve as evidence for intellectual broadmindedness. The only ones who "truly take to heart the implications of" the apparent subjectivity of experience are "ones who have 'traveled' – that is, put themselves in the midst of a culture with radically different premises and tried to comprehend a foreign worldview."[70] More than anyone else, the *ba'al teshuvah* – who had inherited contemporary society's worldview, abandoned it as inadequate, searched for truth, and found it in Torah – can best transcend the subjectivity of opinions and interests. Similarly, according to Tatz, choosing a counter-culture life of Haredi Judaism proves that one is not merely following the crowd, but living as a unique and autonomous individual. The "totally secular person... is the really narrow individual. Such a person may tell you that he rejects religion because it is narrow and limited, that he is broadminded and follows wherever the truth may lead with no limits, but a little thought will show you the falsehood of his position."[71] This rhetoric attempts to undermine the stereotype of Haredi Orthodoxy as philosophically innocent, blindly trusting rabbinic leaders to teach it the truth. Instead, it presents Haredi Jewry as skeptical, questioning, and doubting. "God wants each and every one of us to investigate and ask ourselves: 'How do we know this is true?'"[72] Their counter-cultural, isolationist social condition indicates that Haredim think originally. "Most people are products of their society and their environment. Most people follow; they do not think things out for themselves. But that is not the Jewish way.... Judaism requires the courage to think powerfully about values and it requires the courage to reject values despite their acceptance by society at large."[73]

From this perspective, being a cognitive minority demonstrates one's intellectual clarity, sophistication, and independence. The religious person does not follow the intellectual path of least resistance. Instead, the Haredi status as a cognitive and behavioral minority serves as unspoken testimony to the integrity of its adherents. "Before embarking on a search for truth, you must first determine whether or not you are willing to accept the truth unconditionally. If not, you will see to it that your 'truth' will be based purely on your own comforts and opinions."[74]

Truth and Boundary Maintenance

Haredi emphasis on easily demonstrable proofs helps support Haredi symbolic boundaries, i.e. that sense of distinction and separateness that serves as a key building block of Haredi identity. Scientific proofs and incontrovertible evidence for the truths of Haredi Judaism set up all other ideas, religions, and conclusions as absolutely false. The Haredi community, which emphasizes halakhic authority, conformity in practice, and the individual's attachment to the community, prefers hard and final notions of truth. Conceptions of people acquiring religious commitment in more speculative, unsure, or fuzzy ways might lead to a more individualistic and fluid commitment. If truth is difficult to pin down, or if religious commitments legitimately and sensibly depend on the particular existential situation of the individual, then someone's religious commitments may change dramatically over time, as he or she re-explores and rethinks those commitments and as his or her existential condition changes. Furthermore, less sure notions of truth leave open the door for individualism and decreased conformity to collective norms.

Akiva Tatz's discussion of religious commitment reinforces the preference for firm and unwavering commitment. Writing to hesitant teens about their religious loyalty, he explains that teens legitimately search for their own individuality, but that making a commitment to religion is a once and final decision. "You cannot begin to achieve while you are still exploring." Hence, in the search for self-identity, "You must rapidly decide what is for you, and then get on with it and not look back."[75] A young person should make a once and final commitment to Haredi Judaism. It is easier to avoid rethinking one's commitments if those commitments are grounded in absolute surety and scientific proof.[76]

Proof and Relativism

The Haredi absorption with scientific and objective truth, the view from nowhere, contrasts with the perceived dangers of relativism and unbridled subjectivity which Haredi literature identifies as central negative values in a society where "there are no absolutes."[77] "According to Western ideology, there is no absolute purpose to life. Good and evil... are matters of personal taste."[78] A much publicized book – published not by a distinctively Haredi publishing house, but by the non-Haredi Jewish publisher, Schocken – presents a lengthy exchange of letters between Ammiel Hirsch, a Reform rabbi from New York, and Yosef Reinman, a Haredi rabbi from Lakewood, New Jersey. Reinman opens by suggesting: "Let us begin at the beginning. Let us talk about truth.... We believe without question that there is an absolute Truth, and that it is contained in our holy Torah." For Reinman, this position contrasts with the relativist, and therefore spineless, Reform position. "Do you really believe that there is no absolute truth? That there are many truths?... You have to take a stand.... Everyone cannot be right." By rejecting "absolute truth," Reinman's Reform interlocutor can only "blow hot and cold with the prevailing relativist winds of contemporary society."[79]

R. Yaakov Weinberg, an influential American *rosh yeshiva*, makes the rejection of relativism a central, indeed the central, tenet of Judaism. In a book on Maimonides' thirteen principles of faith, Weinberg asks how Maimonides knew which ideas qualify as fundamental principles of faith and which Jewish ideas are true but not principles. He explains that Maimonides categorized as principles those tenets without which Judaism degenerates into subjectivity and individualism. Without these principles, "a Torah with absolute values cannot exist.... Instead, a Torah with concepts relative to one's situation would exist.... If man is the arbiter, then there exists no good or bad, no right or wrong, only a situation of convenience."[80] Now, it seems likely that Maimonides set down his principles at least in part because he thought that they could motivate the masses to follow the Torah properly and precisely.[81] But Maimonides does not mention the threat of relativism, a more central threat in Weinberg's late-twentieth-century America than in Maimonides' twelftfth-century North Africa.

Weinberg's rejection of relativism links with a rejection of a changing or historically conditioned Torah and hints at a critique of non-Orthodox (and liberal Orthodox) visions of an evolving halakhah. "The Torah cannot be changed. In order for man to be able to serve God, it is necessary to know His Will in absolute, unchanging terms.... When the possibility of change exists, man's priorities and convenience dominate, making him a servant of himself rather than his Creator.... Fortunately, the authority of the Torah itself prevents man from tampering with it."[82] Weinberg links the proclaimed unchanging nature of halakhah with the claim that halakhah contains no ambiguity. "Since only a Torah that is absolute and not open to change can bind man... any ambiguity in the laws of the Torah would render it non-absolute and therefore non-binding."[83]

In light of the theology of unchanging and unambiguous halakhah, contemporary popular books of Jewish law downplay dispute and ambiguity, focusing instead on user-friendly codes that include primarily the binding bottom line. Hence, when Feldheim published an English-language version of R. Yehoshua Neuwirth's influential contemporary code on the laws of Shabbat, *Shemirath Shabbath*, they left out the Hebrew footnotes where Neuwirth deals with disputes, ambiguities, and opinions other than the ones he codifies.[84] R. Shimon Eider's two-volume codification of the laws of *niddah* does include extensive footnotes that deal with ambiguities and disputes, but they are written not in the accessible English of the code itself, but rather in a dense and compact rabbinic Hebrew that would be accessible only to scholars.[85]

Either, Or, and the Middle

Haredi rhetoric benefits from presenting the contrast between absolute truth and moral relativism in this kind of either/or form because that allows maximal contrast between Haredi Judaism and other commitments. Yet, as Chris Gowans points out, "Moral relativism has the unusual distinction – both within philosophy and outside it – of being attributed to others, almost always as a criticism, far more often than it is explicitly professed by anyone."[86] Contemporary culture is not populated by a mass of relativists who have abandoned any attempt to arrive at or abide by firm and binding intellectual or moral conviction. Many claim to know things with a fair measure of certainty, and they try to live up to deeply held values, religious or otherwise. Many work to educate, convince, or even coerce others to follow those convictions and values.

At a philosophical level, there are important middle positions between moral and epistemological absolutism, on the one hand, and relativism, on the other, some of which appear in traditional Jewish sources. Haredi popular literature does not mention them because acknowledging and discussing them would complicate what Haredi popular theology prefers to keep simple. Dovid Gottlieb makes clear that such nuances between absolutism and relativism do not concern him. Any position other than the single, absolute, unambiguous, and authoritative truth of what he claims to be Jewish belief is equally unacceptable. "I am not drawing fine distinctions between relativism, nihilism, subjectivism et cetera. Let's just lump it all together: there is no objective standard of right and wrong."[87]

Gottlieb's rhetoric allows him to maintain sharp distinctions between absolutism and relativism. Yet, note the way Haredi popular literature not only avoids contextualizing its discussions within general philosophy, but even within canonized Jewish philosophy, much of which undermines the absolute/relative dichotomy. One might, for example, distinguish both between different levels of certainty and between different areas of inquiry, claiming that in some areas of inquiry people may have a higher level of certainty than in others. Maimonides, for example, adopts both of these distinctions when he claims that the existence of God can be proven with certainty, but that creation in time cannot be proven in absolute terms and must be known more speculatively.[88]

One might also distinguish between different kinds of ethical norms, claiming that some are absolute, unchanging, and permanent, while others are relative to a given society or condition. R. Yosef Albo (fifteenth century) adopts this position explicitly when he distinguishes between *dat tiv'it*, natural law that governs basic unchanging universal morality, and *dat nimusit*, conventional law, which can legitimately differ from nation to nation or from time to time.[89] One might also distinguish between different periods of time, claiming for example that certain areas of knowledge are knowable today but were not knowable at a different time, or that certain norms are binding today but were not in the past. The sixteenth-century Maharal of Prague, for example, combines the notion that the Torah, in itself, is permanent and unchanging (absolute, in contemporary Haredi lexicon), with the thought that when and how those laws are known and binding is historically conditioned. The Torah's laws were not and could not be revealed at the beginning of creation, but only after the Jewish people were formed into a nation.[90] Similarly, over the course of the Middle Ages, Ashkenazic Jewry gradually adopted monogamy as the only acceptable normative Jewish marriage, modifying the ancient Jewish polygamy – indeed, as noted above, monogamy plays a central role in Haredi images of the supposedly timeless Jewish family.

There are other ways of constructing middle ground between absolutism and relativism. While this middle ground does not (to the best of my knowledge) appear prominently in traditional Jewish sources, at least not the ones canonized by contemporary Haredi culture, Haredi popular literature generally does not raise them as conceptual categories, even in order to reject them. One might, for example, defend a position of fallibilism: despite strong and seemingly compelling reasons for my own convictions, I am aware that those convictions may be flawed, that they might be subject to review, and that reasons to question them may arise at some later time.[91] One might argue for the incommensurability of religious truth claims, arguing that truth claims are accurate and true within the language and categories of a particular religious tradition, but they cannot be compared effectively with one another.[92]

Furthermore, we have seen Weinberg's claim that the integrity of the Jewish tradition depends on strict correspondence between halakhic norms and an unambiguous divine will, as well as the rejection of any ambiguity in the law. Yet some canonized Jewish sources suggest otherwise. There are numerous theories, explanations, and definitions of any halakhic principle, and these translate into an almost endless string of disputes and arguments about every area of Jewish law. As Nahmanides (thirteenth century) explains, "Every student of our Talmud knows that in the disputes of its commentators there are no decisive proofs nor, in the majority of cases, absolute refutations. In this science there are no demonstrative proofs."[93] According to Nahmanides, and contrary to Weinberg, the halakhic system contains significant ambiguity and uncertainty about God's command.

Moreover, other sources emphasize the human input into the unfolding of the law. Some sources suggest that halakhic argumentation depends upon a "correspondence" theory of truth – that a halakhic idea is true when it corresponds to the mind of God or to the natural reality.[94] But others disagree. Many rabbinic thinkers emphasize other notions of halakhic truth, in which the authority vested in the rabbis makes their determination authoritative, whether or not rabbinic opinions correspond to an objective opinion of God. As R. Aryeh Leib HaKohen Heller (18th-19th century), the author of the *Ketzot HaHoshen*, explains, "The Torah was not given to the ministering angels, but rather to man, who has a human intellect. In His great mercy and wisdom, God gave us the Torah in order to decide based on human wisdom, even if it is untrue in a supernal intellectual world.... The truth is what the sages agree to, with their human intellect."[95] As R. Moshe Feinstein, one of the twentieth century's leading halakhic decisors, says in the introduction to his *Iggerot Moshe*: "Whatever the sage determines after having properly studied and analyzed the law, according to the Talmud and codifiers, to the extent of his ability and with fear of God – if it seems to him that that is the decision of the law, it is the truth that should be taught, and he is obligated to teach, even if it is clear in heaven that that is not the correct interpretation."[96]

Differences between contemporary popular Haredi absolutist notions of truth and some canonized Jewish sources with more subtle approaches point to the way in which contemporary popular Haredi literature serves the rhetorical and social needs of contemporary Haredi discourse, particularly the Haredi desire to establish communal authority and boundaries. Exploring the middle ground between absolutism and relativism – either in general philosophical terms or within the Jewish tradition – would force this literature out of the conceptual either/or approach to truth and into an amorphous philosophical discourse. Placing more emphasis on the ambiguity and human input into halakhah would undermine the claim that Haredi Judaism has access to objective and absolute norms, meant to contrast with the subjectivism and relativism that Haredi rhetoric associates with the dominant

secular culture. The rhetoric of a clear distinction between Jewish absolutism and secular relativism helps establish clear lines of demarcation
between "us" and "them."

Homogenization, Totalization, and Purity

The desire for proof and objective truth dovetails with another theme in
Haredi popular theology: that there are no genuinely complex or unsolv-
able spiritual, moral, intellectual, or personal dilemmas. "For every life
problem or issue there is a right Torah solution."[97] "God has the confidence that if we use our minds, ask plenty of questions, and sincerely
seek out truthful answers, then His existence and all of His truths will
be abundantly apparent."[98]

Similarly, Haredi popular literature presents Jewish thought and philosophy as univocal, as reflecting broad agreement about all key issues.
"The sages of the Talmud, the Midrash, Rashi's contemporaries such as
Nachmanides, Ibn Ezra, Rabbeinu Bachya, later commentators such as
Abarbanel, Alshich, Ohr HaChaim, and relatively recent scholars such as
Malbim and Rabbi S.R. Hirsch" have "a consensus of the perspective of
the Scriptures that is shared by all the above and, consequently, shapes
the religious philosophies of the camp of Jews that I am terming as the
chareidim."[99] Presenting Jewish thought as univocal requires Haredi
popular literature to homogenize Jewish intellectual history into a
virtually seamless whole. A biography of R. Shraga Feivel Mendlowitz
describes his lectures in Jewish thought to his students. He would quote
from a broad variety of traditional sources, and his interpretations "demonstrated that the apparent differences [between different theologies]
are primarily ones of vocabulary and expression, not of substance."[100]

Reinforcing Haredi symbolic boundaries, this literature explains that
Torah is not only univocal, but unique and exclusive. Only Torah, and no
other system of ideas or values, no matter how well thought out, can lead
to individual or social happiness. Human reason and conscience provide
no guide, since, "If there is one thing to which the history of mankind
testifies, with the deepest eloquence and without any ambiguity, it is
that dependence on man's sensibilities is a totally ineffective guide for
human actions."[101] More polemically, "It is pathetic to see 'liberals' and
humanists attempting to solve the problems of mankind on an atheistic
basis."[102] Haredi authors often fold the notion of the Torah's uniqueness
and exclusivity into the therapeutic discourse of personal satisfaction.

"Only within the framework of the Torah can a Jew experience real happiness in life."[103] "A Torah framework provides the structure and stability for approaching life... in a meaningful and organized way. Instead of fearing each day's unpredictability and living in a constant vacuum of apprehension, we should... be surging ahead in personal growth.... Such an approach to life generates happiness."[104]

This sentence points to an irony within this popular literature. As noted, Haredi popular theology insists that individuals construct their commitments in purely rational ways, without concerns for emotions or individual self-interest. Furthermore, it argues that when people put self-interest in front of objectivity, this leads to falsehood. Yet, these claims seem inconsistent with the Haredi therapeutic claim that a search for the truth of Torah leads to meaning and happiness. If theological clarity comes as a response to the "anxiety and terror... [of] our generation;" if one searches for truth in response to dissatisfaction with a "modern society that offers no solutions;" and if interests, emotions, and desires destroy objectivity, then perhaps a Haredi Jew, or Haredi Jew in potential, may not be searching perfectly objectively. This tension points to a certain rhetorical goal of Haredi popular literature: presenting Haredi Judaism in the best possible light, one which offers scientifically demonstrable and objective truth, just as it offers happiness and satisfaction.

Be that as it may, in order to maintain sharp boundaries, Haredi popular literature also argues that one should be committed to Torah and to nothing else. Once one has Torah, one needs no other source of knowledge. "There is no question that Torah does not answer."[105] Nor does one need any other sources of guidance, since Torah regulates and perfects every area of human endeavor. "Judaism is a comprehensive scheme which covers all aspects of life; the individual and society, modes of behavior, personal relations, husband and wife, the tax system, ruler and ruled, professional integrity and business ethics, how to run a home, a community, a society, a state. In other words, it embodies the art of living in all its aspects."[106] Or, more concisely, "The Torah itself provides a complete set of values."[107]

As the exclusive arbiter of values, Judaism should take into account no other values, particularly not those drawn from general culture, lest Torah itself become contaminated by the pernicious and pervasive values of general society. Haredi dedication to pure Torah means that

Haredim are not "vulnerable... [to] allowing concepts (read: propoganda) from non-religious sources to influence one's positions on religious issues."[108] Certainly, Torah should not be mixed, merged, or compared to anything else, as it is in the discourse of *Torah UMadda* or *Torah 'Im Derekh Eretz*, in which Torah shares center stage with other values.[109] R. Yisroel Belsky (a Brooklyn *rosh yeshiva*), in his introduction to a work of basic Jewish thought for newcomers to Orthodoxy, explains that when the medieval Jewish philosophers such as Sa'adia Gaon, R. Yehudah Halevi, Maimonides, and R. Yosef Albo borrowed categories from non-Torah sources to explain Torah, they did not do so because they were attracted to those ideas or because they had been influenced to think in the historically conditioned categories of the day. Instead, they "chose to use their opponents' own weapons, such as Aristotelianism, to prove the falsity of their [opponents'] beliefs."[110] Jewish thought remains pure and unsullied by the intrusion of foreign ideas; echoes of non-Torah ideas appear for polemical purposes only.

Today, medieval Aristotelianism no longer poses a threat, but the corrupting influences of contemporary culture do. Kagan, for example, explains that contemporary culture "shuts out Torah" because it produces non-Jewish ways of looking at the world. Under contemporary circumstances, Jews might, tragically, "read the Torah through the eyes of that [gentile] world.... We must realize how permeated we are with... concepts that shut out any connection with true transcendence. We must struggle to understand the ideas of the Torah and not co-opt them to fit our set, limited vision of the world."[111] Another author suggests that the coalescence of Judaism with general culture could spell the destruction of the religion. "If one studies history, in particular Jewish History, one will quickly come to the conclusion that... this path of cultural compromise, of accommodation with the host civilization, is a path which has been tried many times in the past. In each case it has resulted in cultural failure, complete cultural disintegration."[112]

Tatz explains the purity of Torah in linguistic terms. Echoing the distinction between objectivity and relativism, he claims that all language is culturally constructed except for the absolute language of Torah. Words that do not appear in Biblical Hebrew are relative to a particular time, place, and cultural environment. Only Biblical Hebrew gets people in touch with a metaphysical idea-in-itself. "There is a fascinating class of worlds which exist in the language of the secular culture in which we live [but] which have no equivalent in Torah.... Many of these words represent central ideas within society, and yet they exist only outside of Torah.... They convey illusory ideas. They may exist in the imagination of people, they may describe and motivate human behavior and action, but they are essentially of human manufacture." Tatz lists a series of English terms that he believes fit into this category: "Romance, Etiquette, Chivalry, Adventure, and Entertainment."[113] His emphasis on the linguistic purity of Torah captures the paradox of Haredi popular literature. He demands a linguistically pure Torah, one expressed in the idiom of Biblical Hebrew, but he makes that demand in English. Proclamations of uniqueness and distinctiveness stand in tension with a reality of acculturation and similarity.

Intellectual Autonomy and Intellectual Submission

This popular literature's emphasis on a questioning and skeptical attitude that leads to rationalistic proof of the truth of Haredi Judaism seems to work at cross-purposes with another significant aspect of Haredi ideology: intellectual and religious submission, particularly to the superior knowledge and insight of great rabbis. Even after declaring that Judaism demands that each individual think for him or herself, Tatz realizes the limits he must place on the individual's intellectual autonomy and on the independence that he had made so central in other parts of his book. "Self-awareness," he says, "is not enough. No-one can be entirely objective about the self, and therefore you need a guide. The Torah is clear on this: you need a Rebbe [rabbi and teacher]; someone who is greater than you, more objective about life and the world... someone who is ready and able to tell you the truth about yourself."[114] Precisely because self-interest can undermine rationality, precisely because of the importance of objectivity, one must not trust one's own thinking, but rather that of those who are wiser and more objective than oneself, namely the great rabbis. This rhetoric links the desire for objective rationality with submission, since only the great minds are objective and knowledgeable.

Yet others go much further, denigrating the mind and the intellect in principle and rejecting the foundation upon which Haredi rationalistic epistemological discourse seems to rest. Judaism demands submission not because great rabbis are more rational, but because rationality itself is suspect and inadequate. Torah study, for example, requires intellect, but the human intellect cannot truly provide truth and understanding. A proper student of Torah "recognizes the inadequacy of his own intellectual powers and the futility of his efforts, and comes to acknowledge that whatever glimmerings of truth he does perceive are accorded him by Divine Grace alone."[115] Another author indicates that, "If you trust your senses more than your rebbe, then it's a problem."[116] Another source directly combats the suggestion that reason can demonstrate the truths of Judaism. "*Emunah* is not a matter of logic." Hence, a good Jew should have "complete acceptance of the later and present day Torah authorities."[117]

R. Eliyahu Dessler rejects, if not the technology which science has provided, at the very least the reliance on science and reason as sources of wisdom. "The amazing achievements of science have turned it into an idolatry of our age.... Science... soon turns into a curse."[118] After arguing that our motives and desires can easily lead our minds astray, Dessler asks rhetorically, "How can we ever rely on our intellect to give us true conclusions in any matter? There is no alternative. We must admit that the intellect is powerless to produce reliable results in any moral problem."[119] Only the Torah scholar can reach truth, albeit not intellectually. A Torah scholar can transform his personality to the point that he "has imbibed the Torah at such a depth that he arrives at the truth intuitively." The individual Haredi Jew is to rely on "the great Torah-giants of our times," whose "amazing clear-sightedness" leads them to "possess a clarity and truth that border on the miraculous." Hence, an individual should realize that, "My seeing is null and void and utterly valueless compared with the clarity of their [the great rabbis'] intellect and the divine aid they receive." This awareness leads one, in the words of one of Dessler's students, to "submit... in all matters to the moral judgment and outlook, to the clarity of vision of our Sages."[120]

Indeed, in the height of the Slifkin controversy, at least one spokesperson for the anti-Slifkin camp attacked science itself as a tool of understanding.

> There's a tremendous *emunah* that these people have for scientists in the outside world – everything they say is *kodesh kadoshim* [holy of holies]!... These same scientists who tell you with such clarity what happened sixty-five million years ago – ask them what the weather will be

> like in New York in two weeks' time! "Possibly, probably,
> it could be, maybe.".... They don't know. They know every-
> thing that happened 65 million years ago, but from their
> *madda* [science], and their *wissenschaft* [worldview], we
> have to be *mispoel* [amazed]?!¹²¹

Some Haredi theological works argue, as we have seen, that each individual ought to embark on a personal search for truth, one in which he
or she will use science as a background for faith. Yet, other authors reject
the notion that an individual can or should search for truth "objectively"
or that science and reason can provide reliable knowledge. Is this merely
a dispute between different voices within the American Haredi community? Is it only a reflection of the love-hate relationship with science that
characterizes many fundamentalist religious groups?¹²² Fundamentalist
minorities desire the self-confidence that they can earn when hegemonic science supports their values. But they also refuse to acknowledge
sources of knowledge other than their sacred scriptures and traditions.
In the end, contradiction remains.

These suggestions ring true, but I suspect that there is more to it
than that. Context is critical. Outreach-oriented works differ from
works written for the already committed. Kelemen's *Permission to Believe* and *Permission to Receive*, Waldman's *Beyond a Reasonable Doubt*,
Tauber's *Choose Life*, and a *Kiruv* [outreach] *Primer* – all works focused
on bringing outsiders into the fold or strengthening the faith of wavering insiders – emphasize the individual's free and objective search for
truth. They focus on the validity and importance of what these books
perceive as scientific rationality. In contrast, writings such as *The Jewish
Observer*, R. Dessler's *Strive for Truth*, or polemics about the impropriety
of reading certain banned books – various writings created ostensibly
for the enrichment of the religious life of the already committed – put
more emphasis on intellectual submission. A potential recruit into the
Haredi community is praised for his intellectual honesty, his willingness
to buck the trend of contemporary secular culture, and his ability to
adopt a personal rationality. A yeshiva student who insists on his unbridled right to search for truth with rationalistic tools might not be
treated with the same respect.¹²³

One educator highlights the ways in which Haredi society discourages insiders from asking theological questions. A Haredi educator,

Dovid Sapirman, published a short pamphlet through the Haredi educational organization, Torah Umesorah, in which he decries an extant educational policy that views theological questions from Haredi schoolchildren as a threat. "A [Haredi] youngster who is astute will have long sensed that these issues [questions of faith and theology] are not up for discussion. Should he make the mistake of asking" his questions about the truths of Judaism, he will "soon realize that asking such questions is a 'no-no.' At the very least, his question will be rebuffed. 'A *ben Torah* doesn't ask such questions!' There is a good chance that from now on he will be treated as a rebel." Sapirman rejects such an educational strategy, precisely because – echoing themes examined above – educators should find it easy to prove and demonstrate the truths of Haredi dogmas. "The answers to the basic questions that students ask are so compelling, that I cannot envision anyone's faith becoming weakened from hearing the discussion."[124] This polemic against the attitude of discouraging theological questions highlights the existence of such an attitude.

In his guide to doing outreach to the non-observant, Yitzchak Coopersmith makes explicit a similar distinction between insiders and outsiders. After arguing that Judaism, unlike what he takes to be Christianity, is not "anti-intellect and anti-science," he responds to those who claim that teaching scientific "evidence for God's existence" undermines genuine piety since such evidence "reduces the reality of God's existence to a logical theorem and trivializes Judaism." He explains that this is only "true for an observant Jew.... Limiting an awareness of Hashem to 'scientific reasoning' deprives him of a much greater religious experience. However, a Jew who does not believe in God must first be convinced of His existence.... In his case, intellectual evidence is necessary."[125]

By Way of Comparison: Haredi Popular Theology in Context
Comparisons to related but different theological discourses can help highlight the particular characteristics of popular Haredi theology. Identifying how Jews in other contexts construct their faith commitments and theology can throw into relief the contours of contemporary Haredi popular writing, thereby highlighting the particular rhetorical and social functions of popular literature. In the coming section, I will focus on three such comparisons: 1) Haredi popular rationalism differs dramatically from the parallel discourse of medieval Jewish philosophy, even its rationalistic elements. 2) Haredi popular literature differs dra-

matically from Modern Orthodox discussions of the sources of faith. 3) Haredi popular theology's discussion of how outsiders acquire faith differs significantly from the ways that *ba'alei teshuvah* describe their own paths to Orthodoxy.

Haredi popular theology, with its scientifically grounded demonstrations of Jewish dogma, differs from its predecessors in the medieval rationalist Jewish tradition, even as it echoes some of that tradition. Both contemporary Haredi and medieval Jewish theology borrow the scientific idiom of the day to demonstrate the existence of God, and they imagine truth as the outcome of an objective attempt to evaluate the evidence, devoid of subjective elements. Further, both agree that theology could be dangerous, and they discourage at least some already committed observant Jews from studying theology.

Yet, differences between the two remain, differences that at least in part stem from the high-brow, overtly elitist approach of medieval Jewish philosophers, as opposed to the popular writings of contemporary Haredi apologists. To begin with, the medievals conversed with and often authored the hegemonic science and philosophy of the day. Contemporary Haredi apologists, in contrast, largely ignore modern philosophy and borrow much of their science from the fringe of the scientific community, such as Christian anti-Darwinists. Furthermore, the medievals, such as Sa'adia Gaon, couched their proofs for God's existence within a larger epistemological discourse about the nature of doubt, the sources of accurate knowledge, and the challenges and difficulties involved in determining truth. For Sa'adia – and here, broadly speaking, he represents the rationalist medieval Jewish philosophical consensus – reason can lead to the truth of God, but only with great difficulty, lifelong effort, and the danger of error waiting at every step. "The very fact of being created entities necessitates their entertaining uncertainties and illusions."[126] It is difficult for "the seeker of intellectual knowledge [to become] acquainted with the methods of evidence," and it is easy to make mistakes, such that a person "declares a valid proof to be no proof and conversely, he declares what is no proof to be a valid proof." Indeed, according to Sa'adia, God revealed the truth to human beings in the Torah in the form of ready conclusions precisely because attempts to arrive at truth rationally can so easily lead to error.[127] In contrast, contemporary Haredi popular theology postulates that one can easily find truth using reason. Scientific and rational evidence points in a straight and relatively easy manner to the truths of Judaism, and one who does not see that must be blinded by ulterior motives. For the medieval Jewish thinkers, there are a range of reasons why someone, even someone genuine and honest, might not reach correct conclusions.

Moreover, contemporary Haredi presentation of theology as lower on the hierarchy of study than Talmud inverts the attitude of many medieval Jewish philosophers. Sa'adia Gaon, Bahya ibn Paquda, and Maimonides, for example, viewed the rational pursuit of religious truth as a central religious duty, even the pinnacle of Torah study. Bahya ibn Paquda explains that "the science of Metaphysics" is "the supreme wisdom.... It is our duty to seek out this wisdom, in order that we may understand our religion."[128] According to Maimonides, the study of halakhah takes axiological second place to the study of theology (though less experienced and knowledgeable students might need to spend more of their time on halakhah until they develop intellectually).[129] Furthermore, where Haredi popular authors view theology as a prophylactic against loss of faith or as a way of creating faith among the religiously ignorant, Maimonides views it as simultaneously the most important field of study and as potentially dangerous to one's faith. Only the already pious, committed, and knowledgeable should study philosophy, since the ignorant cannot understand it and might be led astray. Contemporary Haredi literature focuses its theological discussion on the ignorant, since such study is not nearly as important as the study of halakhah and Talmud. Haredi popular theology portrays itself as the authentic presentation of the Jewish theological tradition. In fact, it differs in its commitments and presentations from some of its most important predecessors in that tradition.

Haredi Popular Theology and Modern Orthodox Theology

Despite the many similarities in worldview between Haredi Judaism and Modern Orthodoxy, their differing relations with contemporary culture and their different social structures can help explain some of the differences between their respective theological discourses. Modern Orthodoxy, a community that has less invested in boundaries and which sees its boundaries as more fuzzy, presents a very different conception of the sources of religious faith.

Unlike Haredi popular theology, Modern Orthodox theology openly responds to developments in philosophy; thrives on the inherent ambiguity of theology, and hence the difficulty in answering theological questions; openly acknowledges drawing on contemporary values, albeit selectively; admits honesty in the commitments of non-Orthodox Jews; for the most part is not articulated in popular literature; and does not have a primarily inspirational focus.[130] With that, I will focus here on two issues that will help highlight the role of boundaries in Haredi discourse, and the relative lack of importance of those boundaries in the Modern Orthodox parallel. First, Modern Orthodox theology grounds faith in personal experience and intuition, as opposed to scientific reason. Second, Modern Orthodox theology presents disputes in the Jewish theological tradition rather than homogenizing Jewish thought.

Modern Orthodox theology often denies the notion that reason can demonstrate the truths of Judaism. Yeshiva University's David Shatz describes as being on "shaky turf" the notion that people should "filter out the results of upbringing and engage in purely rational reflection on what to believe." Shatz goes further, explaining that despite, or perhaps because of, his training as a philosopher, his "commitment is not rooted in the (naïve) notion that reason vindicates my beliefs."[131]

Modern Orthodox theologians often explain that their religious commitments depend on personal and subjective religious experiences, on intuition, and on the influence of charismatic teachers. For example, R. Aharon Lichtenstein, perhaps the living individual with the most influence on American Modern Orthodox thought, explains that, "The greatest source of faith has been the God Himself. Nothing has been more authentic than the encounter with Our Father." He admits that he cannot easily transmit or communicate this encounter to those who have not experienced it, certainly not by rational proof or demonstration. Shalom Carmy, a leading Modern Orthodox theologian, goes further, responding to a student whose rationalism has led him to skepticism. Carmy does not respond, as the Haredi popular theology might, that rationalism should not lead to skepticism but to a clear awareness of the truth of Judaism. Instead, he explains that rationalism limits people's religious knowing, and on its own it can lead to the conclusion that Judaism is untrue. "Healthy people proceed not by reasoning everything out from scratch or by waiting for undisputed empirical data to accumulate." Instead, they bring all of their personal experiences, intuitions, and spiritual sensitivities to bear on questions of faith. Both Carmy and Lichtenstein admit that their approaches depend on the personal and subjective experiences of the individual, thereby precluding any attempt to demonstrate or prove the truths of Judaism. Experience as a source of faith will "provide little guidance for those to whom attaining [an] encounter [with God] is precisely the problem."[132]

Modern Orthodox theology also has less invested in homogenizing Jewish thought, in seeing all Jewish theologians over the centuries as agreeing with one another. Instead, it plays up the debates between different approaches and the difficulties in clarifying Jewish ideas. Take the example of Norman Lamm's influential book, *Torah UMadda*, which suggests models for the integration of general education into Torah study. Lamm – past president of Yeshiva University and a leading Modern Orthodox intellectual – not only advocates for such a study, against the Haredi consensus, but more importantly acknowledges that not all of the tradition agrees with his position. He sets up numerous alternative models for *Torah UMadda* from within the tradition, focusing on "the variety of responses… and differing orientations" that believing Jews bring to the question.[133] It may not be easy to figure out whether the tradition advocates the integration of general knowledge, since the "intersections of Torah and Wisdom are not always clear; indeed, they are more often than not elusive and indeterminate."[134]

Differences between Modern Orthodox and Haredi popular theology reflect different conceptions of community and its boundaries. The Modern Orthodox project a faith dependent on subjective personal experience, which makes it difficult to imagine clear lines between "our" truth and "their" falsehood. Intellectual boundaries remain more open and blurry. If Jewish ideas are subject to dispute, and if it is difficult to clarify what the tradition requires or allows on any given question, then non-belief becomes more understandable and the boundaries of legitimacy become more difficult to define. Furthermore, authority potentially becomes more diffuse. The subjective nature of the experiences that engender faith might make room not only for an understanding attitude toward non-observance, but it also leaves individuals freer to determine for themselves where they stand on critical issues. Indeed, for these very reasons, Lamm ends his book on the value of general education by advocating a "pluralistic Torah community" that makes room for a range of different commitments and values, and Lamm himself advocates for cooperation between

Orthodox and non-Orthodox Jews on a number of matters.[135] A community's theological commitments coordinate with its desired social conditions.

Between Theology and Lived Experience: Ba'alei Teshuvah Describe Their Own Paths

Haredi popular theology also differs from the voices of *ba'alei teshuvah*, who describe the sources of their own commitments and the paths they took to Orthodox or Haredi Judaism. Actual human beings may construct their commitments differently from the ways that ideologues and theologians say that they should. Studies of *ba'alei teshuvah* by Herbert Danzger, Lynn Davidman, and Debra Kaufman base themselves on individuals' own descriptions of their religious journeys. For the most part, these "returnees" describe themselves in terms echoing only one part of Haredi popular theology: namely, that Haredi Judaism leads to a therapeutic sense of personal meaning and satisfaction. But the returnees did not envision themselves as having participated in a systematic and rational search for objective scientific truth. Instead, they "returned to Orthodoxy primarily spurred by a search for meaning in their lives."[136] Subjects of these studies found themselves attracted to Orthodox Judaism's sense of moral order, in contrast to the moral and existential homelessness that they had experienced in their earlier lives. For some, this homelessness involved disappointment with unfulfilled promises of the youth counterculture. Others rejected the perceived emptiness of a middle class, materialistic lifestyle. "The new recruits felt they were missing a 'core' to their lives, a sense of being rooted in some firm, stable and clearly defined way of being," which pushed them toward Orthodoxy.[137] Yet, Haredi popular theology rejects commitments in which reason is compromised by sociological or psychological forces that make one *want* to believe something. Reason requires cold objectivity. Differences between Haredi rhetoric about how people should construct their faith and the way newly Orthodox people report the sources of their own faith point to the rhetorical function of Haredi proofs for the truths of Judaism. These proofs draw clear boundaries between truth and falsehood and boost the self-confidence of Haredi readers, even if, in practice, recruits to Haredi life are motivated by other things.

Theology as Rhetoric

Differences between Haredi popular theology and medieval Jewish thought focus attention on the ways in which popularizing a tradition inevitably involves modifying and changing that tradition, constructing out of the raw materials of the past something new and innovative. Differences between Haredi popular theology and contemporary Modern Orthodox theology point to the ways in which differing groups, with different ideologies and social structures, create different theological texts. But perhaps something more important and subtle can be learned from the differences between how Haredi outreach literature claims that one *should* construct belief and how newly Orthodox Jews *actually* describe their beliefs. Male rabbis, theologians, and popularizers insist that Jews bracket their emotions so that they can think rationally and systematically, which will inevitably lead them to conclude that Haredi Judaism is true. But newly Orthodox Jews do something different. They make religious commitments based on profoundly psychological and emotional motivations. They violate some of the intellectual rules that the rabbis and authors set for them.

This difference points to the rhetorical function of Haredi popular theology books. These works may or may not prove what they set out to prove, but they certainly set up intellectual and cognitive categories that make clear and sharp distinctions between insiders and outsiders, us and them. As much as they draw outsiders into the unambiguous truths of Haredi Jewry, they help boost the self-confidence and sense of social distinctiveness of authors and readers who are already Haredi.

However, Haredi popular literature does more than boost the self-confidence of its Haredi readers. Often, popular literature serves as a conduit for Haredi internal criticism. Authors of Haredi popular literature not only point out Haredi Judaism's strengths, but also point to its weaknesses. Yet Haredi Jewry criticizes itself cautiously, trying to find the proper balance between internal criticism and self-congratulation. The coming chapter examines some of the rhetorical tools that Haredi authors use to identify communal flaws without undermining the Haredi self-image as superior to others.

Chapter VI:
"WE HAVE BEEN INFLUENCED…": THE RHETORIC OF HAREDI INTERNAL CRITICISM

During the summer of 2009, a scandal rocked the American Orthodox community, when several Haredi rabbis, numerous Orthodox laypeople, three New Jersey mayors, and a number of state legislators were arrested after a Haredi businessman became an informant for the FBI and revealed a web of alleged criminal activity. Charges included bribery, money laundering, and even trafficking in human organs. News of the arrests appeared as headlines in leading newspapers and over the internet. It was not a shining public relations moment for the Orthodox community.[1]

Shortly thereafter, Agudath Israel organized a public meeting under the banner of *"Ve'asisa Hayashar Vehatov"* [and you shall do what is right and good, Deut. 6:18], to address matters of honesty in business in the Orthodox community and its institutions. The meeting called on individuals and institutions to adhere to Jewish and secular law and to be extra careful in their financial dealings, not only because a Jew is obligated to do so, but lest a mistake, honest or otherwise, undercut the public image of Torah as a whole.[2] Shortly thereafter, a satirical "newspaper article" began spreading over the internet, entitled, "Jewish World in Shock as Ultra-Orthodox Admit a Wrongdoing." Authored by a formerly Orthodox Jew who blogs under the pseudonym "Da'as Hedyot" [the layman's opinion, opposite of *da'as Torah*], the article makes thinly veiled references to Haredi organizations and spokespeople, explaining that, "In a stunning reversal of a decades-long policy, the ultra-Orthodox world has publicly declared that they will no longer deny, excuse, cover-up, minimize, whitewash, or rationalize the criminal indiscretions of their community."[3]

The article's satire depends on the assumption that, under normal circumstances, the Haredi community does not criticize itself or police its own wrongdoings. No doubt, Haredi public rhetoric downplays public criticism, for some of the same reasons that the satire identifies: a sense that "Chareidim are so much better than everyone else" and "the *chillul hashem* [desecration of God's name] that will come about when people hear about all the stuff going on." Still, this satire gets something very wrong about how Haredim criticize their own community. Haredi self-criticism most certainly does exist; admitting wrongdoings is not a change of policy. Yet, Haredi Jews, like all other groups, criticize themselves in certain constrained ways. Internal criticism takes very specific rhetorical forms, the contours of which stem from the specific social conditions of and ideological pressures on the Haredi community.

Of course, no group relishes internal criticism. At a psychological level, confronting problems can undercut one's sense of self, and at a social level, raising serious problems and attempting to fix them will inevitably upset the social order, making criticism undesirable, at least to the existing power structure.[4] Several things make it even more difficult for Haredi authors to openly criticize their community. A conservative group like Haredi Jewry, almost by definition, wants to avoid "rocking the boat" by calling for social change. Furthermore, as a minority which perceives itself as embattled and threatened, Haredi Judaism also perceives itself as vulnerable. As Kimmy Caplan points out, this makes Haredim particularly concerned with their public image in the face of the majority culture, and they do not want "dirty laundry" aired in public.[5]

Moreover, Haredi Judaism's self-perception as superior also makes criticism difficult. As noted in Chapter Five, the community's rhetoric defines Torah as perfect and ideal, the guidebook for human happiness and satisfaction at both the individual and collective levels. If the community follows Torah – and the community's popular literature never tires of declaring that no other Jewish community seriously attempts to live up to the Torah's demands – then the Haredi community should not be plagued by significant faults. In addition, an enclave community remains deeply concerned with defection, and the community's rhetoric, therefore, highlights the superiority of Haredi life over and against that which it describes as secular. Significant public criticism of Haredi life might encourage people to look for better things outside of the community's borders.

Internal criticism raises questions of authority and hierarchy. Who possesses the authority to criticize whom, and on what basis? The Haredi community's emphasis on the authority of Jewish law in general and one's rabbis and teachers in particular suggests that laypeople, lower on the communal hierarchy, ought not challenge rabbinic policy and communal norms. The particular doctrine of *da'as Torah* makes this problem more severe, since no community members may challenge or undermine the policy statements of the great rabbis.

Yet, no group is perfect. Like members of every society, Haredi Jews find fault with aspects of their community or its religious life, and, despite limits on their criticism, they find venues to air it. This chapter, then, does not address primarily the "elephants in the room," the open or not-so-open secrets which are not discussed in public, or at least which editorial oversight keeps out of edited venues. Instead, I address the problems that Haredim raise in those venues with significant editorial oversight.[6] While Haredi Judaism has no shortage of external critics, I focus here on internal critics, those who "belong to the community they are criticizing. They have no desire to exit or to distance themselves from that community." They criticize not to undermine their community, but because "they believe that, without internal contestation... the traditions that distinguish that community will decay and atrophy."[7] How can Haredi Jews air criticism of their own culture, out of a real attempt to improve things, without undermining the dogmatic claim that Torah is perfect or undercutting the sense of superiority to general culture?

In this chapter, I claim that Haredi internal critics use specific kinds of language and categories to describe collective faults, and they frame the community's inadequacies in particular ways. Haredi authors and editors have at their disposal a number of rhetorical devices. Haredi rhetoric often identifies communal weaknesses as a collective failing to live up to the Torah's own demands, and these writers often blame communal failings on the damaging influence of general culture. These strategies reinforce rather than undermine the authority of Torah and the community's sense of superiority.

As Caplan points out, the extent and style of Haredi internal criticism depend on venue, language, context, and audience, in addition to idiosyncratic individual personality differences among critics.[8] A rabbinic leader delivering a sermon or *musar* lecture in a language or context that limits the audience to Haredi Jews alone might raise criticism more explicitly and openly than a Haredi journalist writing an op-ed for a non-Haredi newspaper. The rabbi can frame the criticism as Torah-grounded religious guidance and can implicitly reinforce the notion of rabbinic authority over laypeople, without concern that dirty laundry will be aired in public. Further, his rhetoric might maintain continuity with traditional genres of *musar* literature, in which elites provide spiritual guidance for their flocks. In contrast, the journalist will more likely take a cautious or apologetic tone, defending the Haredi community to outsiders rather than raising its faults.

Numerous other factors come into play in how criticism is aired and with what intensity. North American Haredi rhetoric tends to be more open and vocal in its self-criticism than that of Israelis, no doubt related to greater American Haredi openness. Men, who according to official Haredi doctrine are responsible for communal public life, can air more bold public communal self-criticism than can women, whose normative social role involves inwardness and domesticity. On the other hand, women, who are less attached to the power structure and who are outsiders to the male establishment, sometimes maintain a more critical perspective on flaws than do elements within the male power structure. Those born Haredi have a very different perspective than *ba'alei teshuvah*. On the one hand, *ba'alei teshuvah* may have a certain critical distance from the Haredi community, an ability to view the community as both an insiders and outsiders. On the other hand, *ba'alei teshuvah* may sometimes paint Haredi culture as an idyllic alternative to the decadence and moral weakness of the general culture which they have rejected.[9]

In order to examine the rhetorical strategies of Haredi self-criticism, this chapter will focus on *The Jewish Observer*, a monthly magazine which between 1963 and 2009 served as an official mouthpiece for Agudath Israel.[10] Periodicals are particularly interesting venues for examining a group's internal criticism. First, because they appear regularly, they must deal with a broad range of topics from issue to issue. Second, they offer material from more than one author, thus allowing readers access to several voices and therefore a more diverse, nuanced, and subtle picture of the community's discourse. Third, magazines offer a window into the editors' roles as gatekeepers and as the ones responsible for constructing coherent magazine issues out of a chaotic mass of potential material for inclusion.

Primarily designed for internal consumption, *The Jewish Observer* was written in standard English, and therefore reached a population of interested outsiders as well. In addition, the magazine served as an outlet for Agudath Israel ideology. *The Jewish Observer* dealt with many issues at the center of Haredi discourse, and hoped constantly to improve the community's religious life. Improvement requires some attempt to diagnose faults, and diagnosis implies at least some internal criticism. Moreover, periodicals like *The Jewish Observer* have something to gain from controversy. Not only can controversy help to sell more magazines, but it can also increase the magazine's reputation as a serious and front-running venue for communal discussion. In producing *The Jewish Observer*, editors and authors struggled mightily to raise at least some controversial material, even as they worked to frame that controversial material carefully, to embed the criticism within significant amounts of self-congratulatory rhetoric, and to include no small amount of criticism of the non-Haredi "other."

This chapter contains three sections. In the first part, I examine safe, unproblematic criticism, one that reinforces the beliefs of the community. Communal flaws amount to a failure to live up to the Torah or to the instructions of the great rabbis. The critic attributes failures to the influences of secular society or compares communal weaknesses with the high ideals of the Torah. In the second section, I examine a more subversive, dangerous comparison, one in which a Haredi spokesman cautiously and implicitly accepts various aspects of the secular critique of Haredi Judaism. A Haredi writer who makes this dangerous comparison must use careful rhetorical techniques to soften the blow. In the third section, I move beyond the individual author and consider how editors, in composing issues of a magazine, orchestrate patterns of criticism. Editors play a critical role in framing internal criticism by constructing complete magazine issues out of the shorter essays of individual authors.

Critical Distance Measured in Inches

Criticism requires some critical distance. Yet, as Michael Walzer suggests, distance may be best when "measured in inches,"[11] when the critic is part of and identifies with the community he or she is criticizing, such that critics and audience share a moral language and frame of reference. A critic can attack his or her own community for failing to live up to its own values, thereby buttressing other collective values. That is, we criticize by "taking seriously the principles taught us by our own educators and teachers."[12] *The Jewish Observer* makes serious and regular attempts to do just that: identify places where the community's practice does not live up to the community's own passionately held values.

Hence, one common rhetorical strategy for framing Haredi internal criticism involves identifying a gap between what Haredi Judaism demands in theory and what Haredi Jews actually do in practice. Criticism derives from shared Haredi values, thereby pointing to the community's failings while simultaneously reinforcing the authority of Torah. For example, lay leader and educational researcher Marvin Schick published a piece in *The Jewish Observer* chastising Haredi Jews for creating elitist and unaccommodating schools and for not doing enough to support the private day-school system from communal funds. He backed his claim by appealing to the authority of the great rabbis, the supreme representatives of Torah. His article – entitled "The Orthodox Community's Confused Priorities" – claims that R. Avraham Yeshayahu Karelitz, the famed Hazon Ish [1878-1953], rejected elitist schooling. "We dare not pigeonhole students as marked for failure." Schick also recalls an incident involving R. Shneuer Kotler [1918-1982], *rosh yeshiva* of Beth Medrash Govoha in Lakewood, NJ, one of the world's largest yeshivas. While on his deathbed, Kotler asked a student to bring a copy of a letter authored by the same Hazon Ish, in which the latter rabbi argued that communal funds should be spent on elementary schools.[13] By identifying problems as a collective failure to follow the great rabbis, the author not only increases the chances that his voice will gain a hearing, but also reinforces the authority of the rabbis themselves.

Critics also often blame communal faults on imitation of the outside culture, on failure to live up to the community's own isolationist values. This strategy admits a measure of acculturation de facto, but it reinforces the notion of separation de jure and paints the outside culture as a danger. One author, for example, decries trends in the Haredi music industry. "We want to hear *Jewish* music, not just music with *Hebrew* words." He attacks the concerts with "young Jewish boys dancing around the stage like non-Jewish performers, singing holy words of Torah and *tefilla* [prayer], gyrating, as if they were imitating the rock stars of the 60s....We must rise above the albums that are clearly meant to imitate non-Jewish music."[14]

This seems like a relatively uncomplicated example, since, no doubt, much Haredi popular music imitates secular pop and rock, and Haredi concerts look and sound similar to non-Haredi ones. In other examples, critics blame problems on secular influence in cases where such blame seems less compelling. In such cases, attributing faults to secular culture rhetorically grounds the author's potentially controversial position in the agreed-upon value of rejecting secular culture. Sara Medwed, for example, who writes for *The Jewish Observer* on issues related to marriage, explains that a proclaimed rise in the Haredi divorce rate stems from imitation of secular selfishness. "We too much find the prevailing 'me attitude' of today's society – the concern with 'What's in it for me?'... We have been... influenced by a disposable society," and we teach young couples how to lead proper married lives by having them read secular "books like *Men are from Mars, Women are from Venus*."[15] Now, one could blame marital problems on any number of things, and *Men Are from Mars* identifies problems in relationships as stemming not from selfishness necessarily but from innate differences between genders. In fact, some Haredi marriage guides see inherent gender-differences as sources of conflict.[16] But, for *The Jewish Observer*, identifying problems as stemming from the outside culture reinforces boundaries and highlights the sense of Haredi superiority. It makes Haredi Jews feel embattled, and a sense of embattlement is one reason why Haredi Jewry is thriving.

In these examples, identifying communal faults as failures to live up to Torah enables authors to raise criticism. Yet, in some cases, similar rhetoric not only enables criticism, but also serves to limit it. That is to say, criticism itself must also live up to the Torah's demands; those who criticize in ways that Torah does not accept should be silenced. Take the example of an article by Zvi Frankel, who focuses his criticism on Haredi use of the internet. Rather than speaking of the dangers of online access to heretical ideas or to pornography, he focuses on blogs and websites for internal Haredi use – dedicated to information, news, and gossip – some of which raise internal Haredi criticism that might not pass muster in more regulated Haredi media.[17] Haredi online resources are "spreading disease" that could prove "deadly.... Most of these blogs [are] full of... *lashon hara* [forbidden speech]"; "How can thousands of *frum* [devout] bloggers write and comment on forums that are clearly forbidden by the Torah, and then rationalize their major sin by explaining, 'It's all *lesheim Shamayim*' [for the sake of Heaven], thus falsely convincing themselves of their self-righteousness."[18]

Not accidentally, this article appeared shortly after various internet resources helped publicize embarrassing examples of sexual abuse and subsequent cover-ups in Haredi society, and after many websites attacked the Haredi community and its rabbinic leaders for hiding the abuse.[19] And Frankel attacks these blogs precisely because their criticism does not conform to what he considers proper Torah standards. In particular, this author is upset by the way in which the blogs, and the free and anonymous comments on blogs, allow laypeople to attack great rabbis. "These *frum* bloggers criticize and heap scorn on our *gedolei Torah* [great Torah scholars] and *manhigei Yisroel* [Jewish leaders].... Don't you realize that it is forbidden to write any of these posts or add comments on this website? This page is being *mevazeh* [scorning] *gedolim* and *talmidei chachamim*."[20] Frankel suggests an implicit comparison: bloggers criticize wrongly, since they lack the filters and limits on criticism that Torah considers central. But, he suggests, his own internal criticism is valid, precisely because it constructs criticism within the legitimate boundaries of acceptability, as the Torah demands. Haredi Jews criticize their own group for failing to live up to Torah's standards, but they also reject criticism on the grounds that it supposedly fails to live up to proclaimed Torah standards.

I will have more to say below about how *The Jewish Observer* constructs a hierarchy of who is entitled to criticize whom, and how the magazine empowers some voices while limiting or silencing others. Still, Frankel's article raises the possibility that the language of Haredi internal criticism not only enables communal introspection but also stifles it, giving voice only to certain authors and certain ideas but limiting expression of harsher and more subversive internal criticism. Criticism that meets Torah standards should exist; criticism that does not should be abolished. As we shall see below, the internet, with its much more open, free-wheeling, and uncensored expression, gives voice to what magazine editors would not allow.

The Secular Got It Right: A Close Reading of Jonathan Rosenblum
When authors in *The Jewish Observer* do want to present potentially subversive internal criticism, they must proceed cautiously. Yonoson Rosenblum (Jonathan when he writes for non-Haredi venues) is arguably the most popular and influential Haredi journalist writing in English. His works appear continually in Haredi periodicals such as *The Jewish Observer* and *Mishpacha*, as well as in non-Haredi contexts such as *The Jerusalem Post*, Israel's English-language daily newspaper. Founder and director of Jewish Media Resources, a Jerusalem-based journalistic organization with a Haredi agenda,[21] he actively defends Haredi Juda-

ism from its non-Haredi critics, even as he raises internal criticism of Haredi society. As an English-speaking Haredi Jew living in Israel, he often reports on Israeli life in the American Haredi press. Born and educated outside the Orthodox community, he adopted Haredi Judaism as an adult and has a unique ability to speak to the concerns of insiders and outsiders simultaneously and to appreciate some of the criticism which the non-Haredi community levels at Haredim.

In March of 2008, Rosenblum published an essay in *The Jewish Observer* entitled "Growing Pains." The essay amounts to a rather severe critique of Israeli Haredi society, touching on some of the most sensitive issues in Haredi self-definition. At the same time, Rosenblum carefully constructs his argument to present Haredi faults in a relatively flattering light.[22] By doing so, he allows himself to suggest something dramatic and seemingly subversive: secular Israelis who critique Haredi Judaism may be correct. Rosenblum can only make this claim by using subtle rhetorical methods to make his criticism less subversive and to leave some ambiguity about just how right the secular critique might be.

"Growing Pains" focuses on several perceived faults with the Israeli Haredi community: 1) Haredi families and the community as a whole are not economically self-sufficient. In particular, families and institutions remain dependent on government transfer-payments and child subsidies rather than on income derived from participation in the workforce. 2) Haredi schools for males refuse to allow anything but the most basic general education, which leads to unemployment and lack of job skills, which in turn exacerbate the lack of economic self-sufficiency. 3) Haredim do not serve in the Israeli army. 4) Haredi politicians focus on sectarian concerns, those that affect the Haredi community and economy, but remain disinterested in the affairs of the broader Israeli population. According to Rosenblum, Haredi society makes these problems worse by adopting a nonchalant "*yihiyeh tov*' ('it will be alright')" attitude. Instead of thinking ahead about the long-term challenges, Haredim prefer to wait until problems become acute and then "marshal their forces at one minute to midnight."

Rosenblum touches on issues that stand at the center of Israeli Haredi self-understanding, policies perceived as part and parcel of the Haredi "Torah-true" ideology. Few issues matter as much as these ones do for Israeli Haredi self-definition. Context helps ease the brunt of the criticism, for Rosenblum published this article in a venue written not for

Israelis, but for American Haredim. His critique points to Haredi flaws, but also serves as a spiritual and religious vindication of his particular audience and their religious worldview. Draft exemptions hardly matter in the American context, and the American community offers young men much greater leeway regarding general education, vocational training, and working for a living than does its Israeli counterpart, which is much more dependent on government stipends. Hence, the American community suffers from less severe poverty and is not as vulnerable as the Israeli community to the whims, right or wrong, of the non-Haredi majority. Rosenblum's criticism, therefore, subtly reinforces the wisdom and foresight of his own readership and their leaders.

Still, Rosenblum cannot simply announce that Israeli Haredi men should gain general education, join the army, acquire vocational training or higher education, and leave long-term, full-time Torah study for the workplace. Indeed, he does not offer specific policy suggestions at all. After all, according to official Haredi ideology, only great rabbis may make long-term religious and policy decisions; indeed, great rabbis instituted the policies which the article criticizes. Hence, Rosenblum uses a number of rhetorical techniques to moderate and soften, if not the substance of the critique, then at least the tone. He spends much of the article celebrating Haredi successes. He does not want to suggest that existing Haredi leadership and its policies have failed or led the community astray. Hence, he praises the old policies, claiming that their overwhelming successes led to current problems. Change may be necessary, but only because previous communal strategies had succeeded so dramatically. "The rapid growth of the Chareidi population in Israel over the last 60 years is a *nes nigla* – an open, recognizable miracle.... The small, highly committed group of *bnei Torah* [pious male Jews] who fell under the influence of the *Chazon Ish* has today multiplied into a community of tens of thousands.... Societal models that were appropriate [in the past] for the intense core group [of Haredim] will not serve all members of the vastly larger Chareidi society, which in the very nature of things, includes individuals and families of a wide range of abilities and spiritual commitments."

Furthermore, Rosenblum explains that the problems arise due to growing Haredi political influence, rather than from Haredi weakness. The old approach of focusing on sectarian interests was "viable only so long as the Chareidi parties were relatively small." But as "Chareidi political power grows in accord with our rapidly expanding population," it will become more difficult to avoid speaking up on a wide variety of issues, including the "life-and-death security issues." Again, current problems stem from Haredi successes, rather than bad policy.

Rosenblum plays up this narrative of success by peppering his writing with statistics that demonstrate just how strong and numerous the Haredi community has become. "A recent study by the Education Ministry projected that within five years, a full 30% of Israeli students will be in Chareidi educational frameworks." Emphasizing problems that arise from successes reinforces the Haredi sense of superiority and ties into a narrative of inevitable Haredi triumph. Rosenblum also supports a sense of Haredi superiority by blaming problems on imitation of non-Haredi culture. "Some of the 'yihiyeh tov' ('it will be alright') attitude for which secular Israelis are famous has rubbed off on Israeli Chareidim."

In another sentence, Rosenblum introduces another strategy for framing his internal criticism. "One of Rabbi Moshe Sherer's [long-time leader of Agudath Israel, 1921-1998] great strengths as a leader was his ability to understand the point of view of potential adversaries or allies.... Some understanding of secular Israeli society today will similarly help the Torah community to chart a strategy." At one level, Rosenblum gains credibility by citing the authority of one of American Haredi Orthodoxy's most revered political leaders. More importantly, the attitude he attributes to Sherer allows Rosenblum to insist that the Haredi community take secular criticism seriously, if only for tactical reasons. The secular opposition to various aspects of Haredi culture makes those aspects problematic, because the Haredi community depends on making allies of that secular majority.

Rosenblum repeats this strategy throughout the article. "It goes without saying that the goal of the Chareidi educational system, particularly for boys, is to produce talmidei chachamim, not high-tech workers of the future.... But that is a hard sell to Israeli policymakers." Hence, the Haredi community must "begin preparing strategies well in advance" to address the imposition of secular education in Israeli Haredi schools. Rosenblum says something similar about draft exemptions, since, he claims, a high Haredi birthrate will make non-serving Haredim an increasingly large segment of the able-bodied potential draftees. A "draft cohort in which 40%-50% of those eligible for military service are Chareidim and Arabs [who also do not serve]" will force the secular majority to draft Haredi young men. The secular majority's frustration can have a negative impact on the Haredi community, since the secular can impose their will upon it.

Furthermore, Rosenblum's insistence that the Haredi community has something to gain from making allies of the secular allows him to hint, but not state explicitly, that Israeli Haredi Jews, or at least their leadership, ought to gain a broader general education than they currently do. "Some awareness of the impact of large child subsidies and of world economic trends would have shown [the Haredi politicians] why they [the government child subsidies that benefit Haredi families] were vulnerable.... Such understanding could also spare us a lot of futile hopes that child benefits will return to their former levels."

Rosenblum takes this further. He does not claim only that problems ensue because a misguided secular community has the power to impose itself on the Haredi minority. Rather, Rosenblum hints – but only hints – that the secular critique may well be correct. In several places he cites, without comment or response, reasons why secular Israelis might be frustrated with Haredi policy. "In recent years, economists have placed great emphasis on rates of labor force participation.... Large child care benefits are widely viewed as disincentives to labor force participation.... A Treasury Minister with training in economics, like Binyamin Netanyahu, was likely to make good on promises to dramatically cut child benefits." Rosenblum does not offer any argument explaining why not to cut those benefits. He leaves ambiguous whether he considers those economists or Netanyahu correct. Rosenblum says something similar regarding draft exemptions. "The IDF [Israel Defense Forces] does not currently suffer from a manpower shortage. But if the Chareidi draft cohort jumps from 10%-15% of the overall draft cohort to something closer to 30%, as seems possible a decade or two down the line, the situation will look considerably different." Without stating explicitly that they are correct, Rosenblum makes his secular interlocutors seem reasonable. "Israel's economic future is largely dependent on brainpower and an educated workforce. No developed Western economy would calmly accept a situation in which close to 20% of the school age population was not receiving a basic secular education." Nor, Rosenblum seems to imply, should they.

And here, perhaps, is Rosenblum at his most subversive. If this reading is at all plausible, then he is hinting at a much deeper issue. Haredi

Jews, particularly in Israel, should listen closely and carefully to secular critiques of Haredi society, because secular critiques might contain some truth. Rosenblum hints at something similar in another of his columns from *The Jewish Observer*, a review of the book *Real Jews* by non-Haredi journalist and academic, Noah Efron.[23] In this book, Efron lambastes the Israeli secular media for its overly critical, at times vicious, portrayal of Israeli Haredim. This critique, claims Efron, grossly exaggerates Haredi Jewry's actual negative influence and the ways in which low workforce-participation and transfer payments place a drag on the free-market economy.

In reviewing the book, Rosenblum suggests two opposing points to Haredi readers. First, much anti-Haredi sentiment is irrational, hysterical, and overstated, and even an honest secular reader like Efron understands that. Second, some secular observers of the Haredi community may not harbor an anti-Haredi bias, and the Haredi community should listen to them closely. If a relatively honest broker like Efron still airs critiques of Haredi society, perhaps it behooves the community to consider that critique seriously. Here too, Rosenblum follows Efron and chooses issues that stand at the center of Haredi self-definition: exemptions from military service, government financial support for full-time yeshiva students, and Orthodox rabbinical control over marriage and divorce in Israel.

Rosenblum begins by defending the reliability and honesty of Efron and his research, claiming that he "is fair, open minded, [and] skeptical about the claims of his sources." Indeed, the title of the book, *Real Jews*, matches Haredi self-understanding as the only authentic example of true Judaism, thereby making Efron more reliable. "Though Efron details and sympathizes with the litany of grievances [of the secular Israelis against Haredim] he records, he is no hater." Rosenblum then hints that his Haredi audience should understand not only what an honest arbitrator like Efron decries about the secular press, but also what he questions about Haredim. Rosenblum makes this point by quoting more of Efron than he has to. He could have quoted Efron as saying, "When it comes to the ultra-Orthodox, secular Israelis regularly overestimate the threat posed by Haredim, and the injustice perpetuated by them." But Rosenblum insists on quoting Efron's full paragraph. "There are innumerable good, objective reasons to fight ultra-Orthodox political initiatives, begrudge the money they get from the government, and resent the fact that they don't serve in the army." Rosenblum also summarizes Efron's criticisms of Haredi exemptions from the military. "While he [Efron] is convinced the chareidi ideal of full-time learning for all men can no longer be sustained, and that it is 'graceless' to insist that secular Israelis, who do not share that ideal, sacrifice on its behalf, Efron nevertheless recognizes that it is a 'lovely ideal.'" Rosenblum goes further, recording Efron's citation of "the Chief Rabbinate's control over marriage and divorce" as the one context where Orthodox power "impinges on the lifestyles of secular Israelis." Without rebuttal or disagreement, Rosenblum cites Efron's claim that "women frequently have to renounce all right to child support in order to obtain a *get* [religious divorce], and that many women are sent back to attempt reconciliation with violent husbands." Rosenblum does not respond to these claims, hinting that they contain some truth.

Efron's book, then, "provides the chareidi readers with a glimpse into a mirror – albeit a distorted one – into which we rarely peer." It seems that Rosenblum would like Haredi Jews to look in that mirror, perhaps longer and harder than seems comfortable. It is easier to have Efron call for that long hard look in the mirror than for Rosenblum to do so himself. It seems likely that Rosenblum sympathizes with these criticisms, at least up to a point, but prefers to have Efron voice them rather than voice them himself. This example could add a layer to Walzer's suggestion that internal criticism matters most since outsiders have little influence on an existing culture. Here, the outsider critique matters when it influences an insider cultural agent, who then translates the outsider critique into the language of insiders.

Delinquency, Dropout, Definition, and Discourse

So far, we have examined only individual authors and the strategies that they use to frame their internal criticism. However, the writings of particular authors reach the readers within broader literary constructs. In the case of *The Jewish Observer*, the articles appear within the pages of magazine issues that include articles, artwork, advertisements, photos, and graphics, which together constitute the product which the reader takes in. Hence, the editorial staffs of *The Jewish Observer* or other venues play crucial roles in constructing how particular kinds of criticisms appear to the reader. They may frame or define a subject in a particular way, choose which authors to publish and which authors not to publish, or provide editorial commentary – explicit or implicit – on the material that they do publish. Even when they introduce debate and differences of opinion, they may give priority to some voices, while downplaying or marginalizing other ones.

One fascinating example of editors' roles in constructing public debate involves *The Jewish Observer*'s two special issues on a very tense and potentially threatening topic: teens who drop out of Orthodox observance. Defection raises significant concerns for a community that values boundaries. Youth who drop out threaten to breach those boundaries, and they undermine the claim that life inside is vastly superior to that on the outside. After all, if life in the Haredi enclave is superior to non-Haredi life, why would anyone leave?

In November 1999, *The Jewish Observer* devoted an entire issue to what it called "Children on the Fringe . . . and Beyond." The magazine was concerned with what it referred to as "kids-at-risk": a perceived increase in dropout teenagers who reject communal norms and abandon Orthodox practice, dropping out of school and falling into delinquency, sexual promiscuity, substance abuse, and petty crime. The publication struck a raw nerve, and the publishers quickly ordered a second print run, making this issue the most widely circulated in the magazine's thirty-plus years of existence.[24] A few months later, in March 2000, the magazine dedicated another issue to follow-up and readers' responses. These special issues make an intriguing case study in Haredi internal criticism, because the magazine cannot address a perceived growth in dropout youth without considering the community's contribution to the problem. Further, any thorough discussion demands input from a variety of stakeholders: educators, mental-health professionals, parents, young people, and communal leaders. Editors must weave together a great deal of material from different voices. They must make decisions about whose opinions to publish, how to present the problem to the public, and how to frame the conversation. In preparing these magazine issues, the editors, as "purposeful, reasoning, and well-intentioned actors... [are] latently serving ideological functions at the same moment that they are seeking to alleviate some of the problems facing individual students and others."[25]

For example, the editors chose a specific definition of the topic that has a side effect of supporting the community's sense of superiority and moral supremacy. Abandonment of observance on the part of those born into observant families has been a significant challenge since the founding of Orthodoxy in the early nineteenth century, if not earlier. "Kids-at-risk" represent a specific subset of the larger problem. After all, one could leave the Haredi community in any number of fashions, and one need not go through a stage of substance abuse or delinquency while leaving a Haredi life. The magazine does not focus on ideologically and intellectually committed secularists, who might have compelling rational reasons for abandoning Orthodoxy. Nor does the magazine discuss those who drift out of Orthodoxy for alternative lives as upstanding, well-adjusted, non-Orthodox Jews. Certainly, examples of both kinds of dropout exist in today's Orthodoxy, as they have in the past.[26] Instead, *The Jewish Observer* discusses youth who fell into substance abuse and delinquency.

Kids-at-risk offer a comparatively comfortable way for the community to reflect on the fragility of its commitments. Delinquent youth represent a powerful and compelling "other" against which to define normalcy and health. In this discussion, Haredi observance becomes associated with health and satisfaction, while leaving Haredi Jewry becomes associated with illness and pathology. Lack of observance itself constitutes illness. Indeed, many authors assume that a young person could not recover from an addiction or from other psychological problems without also re-adopting observance. One mother explains that her dropout son "can only be happy (and productive and a *mentch* [upstanding person], *et al.*) if he is connected to *Hashem* and (dare I say it) a true *ben Torah*."[27]

A comparison to an article on a related topic during a somewhat different historical period supports this suggestion. In 1964, a year after the founding of *The Jewish Observer*, an article on yeshiva dropouts was not about delinquency, but about the fact that many students enrolled at the time in Orthodox elementary schools were not dedicated enough to observance or to parochial Orthodox education to continue through high school. Many parents sent their children to day schools even if the home was less than fully observant. Hence, "Large numbers of students with superior ability drop out at the high-school level." Editor Nisson Wolpin speaks of the "predestined dropout" of youngsters whose religious background and early-childhood educational experiences make their dropout predictable. In 1964, the phenomenon of dropout did not mean delinquency, but a conscious choice, often supported by parents, to prefer public school to the yeshiva alternative.[28]

During the 1960s, when America's Haredi community was smaller and considerably less self-confident than it is today, when it could not reasonably be referred to as an enclave community, when it had less confidence that the next generation would follow in its path, when borders were more porous and ill-defined than they are today, it was possible to speak of desertion as something unfortunate and inevitable but not pathological.[29] Some three-and-a-half decades later, when a self-confident enclave community had come into being, a discussion of dropout refers to it as a kind of pathology.

Editors and Authors in Dialogue: Defining the Right to Criticize
Equating dropout with delinquency is not the only way in which the editors guide the conversation. Editors also play an important role in a complex attempt to deal with this potentially painful topic in a way that balances the necessity of internal criticism with the preservation of the community's superior self-image. Editors possess at least four tools for inserting their opinions and agendas into this issue and for presenting internal criticism in ways that meet their standards. First, editors choose what to include in the issue. They have the privilege of soliciting or not soliciting articles by particular authors or on particular topics, and they must choose the material to publish from among the submitted articles and letters. Second, they structure and organize the issue, thereby implicitly commenting on what they have included. Third, with their introductions and marginal comments, they frame and present matters in ways that are in line with their larger ideological agenda or economic interests. Fourth, they explicitly respond to material that they publish by inserting editorial comments or by inviting (or not inviting) responses from countervoices.

The two magazine issues on dropout discuss many topics: the propriety of expelling problematic students from school, advice for finding a good match between a family and a therapist, diagnoses of reasons for youth problems, suggestions for interventions at the school and individual levels, descriptions of treatment programs, and even suggestions for better and more appropriate teaching. These discussions contain no small measure of internal criticism. Most take the form of attacks on the negative influence of secular culture, suggesting that the "unraveling of the moral fabric of secular society" has had an "effect on (even) our insular community."[30] Some criticism goes further, attacking the community for its materialism and conspicuous consumption and for being too focused on people's public reputations rather than with the substance of their religious lives.[31]

In building magazine issues out of this mass of material, editors struggle not only with what kinds of criticism to raise and how to frame that criticism, but also with the larger question of who ought to advise and criticize whom. In the case of a troubled educational system, rabbis, teachers, and the educational establishment may have different perspectives than parents, laypeople, and students. Who earns the status of expert, and how does the magazine present them as such? Who claims the task of identifying others' mistakes and correcting them? And who, in contrast, has the status of one to be taught, advised, directed, and criticized? How are those roles assigned by the magazine and encoded on the page? How can the magazine play a role in constructing and reinforcing a sense of communal hierarchy and authority? Put somewhat differently, the question of who is entitled to criticize whom becomes a kind of "constitutional" question, highlighting legitimate and illegitimate uses of power within the communal hierarchy.

One would expect *The Jewish Observer* to present rabbis and Torah educators as responsible for identifying the causes of dropout and for explaining to laypeople how to better educate their children. This would fortify the Haredi ideology of strong rabbinic authority, according to which Torah as interpreted by rabbis and communal leaders is the sole authority. Moreover, one would expect that laypeople, parents, and students should not criticize the wisdom and Torah-based decisions or advice of the educators and rabbis.

Yet, several factors make it difficult to adopt that strategy exclusively. To begin with, laypeople and students have a lot to say about the quality of education, and they may be dissatisfied with some of the work done by the rabbis and leadership. Moreover, magazine editors must be sensitive to the opinions and voices of laypeople, who, in the end of the day, make up the readership. Ignoring their voices could alienate readers. Furthermore, including disagreement and dispute makes for more interesting reading and can boost sales and readership. Lay criticism of rabbinic authority has the potential to create interest and even scandal, precisely because it is somewhat transgressive. Finally, editors may genuinely believe that open dispute and disagreement will lead the conversation toward truth. Silencing laypeople entirely does not serve the interests of the editors.

Still, how can one reasonably raise parent and student criticisms of the educational system, the teachers, or the rabbis without implicitly or explicitly undermining rabbinic authority? This question is made more challenging because Haredi educational discourse considers it very important to create and maintain a united front between schools and homes. Uniformity between families and educational institutions makes it easier to socialize students into communal norms. Numerous Haredi parenting guides explain that parents must always support the teachers in the presence of their children, and that in conflict between homes and schools the "child should never see himself as in the right."[32] Or, as Rabbi Shimon Schwab puts it, "Parents who expect the best kind of education for their sons and daughters can do very little without the proper school. Yet even the best school will accomplish next to nothing without the cooperation of the parents."[33] Lay criticism of educators or rabbis could undercut that image of cooperation. How, then, can authors and editors work together to construct a plausible and effective communal self-examination, one that includes critical voices from laypeople, while at the same time presenting parental and student voices as possessing weak authority? As we shall see, the editors of *The Jewish Observer* solved this problem in one way in their initial foray into the discussion, but they quickly adopted a different strategy in the follow-up issue.

The two issues on kids-at-risk, November 1999 and March 2000, differ dramatically from one another. The clearly structured and organized first issue expresses the idea that experts, rabbis, and educators must explain to parents how to educate and raise their children. The second issue, more chaotic and democratic in tone, allows a much freer flow of opinion and criticism. Even there, however, the editors play an active role in defining the contours, tone, and structure of the internal critique, and they do not give laypeople free reign to voice potentially subversive opinions.

In the November 1999 issue, the editors construct a "top-down" approach toward authority. An expert class explains to laypeople how to act and parent properly. The first issue, with its expert advice for parents, explains throughout that problems stem from bad parenting, or at least that improving parenting is the key solution. Editors effectively silence the potential criticisms that parents and youth might raise, encoding parents as objects of advice rather than as subjects who might raise their own critical voices. Experts explain what ought to occur; students keep silent; and parents worry, pray, and try to improve themselves in light of the experts' advice.

Experts dominate the first issue, which includes articles by great rabbis (*gedolei Yisrael* in the magazine's lexicon, 3 articles), rabbis and educators (10 articles), and mental-health professionals (4 articles). As we shall see below, only two articles are presented as being authored by parents, and only one of those is actually written by a parent. The other is a pseudonymous account, authored by a mental-health professional, of what a parent might or should write. No articles appear by students, young people, or dropouts themselves.

Even within the expert class, editors create a hierarchy of authority, according to which great rabbis are authoritative, with educators and mental-health professionals below them. One sentence in the editors' introduction directly reflects on the relative authority and roles of different groups in the hierarchy. "In preparing this issue, we have drawn on the insights and guidance of *Gedolei Torah*, benefited from the experience of *mechanchim* (Torah educators), invited the comments of mental-health professionals, and shared the anguish of parents."[34] The order and language here is quite precise. Great rabbis, at the top of the pyramid, provide guidance; educators bring their experience; mental-health professionals, when invited, are entitled only to comment; parents, however, have nothing to offer but their own suffering.

Editors make sure to heap praise on the great rabbis. One article, summarizing the position of the Chazon Ish, begins with an editorial comment explaining that the rabbi is "one of the greatest Torah luminaries of recent times" whose "views, actions, halachic rulings and writings continue to have a major influence on the fabric of Torah life everywhere."[35] Similarly, the biography describing Rabbi Shlomo Wolbe explains that he is "one of the foremost living educators and musar personalities."[36]

While articles by educators (*mechanchim*) are generally left without such editor-authored praise, the editors explicitly define mental-health professionals as being lower on the hierarchy. Indeed, the editors feel the need to defend the very inclusion of such professionals in the discussion. After all, "modern psychology," a member of the editorial board explains, has rejected the notion of a God-given soul, abandoned the notion of free will, and adopted an atheistic stance. Editors would have left mental-health professionals out of the conversation were it not for "alternative approaches" such as "cognitive/behavioral techniques" and other less problematic methods that have appeared on the scene. These newer approaches "are acceptable – indeed, laudatory – when administered in a Torah-true environment by a therapist who is steeped in Torah values and uncompromising *gestalt* immersed in Torah *hashkafah*." The legitimacy of these mental-health professionals depends upon their "work[ing] in tandem with their own carefully selected *Rabbanim/Poskim* who mentor the therapeutic process and ensure its fidelity to *halacha* and Torah *hashkafa*."[37]

Whatever the internal hierarchy within the class of leaders, editors fill this magazine issue with advice, suggestions, and criticism by members of the leadership group aimed at parents, who are treated as passive recipients of the leaders' guidance. The articles collectively imply that bad parenting causes the problem, and that improving parenting through expert advice can help solve it. "Parents often act toward their children in a way they think is educational, but which, in reality, hasn't the slightest connection to their children's behavior." Parents should turn to experts to help control the dangerous parenting emotions of "jealousy... honor seeking... and anger."[38] The seventeen articles by the expert class include one summarizing Wolbe's "Basic Principles of Parenting." A teacher, in a section on "The Mechanech's Perspective," explains that "mandatory parenting groups under the auspices of our yeshivas are vital."[39] Rabbi Yakov Horowitz, director of Agudath Israel's Project YES for dropout youth – an individual who has emerged as one of the leading Haredi spokespeople regarding this issue, and who, in other contexts, has raised biting criticism of the community and its educational system[40] – in this context focuses on the "need to improve the overall quality of our home life," by offering "*Shalom Bayis* [marital harmony] classes" and "parenting classes."[41] The magazine includes a discussion of what to do "when conventional parenting is not enough," as well as a "guide to therapy" for parents.[42]

In the first issue, nobody suggests that schools and educators might learn from having parents and students critique or offer advice about the curriculum or educational program. Schools appear as locations for solving educational or emotional problems, but not as locations that cause such problems. "Schools" must work to "diagnose and remediate any learning difficulties" and can offer "a tutor/mentor for a child experiencing academic failure," all in order to prevent future dropout. Indeed, schools, rabbis, and educators have the task of explaining to parents what the latter currently do wrong and what they can do to improve their parenting. "*Mechanchim* [educators]... often are in the unenviable position of regularly pointing out to parents their children's problems."[43] Schools can help diagnose problems, but they do not, in this discourse, create them.

One educator in the issue more explicitly undermines the legitimacy of parental criticism of the educational system – thereby, perhaps unwittingly, informing readers of various criticisms that parents might raise were they given the opportunity to do so. When parents criticize the educators, this undermines the educational system as a whole and leads to dropout and delinquency. "Only when parents work together with the *Rebbe* can the child's full potential be achieved.... When a parent questions the integrity of a *Rebbe* or *Menahel*, and accuses the *hanhala* [administration] of making its primary concern the reputation of their institution or their egos and not working with *mesiras nefesh* [dedication] and concern for the welfare of the child, they are damaging the relationship between the child and *Rebbe*, between *talmid* and yeshiva.... This will cause the *talmid* to seek identity and support amongst peers outside the yeshiva whom he mistakenly perceives to be friends who care."[44] This first issue does not include parental criticism of educators because such criticism (even when true?) itself causes delinquency.

The first and last articles in the issue appear to be authored by parents, and both reinforce the idea that parents should not criticize the educational system. They focus on the highly personal, and both authors avoid criticizing anyone but themselves. The first, "Thoughts of a Mother" – authored by a pseudonymous, anonymous, and therefore largely powerless mother – opens the issue and "set[s] the scene"[45] for the rest of the issue. It articulates the pain and suffering of a mother of a delinquent child. "Nowadays I'm sleeping through the night – mostly. Last year, and two years ago, (and three and four also) I didn't sleep as well. Often I would wake up in the middle of the night – find my face wet from tears – my lips moving even as I slept. 'Please, *Hashem* – help us. Help him. Protect him from himself.'... The horror of those nights. I would sit up in the living room – saying the whole *Tehillim* [Psalms] – and sobbing out loud." The language and style work to elicit an emotional response from the reader, both of personal identification with the suffering but also with the gravity and seriousness of the problem.

The anonymous mother makes no attempt to diagnose the reasons for dropout, neither in terms of her individual son nor regarding the perceived problem with Haredi education as a whole. In fact, she sees herself as unqualified to diagnose. "I used to think that I knew the 'reason' for kids like mine.... It's a dysfunctional home.... Too rigid or too loose. No money, or too much money.... Too liberal-modern. Too frumfanatic.... And then all of the sudden the kid was mine," and none of the older explanations made sense anymore.[46] Any attempt to explain why and how this happens is doomed by an equal and opposite, but mutually exclusive counter-explanation.

The issue closes with a second article, entitled "Hereby Resolved: A Father's *Kabbalos* [resolutions]." It presents parents as submissive. The article speaks in the name of a father of a delinquent child, as he introspects and plans for the future. Each paragraph begins "I will..." and continues with a resolution that the father intends to keep in order to help his troubled child. "I will not degrade you, laugh at you, ridicule you in any way.... I will smile more to you. I will smile more, period." This "father's" resolutions close the issue perfectly, translating the experts' advice into a practical to-do list of activities. The crisis can be solved if deferential parents attempt to live up to the experts' demands. Even here, however, the editors have not given a real father a voice. The article was written by a clinical psychologist, role-playing the father and imagining what a troubled father *ought* to say to himself. It is not clear how to parse this editorial decision. Were no actual parents available to write? Did editors not want to risk a father who would not toe the editorial line and might have more critical and less submissive things to say? Or, was it simply easier to commission the "right" parental voice from an expert?

Be that as it may, the first issue proved a remarkable success. "After the initial press run (plus 1000 extra for Agudath Israel convention delegates) was released, and newsstands' and bookstores' copies were snapped up, the editorial office was inundated with requests for more copies as well as multiple orders. A second press run was ordered, and almost completely sold out."[47] As a result, the editors chose to release a second, follow-up issue to further explore the matter. The tone and structure of the second issue differ dramatically from those of the first, in large part because the editors dedicated the latter issue extensively to readers' responses and letters to the editor. The issue has a frenzied tone, with short letters to the editor by different parties, several on a page, interspersed with editorial comments and clarifications of points, together with some longer, more systematic articles. Unlike the first issue, it includes significant "bottom-up" critique of the Haredi educational system. Editors also included the voices of young people themselves: dropouts, former dropouts, and normative Haredi youth, who had experienced the educational system from a perspective different from that of the teachers and parents. If the first issue contains measured advice from experts to help parents do a better job of raising their children, the second issue contains smatterings of a great deal more – attacks on schools and educators, criticism of parents, angry tones, individual hand-wringing, and collective introspection – all in less measured, more rapid-fire writing. A letter writer, for example, asks a quick series of rhetorical questions: "Are we catering enough to the below ninety student?... Are we guiding our students who cannot for whatever reason become *Roshei Yeshiva* to some vocational studies? What are we doing to build the self-esteem in a student? Are we adhering to the well-known concept of '*Chanoch lana'ar al pi darko*' [educate the youth in his own path, Proverbs 22:6]?"[48] The implicit answer is, "no."

The letters to the editor, shorter articles, letters from students and laypeople, and more open criticism all leave an impression of a democratic tone, as if the editors have opened the floor to the public to raise their voices about an issue of such great concern. But even in the second issue, editors structure and regulate the seemingly open discussion. They choose what to publish and how to frame what is published, and they intersperse their own editorial insertions between the authors' writings. As the editors state explicitly, "After selecting articles and letters for publication, we have grouped them according to the categories indicated in the table of contents.... On the pages that follow, we present introductions to specific sections along with some readers' responses, full-length articles, and comments of our own."[49]

For example, after a one-page editors' introduction, the issue opens by shoring up the community's and magazine's collective self confidence, in the form of several letters congratulating *The Jewish Observer* for its willingness to open the issue to public discussion and applauding the community for taking the issue so seriously. "I am very impressed with the November issue of the *The Jewish Observer*…. I see a *tzibbur* [community] that is facing the problem head on – and investing minds and money in efforts to solve it."[50] Support for the community's positive self-image, along with some self-congratulation on the part of editors, appear front and center.

Editors work to maintain the hierarchical authority within the community and prevent lay criticism from undermining the rabbinic leadership. The editors make clear that they did not, and would not, publish everything that the community had to say, precisely because open criticism of the school system is unacceptable. "Some letter-writers faulted the *chinuch* system for children's difficulties and their ultimate defection – too high standards; too little allowance for variations in strengths and weaknesses, in intelligence, in areas of interest, in mental processing, or in ability to concentrate; no accommodation for individuality of expression…. The pages of this magazine are not the forum for their publication."[51]

Notice the editors' careful use here of paralipsis: the rhetorical strategy in which a speaker brings up a topic by denying its importance or relevance (such as when someone mentions a topic by saying, "not to mention X"). The editors actually give voice to those critics by summarizing their claims, even admitting that "some of the observations might be valid." At the same time, the editors undercut the legitimacy of that critique by declaring explicitly that they would not print it. They hint that a deeper critique might have its place, but not in this venue. Echoing themes mentioned above in the discussion of Haredi historiography, the editors suggest that the education system is sacrosanct, grounded in the idyllic world of East European Jewry. "Our contemporary yeshiva system has its roots in the vision of Rabbi Chaim Volozhiner, which was based on the directives of his *Rebbe*, the Vilna Gaon."

But history is not the only matter at play. After all, the contemporary American Haredi educational system – with its network of high schools that combine Jewish and general studies, its advanced academies for girls and women, and its allowance if not at times encouragement of college attendance – differs radically from that of Eastern Europe as envisioned by contemporary Haredi society. Hence, editors provide another reason for not publishing such critical letters, one directly related to the communal hierarchy. Suggestions for institutional change in the school system cannot come from laypeople, but only from great rabbis. "Letters with questions, criticisms and suggestions regarding *chinuch* have been referred to a group of *Roshei Yeshiva* with the confidence that... they will evaluate these issues and will א"יה [God willing] share their suggestions for how to deal with them."[52]

If editors shield the educational system and its supposedly tradition-bound institutions from public criticism, they do the same for teachers and professional educators, and use the same ironic strategy of announcing a certain criticism by declaring a refusal to print it. They leave critical letters out of the issue, even when the criticism seems valid. "Some [unpublished] letters directly faulted teachers, *rebbeim* or principals for a variety of shortcomings – some probably real, others imagined, and yet others irrelevant."[53] Don't critique teachers, say the editors, since, for the most part, they are talented, dedicated, idealistic, and motivated. As much as this magazine issue seems to celebrate an open, democratic discourse, in practice editors have subtly silenced much of a bottom-up critique of the expert class.

Yet, lay voices and lay criticism remain. Declarations notwithstanding, editors did include quite a bit of material, even by laypeople, that criticizes educators, teachers, and schools. Laypeople suggest that schools do not provide enough individual attention, are too elitist, and force students to fit into a single and difficult mold. The supportive "webbing in our 'mainstream' *yeshivos* has become too loosely woven.... It is not difficult to suggest that a new *yeshiva*, a new string of *yeshivos*, should be supported, *yeshivos* that are truly sensitive to and address the strengths and weaknesses of the individual *talmid* [student].... When we are truly prepared to reach and to teach *al pi darko*... then we can begin the process of reclaiming our own."[54]

Editors included two particularly harsh letters from parents. One mother places the blame firmly on "the conventional mainstream yeshiva system," which, she claims, "nearly made rejects of my sons. Not until my husband and I transferred our boys into more nurturing and flexible *yeshivas*, which made the *Rebbe-talmid* relationship the main concern, not the number of *blatt Gemora* [pages of Talmud] learned, did our boys return to *Yiddishkeit*."[55] Here, the mother goes beyond a critique of the overemphasis on academics in a given school. She diagnoses not a local, but a systemic problem. Another parent praises the "awe inspiring" advice of Rabbi Wolbe from the first issue, which insists on a warm, caring educational approach. But the parent then points to schools that pay mere lip service to that ideal rather than living up to it. "If only I could have that skillful blend of gentle and caring educational experience for my child in his elementary *cheder* [school]. At home I use many of" R. Wolbe's suggestions to help my son. "But, oh, what he is up against once he's in school, dealing with his '*frum*' English teachers and administration. I feel like he comes home battle scarred each day and indeed I have to bandage his wounds."[56]

These parents exemplify a "bottom-up" parental critique of the schools and the school system, precisely what the editors excluded from the first issue and what they said that they would not publish in the second. For whatever reason, the editors chose to include some of the material that they themselves indicated they would not. Still, the editors have various ways of countering the implicit subversiveness in these letters. To begin with, these parents, at least one female, appear anonymously, presumably to protect their privacy. However, the anonymity also functions to weaken the authority and power that their voices carry. Furthermore, editors counter the letter-writers explicitly, explaining that, "We do not endorse every opinion expressed in the letters."[57] The editors scattered throughout the issue a series of editorial responses, which explicitly reply to potentially subversive critiques. These responses are authored by named, and therefore more authoritative, male rabbis and educators, and they inevitably defend teachers and schools. "The experts' consensus is that most teachers are not to blame, working as they do in next to impossible conditions."[58] The editors themselves declare on the inside of the front cover of the first issue that, "There are those who claim – inaccurately and unfairly – that fault lies with our heroic *mechanchim* [educators]. We reject that claim. Most *rabbe'im* and *morahs* [female teachers] are overworked, underpaid, underappreciated – and, yet, notably effective. Are they perfect? No. But they are far more devoted and caring than most of their detractors. And if all the critics of 'the system' would focus their energies on ensuring the financial viability and societal prestige of the *chinuch* profession in America, the face of Orthodox Jewry across the country would be unrecognizable."[59] These editors' responses to critique of teachers retain some ambiguity, since they suggest both that teachers do not deserve the blame and, simultaneously, that teachers may contribute to the problem. Still, the more authoritative editors' voices protect the educators and push laypeople to expend their energies not criticizing schools but improving the financial conditions and social status of the educational profession.

Similar patterns of editorial oversight appear regarding the voices of the teens themselves. Editors included some letters from teens in a special section entitled "The Kids Speak." Here again, the most critical voices are anonymous, written by "A Student," "A Teenager," or "The Next Generation." Several other letters are in fact authored not by teens, but by rabbis and educators retelling what young people "really" think. And, here too, the editors explain that "some" of the letters "by teenagers... have been deliberately omitted." Editors, it seems, respond in advance to their own critics, who might argue that the editors should not publish these subversive letters. The editors explain that they have published only the softer versions. At the same time, the editors articulate to the careful reader that the extent of teen anger and frustration runs deeper than these published letters.

Moreover, in the case of student letters, editors wrote and published their own responses to individual students, making the editors' defenses of the community more direct and targeted. One teen, for example, leveled a blistering attack on the Haredi community for its extra-legal stringencies and for its insistence on a conformity that does not leave room for individualism, particularly when it comes to matters of dress. "I know a number of people who are 'on the fringe and beyond'... [because] they feel that their parents/teachers/schools etc. are too demanding with them on issues that are not *halachos* [laws], but rather *chumros* [stringencies].... We live in a society that judges people only by the way they look. Did you ever notice that when you ask someone about someone else, they almost always describe the way the person dresses?"[60] The editors respond directly to this young man. They agree with the first point, that insisting on stringencies can, at times, prove counterproductive. Yet, when it comes to conformity in dress, they are less accepting. "There is some inherent value in the issue of dress.... It sets us apart from the immoral and hedonistic society that surrounds us.... Dress is a form of symbolic speech. It often signals to the world what values we embrace and, even more important, which values we reject.... When one abandons the white shirt for the blue, it may signal that something is amiss."[61]

These two issues of *The Jewish Observer* exemplify the role of editors in simultaneously opening and closing lines of discussion. These magazine issues about dropouts, as well as numerous other issues of *The Jewish Observer*, could supply endless examples of explicit and implied communal self-criticism, balanced with numerous mechanisms and rhetorical strategies for framing and limiting that criticism, thereby both maintaining the community's internal hierarchy and supporting the community's superior self-image. Editors work hard to find the right balance, and when they succeed – as they seem to have regarding these issues – the community begins to change aspects of its policy and practice. These magazine issues opened a wellspring of conversation, institution building, introspection, and communal improvement. The relatively open and heated debate regarding issues of teen dropout has created increased awareness of the problem and led to significant changes and innovations in Haredi education in the past decade. Several attempts have been made to survey the extent of the problem.[62] New organizations and programs, such as MASK (Mothers and fathers Aligned Saving Kids), have been founded to provide resources to struggling parents. Nefesh, the organization of Orthodox mental-health professionals, has placed the problem of at-risk youth at the center of its agenda.[63] Furthermore, the community has created numerous programs, like Camp Extreme and Project YES of Agudath Israel, in addition to new schools and educational institutions, to help these struggling youth find a place for themselves. Social support and psychological services, as well as drug counseling, rehabilitation centers, and other resources have become increasingly available within the Haredi community. Perhaps most importantly – though this is difficult to measure – parents and educators have become progressively more sensitive to signs of at-risk behavior, and have, it seems likely, become more astute and sensitive in their responses to children with adjustment issues. While some suggest that this topic "needs to be addressed, but not in the public arena," others, including the editors of *The Jewish Observer*, believe that "these problems can and will be addressed" only if there is public debate.[64]

The Internet as Sea Change?

Something has changed dramatically in the decade since *The Jewish Observer* addressed the matters of dropout and delinquency: the internet. Editors worked hard at the turn of the millennium to ensure that internal criticism remained within acceptable boundaries, and editors of Haredi magazines and publications continue to do so. But in the years since, an important segment of the Haredi community's internal conversation has moved to "web 2.0," where blogs, unmoderated comments, and ease of instantaneous publication allow vocal Haredi internal criticism, all relatively free of editorial oversight. Any Haredi Jew with a relatively inexpensive internet connection and a minimum of computer savvy can publish to the world any thoughts, criticisms, and attacks on his or her own community.

In the process, the discourse has changed. Lay criticism, even of the great rabbis, abounds, juxtaposed with no less vigorous defense of those rabbis and denouncement of critics. In some cases, news websites created by and for Haredim allow relatively unmoderated commenting, giving voice to laypeople to say what is on their minds. And so, readers of vosiznaiz.com or "Yeshiva World News" can post comments on the latest news or scandals in the community, or enter the "coffee room" to exchange ideas and debate with anybody interested in discussing the strengths and weaknesses of Haredi life. Topics range from outrageously priced groceries before the Passover holiday to attempts to cover up sexual abuse in Haredi schools.

Disgruntled Haredim and ex-Haredim have also created their own websites, chat forums, and blogs to articulate their frustrations. The website unpious.com, written mostly by and for those on or beyond the fringes of the Hasidic community, regularly blasts Haredi Judaism for its alleged hypocrisies, obscurantism, ignorance of the wider world, misogyny, and sexual repression. The (in)famous failedmessiah.com, founded by a no-longer Hasidic Jew Shmarya Rosenberg, dedicates itself to muckraking about the dark underbelly of Haredi life. Whether these criticisms are right or wrong, fair or unfair, editors can do little to regulate the discourse or to prevent laypeople – those still within the community and those who have left – from attempting to undermine the communal rabbinic hierarchy. These websites have significant influence, most apparently in their roles in publicizing sexual abuse in the Orthodox Jewish community. The web has given voice to victims and activists who could not have their opinions published in the mainstream Haredi press.

Many Haredi rabbis, educators, magazine editors, and gatekeepers would like nothing more than to return the genie to the bottle. Israeli rabbis have had greater success than American ones in encouraging Haredi Jews to use "kosher" cell phones, which do not have internet access. But even in Israel, many Haredi Jews continue to use regular phones.[65] In December 2009, prominent Haredi rabbis attempted to ban Haredi websites.[66] The attempt gained much publicity but had little effect on Haredi online life; chat rooms, blogs, and news sites remain, read, no doubt, by many within the Haredi community. Zvi Frankel got it right in the above-cited article in *The Jewish Observer* when he claims that blogs threaten the existing Haredi power structure.[67] For some observers, the internet represents a sea change in Haredi internal discourse, permanently and enduringly empowering laypeople at the expense of the older establishment. For other observers, hegemonic Haredi gatekeepers may well succeed in limiting the internet's impact on Haredi discourse and society or in co-opting it for their own purposes.[68] Perhaps both are correct, but only time will tell.

Chapter VII:
TRUTH, FICTION, AND NARRATIVE

> Shall we therefore readily allow our children to listen to
> any stories made up by anyone, and to form opinions
> that are for the most part the opposite of those we think
> they should have when they grow up?... Then it seems
> that our first business is to supervise the production of
> stories, and to choose only those we think suitable, and
> reject the rest. We shall persuade mothers and nurses to
> tell our chosen stories to their children, and by means
> of them to mold their minds and characters which are
> more important than their bodies. (Socrates, in Plato's
> *Republic*, 377, d-e)

Plato famously wanted to banish poets because poets lie. Fiction, after
all, means a kind of untruth. Specifically, Plato felt that poets lie about
the divine. Greek poets told stories in which gods behave like powerful and amoral humans, not worthy of worship, not transcendent. We
should take care to teach correctly, especially when we teach about matters of ultimate religious importance. Cynthia Ozick made a particularly
Jewish extension of Plato's objection. The true Creator has created the
universe. Fiction writers create a pretend universe. They lie about the
universe, and so they lie about God.[1]

However, as both Plato and Ozick understood quite well, there is good
reason to suspect that simple dichotomies between truth and falsehood,
fiction and non-fiction, do not neatly apply. Plato himself embedded his
critique of poets within a fictional dialogue about the nature of the good
republic. His subtext suggests that we need fiction, perhaps even lies, to
construct our communities. Individuals and communities do not build
their self-understandings on the basis of pure, unadulterated truth. Instead, people build a sense of identity and solidarity through narratives.

Narratives tell stories with characters and events. As such, they involve characters who relate to other characters and the world around

them, succeed or fail, emerge as heroes or villains, imagine a past or envision a future. Narratives ask an interpretive community to identify with certain characters or groups and not with others, and to follow the guidelines implicit in the stories. The events that make up a narrative implicitly or explicitly divide the world and its people into categories, assign attributes and values to those categories, explain how people of different kinds do or should behave, and envision the ways in which things or objects in the various categories do or should interact. Narratives explain who "we" are and who the "others" are, how we can and should react to them, and how they can and should react to us.

But narratives do not do this by explicitly stating answers to these questions. Instead, they call on listeners to imagine themselves as part of ongoing described events, to intuit their roles in the world by identifying with some characters and by living up to the values implicit in those characters and the events surrounding them. More, listeners identify themselves with the past, present, and implied future of the characters in the narrative. That is to say, people and groups appear as characters in their own narratives, because narratives inevitably describe the place of the "self" within a larger image of the world. As such, narratives not only provide individuals and groups with ways of organizing information; they offer ways of thinking about how to live and what to strive for. They offer images not only of how things are and were, but how they ought to be.[2]

The narratives around which communities build their values inevitably combine elements of truth and fiction. Or, to be more precise, human beings, as individuals and collectives, inevitably embed even true statements – even statements that correspond directly to a reality "out there" – within more complicated cognitive constructs: stories, moral maps, and pictures of the universe that position facts within a context. That context involves picking and choosing which facts to include and which to exclude. And the narrative inevitably involves interpretations and value judgments about the characters and groups in the narrative. Sometimes, this involves misrepresenting facts and creating fictions instead of sticking to verifiable facts. It always involves creatively interpreting and organizing material in ways that go beyond "just the facts." People relate to the world by positioning their facts within implicit answers to questions such as: What matters? What is worth knowing? Why do I/we care about these facts? How do these facts help me/us navigate the world? In what contexts do these facts matter? What kinds of behaviors do these facts call for? Ultimately, people cannot answer these questions only descriptively. As the expression goes, no "is" implies an "ought." Consequently, no description of things, no matter how detailed and precise, can tell me how to live. One cannot build a republic on the basis of pure fact; one must build it also on the basis of imagination. People need fiction, poetry, and narratives to make sense out of themselves and their environments. In short, people come to know themselves by placing themselves within the context of socially constructed facts and fictions about the past and the present, about the self and others, about in-group and out-group, about what was and what will be, about the good and the bad.

A Haredi Narrative

Very often, narratives remain implicit. In the course of this book, I have tried to tease out and make explicit some aspects of the narrative around which the contemporary Haredi community organizes itself. According to this story, Haredi Judaism begins with God's creation of the world and his revelation of the Torah to the Jewish people at Mount Sinai. This Torah, unique and unchanging, contains all the wisdom one needs to live well. Moreover, the truth and validity of Torah can be absolutely demonstrated, proven rationally. Unchanging Judaism requires male followers to study Torah intensely and constantly. It requires all Jews to observe the mitzvot down to the last detail and to submit to the authority of the great rabbis, the *gedolim*, who have a unique window into truth and God's will. Judaism must never become mixed, influenced, or coalesced with gentile culture, lest it deviate from its perfect and unchanging form. Pious Jews have always made genuine and good-faith attempts to live up to Torah, and their communities have, with rare exceptions, followed the lead of great rabbis. No community exemplified these values more than did modern Eastern Europe, particularly its yeshiva-centered and Hasidic-oriented *shtetl*. Materially poor, but with great spiritual richness, its residents lived in splendid isolation from outside culture, observed Jewish law scrupulously, studied Torah intensely, and viewed great rabbis as the ultimate decision makers and leaders. Today's Haredim cannot hope to surpass that Eastern European Jewish ideal, but they can do their best to imitate it. Contemporary Haredi Judaism today follows the timeless sources, unchanged in any significant way.

Today, Haredi life differs in profound ways from the lives of non-Haredi neighbors, so much so that Haredim must establish separate enclaves to avoid the dangerous outside influences. Consequently, the Haredi way of life is vastly superior to that of the surrounding culture. By caving in to the influence of the zeitgeist, all other groups of contemporary Jews abandon an attempt to live up to what Judaism has always stood for. Haredi life today represents the only authentic Judaism, and it will inevitably triumph into the future.

In the course of this book, I have attempted not only to describe this narrative, but also to interrogate it, to demonstrate the difficult, complex, and subtle work that Haredi Jews must do to build this narrative by combining facts and fictions and weaving them into a coherent story. I have tried to show gaps between facts and fictions in this Haredi narrative, such as attempts to view modern, contemporary parenting advice as grounded in supposedly unchanging Jewish sources. *Strictly Kosher Reading* attempts to describe some of the literary tools that Haredi popular literature uses to cover over or explain those gaps, including at times denying and at times admitting borrowing from contemporary culture. I have also tried to explain the interpretive principles that Haredi authors use to distinguish what is important to them from what is unimportant, the imaginative work they must do to weave their facts and purported facts into a narrative, such as presenting Haskalah as the antithesis of Torah while ignoring the more complex relations between Haskalah and observance in Eastern European Jewry. Haredi popular literature drafts everything from diet guides to proofs for the existence of God into an attempt to construct and transmit the Haredi narrative. Moreover, I have tried to identify ways in which Haredi popular literature tries to make this narrative plausible, for example by limiting internal criticism to topics and matters that do not undermine the narrative. In short, I have tried to describe the complexities of the task of Haredi meaning-making and storytelling.

In this book, I have also tried to say something about the role of popular literature in spreading this narrative. By creating mass-produced, accessible print matter with shared values, priorities, and cultural narratives, and by distributing these books widely within the Haredi community, ArtScroll, Feldheim, Targum Press, and other publishers help unify a community around these shared values.[3] People, at least in part, come to understand what Haredi Judaism is and what it demands of them by reading these popular books. Some observers have even traced the so-called "shift to the right" in American Orthodoxy to ArtScroll's influence.[4]

In the end, I am trying to make a larger point about contemporary Haredi identity. Haredi self-understanding to the contrary, Haredi Judaism is not and probably could not be a simple continuation of ancient Judaism, not only because Judaism itself had changed over the course of centuries and millennia, but because contemporary Haredim are profoundly acculturated. That is, Haredi Judaism is modern not only in the sense that any rejection of modern conditions requires engagement with modernity and a self-understanding constructed around modernity,[5] but also because the particular ideas, values, and social behaviors of Haredi Jews share a great deal with the culture around them and differ from much of the ancient tradition. We should understand Haredi distinctiveness from non-Haredi outsiders not entirely in terms of different values and cultural patterns, but also and perhaps primarily in terms of symbolic boundaries: ways of making Haredi Jews feel different even under circumstances in which, in fact, they are very much the same. Moreover, we should view Haredi popular literature not only as the literary evidence of existing differences between Haredi Jews and others. We should also view it as a way of forming Haredi identity, as a purveyor of prescriptions that operate especially when and where Haredi Jews do resemble the culture around them. Creating such a sense of difference and distinction – that is, creating the symbolic boundaries without which no community or identity can exist – is hard and ongoing work, and popular literature plays a role in Haredi identity-construction.

All There is in the World is the Torah

An otherwise unremarkable sentence, buried in an otherwise unmemorable article in *The Jewish Observer*, captures this tension precisely, even if unintentionally. "All there is in the world is the Torah."[6] This statement could mean one of two contradictory things, and I suggest that we will learn something important about the paradoxical nature of contemporary American Haredi Jewry if we take it to mean both.

The simplest meaning suggests that Torah is the only worthwhile thing in the world, which is why the author follows up by explaining that, "Everything else is meaningless." Yet, the sentence could also mean exactly the opposite, something that the author no doubt does not intend. It could mean that everything in the world, no matter how secular, is actually Torah. On the surface, this reading appears entirely implausible, since it seems like heresy of the worst kind. But I have claimed in *Strictly Kosher Reading* that if we look closely at contemporary Haredi culture and its popular literature, we discover that Haredi Jewry has converted many aspects of general culture, koshering them, turning them into Torah.

These two interpretations of the sentence stand in tension with one another. The first interpretation focuses on boundaries. Those within the Torah's protective envelope have access to everything important or valuable; they need nothing else. The second interpretation blurs those boundaries, suggesting an ongoing interaction between Torah and that which, on the surface, comes from outside Torah. Both mutually exclusive interpretations contain truth. The Haredi community works extremely hard to reinforce its carefully constructed boundaries, protecting itself from what it perceives as the damaging influences of the outside. At the same time, the Haredi community works extremely hard to introduce itself to broad aspects of general culture, indeed to convince itself that many aspects of general culture are in fact Torah.

PREFACE

1   Baruch Chait, *The Lost Treasure of Tikkun HaMiddos Island* (Jerusalem: B and B Septimus Educational Publications, 2001), 26-27, 30. In quotations, circular parentheses appear in the original while square brackets indicate an addition to the original text.

2   This illustration does not depict at least one decadent practice generally associated by Haredim with non-Haredi culture: sexual promiscuity. Presumably it would be considered immodest to even draw such sins, and depiction of such activities might also make the sinners' world seem not only immoral but also enticing.

3   Ibid.

4   Strictly speaking, I refer to matters of cultural or group acculturation rather than to individual or psychological acculturation. Popular literature provides some access to a group's culture, but provides much less information about individuals and their subjective attitudes. See Theodore Graves, "Psychological Acculturation in a Tri-Ethnic Community," *South Western Journal of Anthropology* 23 (1967), 337-350, and John W. Berry, "Immigration, Acculturation, and Adaptation," *Applied Psychology: An International Review* 46 (1997), 7.

5   On the notion of symbolic boundaries as distinct from social boundaries, see Michele Lamont and Virag Molnar, "The Study of Boundaries in the Social Sciences," *Annual Review of Sociology* 28 (2002), 167-195.

CHAPTER ONE

1   For examples of such works, see Abraham Joshua Heschel, *The Quest for Certainty in Sa'adia's Philosophy* (New York: Feldheim, 1944); Louis Finkelstein, *Jewish Self-Government in the Middle Ages* (New York: Feldheim, 1964); Noah J. Cohen, *Tsa'ar Ba'ale Hayim: The Prevention of Cruelty to Animals, Its Bases, Development and Legislation in Hebrew Literature* (Jerusalem and New York: Feldheim, 1976); Leon Stitskin, *Eight Jewish Philosophers in the Tradition of Personalism* (New York and Jerusalem: Feldheim, 1979).

2   Meir Zlotowitz, Ed. *The Megillah* (Brooklyn: ArtScroll, 1976).

3   For a quick overview of their literary output, see www.artscroll.com; www.feldheim.com; www.targum.com.

4   Jeremy Stolow, *Orthodox by Design: Judaism, Print Politics, and the ArtScroll Revolution* (Berkeley, Los Angeles, and London: University of California Press, 2010).

5   Joseph Berger, "An English Talmud for Daily Readers and Debaters," *The New York Times*, February 10, 2005, available at http://www.nytimes.com/2005/02/10/books/10talm.html?pagewanted=all&position=, viewed November, 2010.

6   ArtScroll Publishers, *The Schottenstein Edition of the Talmud* (Brooklyn: Mesorah, 1990-2004), 72 volumes.

7   Susie Fishbein, *Kosher By Design: Picture Perfect Foods for the Holidays and Everyday* (Brooklyn: Mesorah, 2003) as well as the other books in the series.

8   See B. Barry Levy, "Our Torah, Your Torah and Their Torah: An Evaluation of the ArtScroll Phenomenon," in *Truth and Compassion: Essays on Judaism and Religion*, Eds. H. Joseph, et al. (Waterloo, Ontario: Wilfrid Laurier University Press, 1983),

137-189; idem. "ArtScroll: An Overview," in *Approaches to Modern Judaism*, Ed. Marc Lee Raphael (Chico, CA: Scholars Press, 1983), 111-140; idem. "Contemporary Jewish Booklore: The Exegetical and Editorial Work of Rabbi Meir Zlotowitz and Rabbi Nosson Scherman (or The ArtScroll Phenomenon, 2005)," unpublished manuscript; Jacob J. Schacter, "Facing the Truths of History," *The Torah U-Madda Journal* 8 (1998-1999), 200-276; Jonathan Helfand, "Striving for Truth: Struggling with the Historical Critical Method," *The Edah Journal* 2:1 (2002), unpaginated, available at http://www.edah.org/backend/JournalArticle/helfland2_1.pdf, viewed October, 2010; and Zvi Zohar, "*VaYivra ArtScroll et Haleb Betzalmo: Itzuvah Shel Haleb KaKehilat Kodesh Haredit*, in *Kehilat Yehudei Haleb*," Ed. Miriam Frankel (Jerusalem: Makhon Ben Tzvi, forthcoming).

9   Marshall Sklare, *Conservative Judaism: An American Religious Movement* (Glencoe, IL: Free Press, 1955), 43.

10   Charles Liebman, "Orthodoxy in American Jewish Life," *American Jewish Year Book* 67 (1966), 34-36.

11   The National Jewish Population Surveys indicated that Orthodox Jews made up some 11% of the Jewish population in 1971, 7% in 1990, and 10% in 2001. There has been some debate regarding the precision of all of these numbers, particularly the low number in 1990. For more recent data, see United Jewish Communities, *American Jewish Religious Denominations* (New York: National Jewish Population Survey, n.d.), available at http://www.jewishfederations.org/local_includes/downloads/7579.pdf, viewed August, 2010.

12   Etan Diamond, *And I Will Dwell in Their Midst: Orthodox Jews in Suburbia* (Chapel Hill and London: University of North Carolina Press, 2000). On the rise of day schools, see Gil Graff, *"And You Shall Teach Them Diligently": A Concise History of Jewish Education in the United States, 1776-2000* (New York: Jewish Theological Seminary, 2008), in the index under "day schools."

13   Samuel G. Freedman, *Jew vs. Jew: The Struggle for the Soul of American Jewry* (New York: Touchstone, 2000), 338. For a less optimistic take on Orthodox triumphantalism, see Jonathan Sarna, "The Future of American Orthodoxy," *Sh'ma* (February, 2001), available at http://www.shma.com/feb01/sarna.htm, viewed July, 2008.

14   On this group and their limited acculturation, see most recently Ayala Fader, *Mitzvah Girls: Bringing up the Next Generation of Hasidic Jews in Brooklyn* (Princeton and Oxford: Princeton University Press, 2009).

15   Samuel Heilman and Steven Cohen may not have drawn their sample from the most representative community of Modern Orthodox Jews, but their points about levels of halakhic observance in the Modern Orthodox and more isolationist Orthodox communities are well taken. See their *Cosmopolitans and Parochials: Modern Orthodox Jews in America* (Chicago and London: University of Chicago Press, 1989).

16   See Alan Brill, "Judaism in Culture: Beyond the Bifurcation of Torah and Madda," *The Edah Journal* 4:1 (2004), 1-26, http://www.edah.org/backend/JournalArticle/4_1_brill.pdf, viewed July, 2010.

17   My use of the term Haredi to refer to "Black Hat" Jews and not Hasidic ones is somewhat idiosyncratic. In other contexts, the term Haredi would include both groups.

18   On "yeshivish" jargon, see the tongue-in-cheek dictionary, Chaim M. Weiser, *Frumspeak: The First Dictionary of Yeshivish* (Northvale, NJ: Jason Aaronson, 1995), and Sarah Bunim Benor, "Second Style Acquisition: The Linguistic Socialization of Newly Orthodox Jews," Ph.D. Dissertation, Stanford University, 2004.

19   William B. Helmreich, *The World of the Yeshiva: An Intimate Portrait of Orthodox Jewry* (New Haven and London: Yale University Press, 1982), 54.

20   On Agudath Israel and its role in forming Haredi identity, see Jeremy Stolow, "Trans-

nationalism and the New Religio-Politics: Reflections on the Orthodox Jewish Case," *Theory, Culture and Society* 21:2 (2004), 109-137.

21 See Helmreich, *The World of the Yeshiva*, for a discussion of American yeshiva life.

22 Yoel Finkelman, "Ultra-Orthodox/Haredi Education," in *The International Handbook of Jewish Education*, Eds. Helena Miller, Alex Pomson, and Lisa Grant (Dordrecht, Heidelberg, London, and New York: Springer, 2011), Vol. 2, 1063-1080.

23 Kimmy Caplan, "Haredim and Western Culture: A View from Both Sides of the Ocean," *Middle Eastern Societies and the West: Accommodation or Clash of Civilizations?*, Ed. Meir Litvak (Tel Aviv: The Moshe Dayan Center for Middle Eastern and African Studies, Tel Aviv University, 2006), 269-288.

24 Many have described these changes, each with slightly different emphases. See Jeffrey Gurock, "The Winnowing of American Orthodoxy," in his *American Jewish Orthodoxy in Historical Perspective* (Hoboken, NJ: Ktav, 1996), 299-312; idem, *Orthodox Jews in America* (Bloomington and Indianapolis: Indiana University Press, 2009), Chap. 9-10; Haym Soloveitchik, "Rupture and Reconstruction: The Transformation of Contemporary Orthodoxy," *Tradition* 28:4 (1994), 64-130; Samuel Heilman, *Sliding to the Right: The Contest for the Future of American Jewish Orthodoxy* (Berkeley: University of California Press, 2006).

25 Tehilla Abramov, *The Secret of Jewish Femininity: Insights into the Practice of Taharat HaMishpachah* (Southfield, MI: Targum/Feldheim, 1988), 29.

26 From the approbation of R. Shlomo Wolbe to Shimon Hurwitz, *Being Jewish* (Jerusalem: Feldheim, 1979), 2; Pesach Eliyahu Falk, *Modesty: An Adornment for Life* (Jerusalem: Feldheim, 1998), 3.

27 Berry, "Immigration, Acculturation, Adaptation," 10-11.

28 Jacob Katz, "Da'at Torah: The Unqualified Authority Claimed for Halakhists," *Jewish History* 11:1 (1997), 41-50; Lawrence Kaplan, "Daas Torah: A Modern Conception of Rabbinic Authority," in *Rabbinic Authority and Personal Autonomy*, Ed. Moshe Sokol (Northvale, NJ: Aaronson, 1992), 1-60; Binyamin Brown, *"Doktrinat Da'at Torah: Sheloshah Shelavim,"* *Jerusalem Studies in Jewish Thought* 19 (2005), 537-600.

29 Will Herberg, *Protestant-Catholic-Jew: An Essay in American Religious Sociology* (Garden City, NY: Anchor Books, 1955), Chap. 5.

30 R. Stephen Warner, "Work in Progress: Toward a New Paradigm for the Sociological Study of Religion in the United States," *The American Journal of Sociology* 98:5 (1993), 1044-1093; William H. Swatos and Kevin J. Christiano, "Secularization Theory: The Course of a Concept," *Sociology of Religion* 60:3 (1999), 209-228.

31 Wade Clark Roof, *A Generation of Seekers: The Spiritual Journeys of the Baby Boom Generation* (San Francisco: Harper, 1993).

32 Christian Smith, *American Evangelicalism: Embattled and Thriving* (Chicago and London: University of Chicago, 1998), Chap. 4.

33 Emmanuel Sivan, "The Enclave Culture," in *Fundamentalisms Comprehended* (Chicago and London: University of Chicago Press, 1995), 11-68.

34 Anthony Cohen, *The Symbolic Construction of Community* (London and New York: Tavistock Publications, 1985); Lamont and Molnar, "The Study of Boundaries in the Social Sciences."

35 See Murray I. Friedman, "What is Our Historical Imperative? On the Function of Torah-True Literature in Our Times," *The Jewish Observer* 1:1 (September, 1963), 19-20.

36 To paraphrase Colleen McDannell, *Material Christianity: Religion and Popular Culture in America* (New Haven and London: Yale University Press, 1995).

37 Kosher Care over-the-counter pain-relief and cold medicines are available in pharmacies in Haredi neighborhoods. See http://www.hitechcomputers.com/kcare/index.htm, viewed August, 2007.

38 To a lesser degree, similar patterns also exist within America's Muslim community. See Lynn Schofield Clark, "Identity, Belonging, and Religious Lifestyle Branding (Fashion Bibles, Bhangra Parties, and Muslim Pop)," in *Religion, Media, and the Marketplace*, Ed. Lynn Schofield Clark (New Brunswick, NJ and London: Rutgers University Press, 2007), 1-36.

39 McDannell, *Material Christianity*, Chap. 8.

40 See some of the relevant statistics in Heather Hendershot, *Shaking the World for Jesus: Media and Conservative Evangelical Culture* (Chicago: University Of Chicago Press, 2004), 21-22 (also see 56-58), as well as Mara Einstein, *Brands of Faith: Marketing Religion in a Commercial Age* (London and New York: Routledge, 2008), Chap. 3. William D. Romanowski, "Evangelicals and Popular Music: The Contemporary Christian Music Industry," in *Religion and Popular Culture in America*, Eds. Bruce David Forbes and Jeffrey H. Mahan (Berkeley and Los Angeles: University Of California Press, 2000), 103-124; Carol Flake, *Redemptorama: Culture, Politics, and the New Evangelicalsim* (n.p.: Penguin, 1984), Chap. 8.

41 If the CBA (formerly the Christian Booksellers Association) keeps systematic data on the Christian product industry, the much smaller Haredi community keeps no such records, and insiders with whom I spoke were less than enthusiastic about sharing what they know.

42 On these and other forces in the growth of American Protestantism, see Nancy T. Ammerman, "North American Protestant Fundamentalism," in *Fundamentalisms Observed*, Eds. Martin Marty and R. Scott Appleby (Chicago and London: University of Chicago Press, 1994), 38-42.

43 Warner, "Work in Progress"; R. Laurence Moore, *Selling God: American Religion in the Marketplace of Culture* (New York and Oxford: Oxford University Press, 1994); Roger Finke and Laurence Iannacone, "Supply-Side Explanations for Religious Change," *Annals of the American Academy of Political and Social Science* 527 (1993), 27-39; Einstein, *Brands of Faith*. Regarding these patterns in the contemporary Orthodox Jewish book market, see Stolow, *Orthodox by Design*.

44 Heilman, *Sliding to the Right*, 75-76 puts the number at approximately 200,000, including what I have called both Haredi and Hasidic Jews. His estimate may be quite low.

45 Eric Gormly, "Evangelizing through Appropriation: Toward a Cultural Theory of the Growth of Contemporary Christian Music," *Journal of Media and Religion* 24:4 (2003), 251-265. For a related attempt by Israeli Religious-Zionists to re-create modern national culture in a religious image, see Yoel Finkelman, "It's a Small, Small World: Secular Zionism through the Eyes of a Contemporary Religious Zionist *Parshat Hashavua* Pamphlet," in *The Relationship of Orthodox Jews with Believing Jews of Other Religious Ideologies and Non-Believing Jews*, Ed. Adam Mintz (New York: Yeshiva University Press, 2010), 313-350. In this sense, both some circles of American evangelical Christianity as well as Israeli Religious-Zionism adopt something akin to what Almond, Appleby, and Sivan have referred to as a "world transformer" type of religion, one that hopes to partially emerge from its isolated enclave and have a broad impact in the wider culture. See Gabriel A. Almond, R. Scott Appleby, and Emmanuel Sivan, *Strong Religion: The Rise of Fundamentalisms around the World* (Chicago and London: University of Chicago Press, 2003), 168-179.

46 A vast discussion within the field of culture studies struggles with the definition and even the very usefulness of the term "popular literature" and "popular culture." In this context, I use the term to mean cultural products meant to be accessible and appealing to a broad common denominator of people and which succeeds in reaching a wide audience. See Daniel Stout, "Beyond Culture Wars: An Introduction to the Study of

Religion and Popular Culture," in *Religion and Popular Culture: Studies in the Interaction of Worldviews*, Ed. Stout and Judith M. Buddenbaum (Ames, IO: Iowa State University Press, 2001), 5.

47   Jacket covers from Aryeh Striks and Shimon Zehnwirth, *Pinnacle of Creation: Torah Insights into Human Nature* (Brooklyn: Mesorah, 2007); Yaakov Wolfson, *All I Needed to Know I Learned in Yeshiva* (Southfield, MI: Targum Press, 1995); Zelig Pliskin, *Gateway to Self-Knowledge* (Jerusalem: Aish Hatorah Publications, 1986).

48   Simcha Bunim Cohen, *The Shabbos Kitchen: A Comprehensive Halakhic Guide to the Preparation of Food and Other Kitchen Activities on Shabbos and Yom Tov* (Brooklyn: Mesorah Publications, 1991); idem. *Children in Halachah: Laws Relating to Young Children* (Brooklyn: Mesorah Publications, 1993). A pioneer in this regard is certainly R. Yehoshua Neuwirth's influential *Shemirath Shabbath: A Guide to the Practical Observance of the Sabbath* (Jerusalem and New York: Feldheim, 1984). Though the organization of the latter book follows legal-halakhic categories, the index is organized based on the realia of the contemporary nuclear family and its Shabbat observance.

49   For more on this tension, see Anne L. Borden, "Making Money, Saving Souls: Christian Bookstores and the Commodification of Christianity," in *Religion, Media and the Marketplace*, Ed. Lynn Schofield Clark (New Brunswick, NJ: Rutgers University Press, 2007), 67-89.

50   Such a "non-confrontational" model is suggested in J.D.J. Waardenburg, "Summaries of the Contributions," in *Official and Popular Religion: Analysis of a Theme for Religious Studies*, Eds. Pieter H. Vrijof and Jacques Waardenburg (The Hague: Mouton Publishers, 1979), 636-637. For further discussion of the lack of tension between elite and popular religion, see David Hall, *Worlds of Wonder, Days of Judgment: Popular Religious Belief in Early New England* (Cambridge: Harvard University Press, 1989), Introduction. In this, I disagree with Kimmy Caplan, who identifies more tension between elite and popular Haredi culture. See his *Besod HaSiah HaHaredi* (Jerusalem: Zalman Shazar Center, 2007), Introduction.

51   This is a variation on Mary Douglas' notion that enclave cultures tend to be non-hierarchical. The Haredi enclave is a partial counterexample to that claim, to the extent that political and social hierarchy is very important within it. Still, the lack of tension between elite and popular culture moves in Douglas' direction. See her *Natural Symbols* (London: Barrie and Rockliff, 1970).

52   Perlmutter, *Tools for Tosafos* (Southfield, MI: Targum/Feldheim, 1996); idem., *Grow with Gemara* (Southfield, MI: Targum/Feldheim, 2005).

53   Ehud Tokatly, Shmuel and Judy Klitsner, *The Lost Children of Tarshish* (Southfield, MI and Lakewood, NJ: Targum Press and CIS, 1989); Shmuel Klitsner, *Wrestling Jacob: Deception, Identity and Freudian Slips in Genesis* (Jerusalem and New York: Urim Publications, 2006); Judy Klitsner, *Subversive Sequels in the Bible: How Biblical Stories Mine and Undermine Each Other* (Philadelphia: The Jewish Publication Society, 2009). The latter book won a prestigious National Jewish Book Award.

54   Soloveitchik, "Rupture and Reconstruction."

55   Regarding these factors in the religious marketplace, see Moore, *Selling God*; Einstein, *Brands of Faith*. Regarding Orthodox publishing, see Stolow, *Orthodox by Design*.

56   Yechezkel Hirshman, *One Above and Seven Below: A Consumer's Guide to Orthodox Judaism from the Perspective of the Chareidim* (Jerusalem: Mazo, 2007), 69.

57   See McDannell, *Material Christianity*; Hendershot, *Shaking the World*; Borden, "Making Money, Saving Souls"; Gordon Lynch, Ed., *Between Sacred and Profane: Researching Religion and Popular Culture* (London and New York: I.B. Taurus, 2007), and the diverse literature cited there; Edward Croft Dutton, "Crop-Tops, Hipsters and Liminality: Fashion and Differentiation in Two Evangelical Student Groups," *Journal of Religion*

and Popular Culture 9 (2005), available at http://www.usask.ca/relst/jrpc/art9-fashion. html, viewed April, 2007.

58   Stolow, *Orthodox by Design*; idem. "Communicating Authority, Consuming Tradition: Jewish Orthodox Outreach Literature and Its Reading Public," in *Religion, Media and the Public Sphere*, Eds. Brigite Meyers and Annelies Moors (Bloomington: Indiana University Press, 2006), 73-91; Hillary Warren, "'Jewish Space Aliens Are Lucky to Be Free': Religious Distinctiveness, Media, and Markets in Jewish Children's Culture," in Clark, Ed. *Religion, Media, and to the Marketplace*, 90-101.

59   Binyomin Forst and Aaron D. Twerski, *The Laws of B'rochos: A Comprehensive Exposition of the Background and Laws of Blessings* (Brooklyn: Mesorah, 1990). Note that such a work reflects a situation in which educated Haredi Jews may prefer an accessible English-language format to the traditional language of halakhic discourse. See Soloveitchik, "Rupture and Reconstruction."

60   Hendershot, *Shaking the World*, 11-12. Also see Amy Johnson Frykholm, *Rapture Culture: Left Behind in Evangelical America* (New York: Oxford University Press, 2004) 160-161, and Hillary Warren, "Southern Baptists as Audience and Public: A Cultural Analysis of the Disney Boycott," in Stout, Ed. *Religion and Popular Culture*, 169-186.

61   On the distinction between encoding and decoding, see Stuart Hall, "Encoding, Decoding," in *The Culture Studies Reader*, Ed. Simon During (London: Routledge, 1990), 507-517. The distinction between what is "ascribed" to religion by popular culture in contrast to what readers "achieve" as they read, comes from Stewart M. Hoover, "Religion, Media, and the Cultural Center Of Gravity," in Stout, Ed. *Religion and Popular Culture*, 58. More broadly, one might understand my approach as a combination of what Gordon Lynch refers to as "author focused" and "text based" approaches to religion and popular culture, while ignoring his "ethnographic approach." See his *Understanding Theology and Popular Culture* (Oxford: Blackwell, 2005). For an example of what such a reception study might look like, see Frykholm, *Rapture Culture*. Stolow pays some attention to reader reception in his *Orthodox by Design*, and his "Communicating Authority."

62   My choice to examine these books as collective cultural products also means thinking less about the physical geography of an individual author and more about the cultural milieu. An American expatriate author living in Israel belongs, in many ways, to the collective American-style Haredi community.

63   For a discussion of such a dynamic within the Christian fiction market, see Jonathan Cordero, "The Production of Christian Fiction," *Journal of Religion and Popular Culture* 6 (2004), available at www.usak.ca/relst/jrpc/art6-xianfiction-print.html, viewed September, 2008.

64   Tony Bennett, "Series Editor's Preface," in *Popular Fiction: Technology, Ideology, Production, Reading* (London and New York: Routledge, 1990), ix.

CHAPTER TWO

1   Akiva Tatz, *Worldmask* (Southfield, MI: Targum/Feldheim, 1995), 84.

2   Sylvia Barack Fishman, *Jewish Life and American Culture* (Albany, NY: State University of New York Press, 2000), 10.

3   Ibid.

4   Ibid.

5   Haym Soloveitchik, "Rupture and Reconstruction," 75. For internal Haredi discussion regarding this issue, see Mordechai Schiller, "Chasidus in Song – Not for the Record," *The Jewish Observer* 10:8 (March, 1975), 21; Breindy Leizerson, "Set the

Record Straight," *The Jewish Observer* 20:4 (May, 1987), 40-41; Dovid Sears, "Who Took the 'Jewish' Out of Jewish Music?" *The Jewish Observer* 29:10 (January, 1997), 12-16; Yosef C. Golding, "How to Get the Entire Jewish Music World Angry at Me... Or a Parents' Guide to What Your Children Listen To," *The Jewish Observer* 40:4 (May, 2007), 36-37.

6   Stolow, *Orthodox by Design*, 132-142; Andrew R. Heinze, "The Americanization of 'Mussar': Abraham Twerski's Twelve Steps," *Judaism* 48:4 (1999), 450-469. On the self-absorption of this therapeutic self-help literature, see Wendy Kaminer, *I'm Dysfunctional, You're Dysfunctional: The Recovery Movement and Other Self-Help Fashions* (New York: Vintage Books, 1993).

7   See below and Yoel Finkelman, "Medium and Message in Contemporary Haredi Adventure Fiction," *The Torah U-Madda Journal* 13 (2005), 50-87.

8   The academic literature has focused on this trend primarily regarding the development of Orthodox historiography. See below, Chapter Four, n. 4.

9   Yaakov Levinson, *The Jewish Guide to Natural Nutrition* (Jerusalem and New York: Feldheim, 1995), 4-5. Much of the following analysis could be duplicated for the issue of *The Jewish Observer* entitled "A Healthy and Productive Life as a Torah Jew," 40:8 (November, 2007) and for David J. Zulberg, *The Life-Transforming Diet: Based on the Health and Psychological Principles of Maimonides and Other Classical Sources* (Jerusalem and New York: Feldheim, 2007).

10 Levinson, *Natural Nutrition*, 5. Zulberg, *The Life-Transforming Diet*, quotes more extensively from selected passages from Maimonides' medical writings, those in line with contemporary sensibilities.

11 Unpaginated approbation of Prof. Leon Epstein.

12 Maimonides, *Mishneh Torah, Hilkhot De'ot*, 4:1; Levinson, *Natural Nutrition*, 128.

13 Levinson, *Natural Nutrition*, 136.

14 Ibid., 4. Maimonides did advocate eating until not fully satiated, though Levinson's language, as noted, derives from modern, not Maimonidean categories. See Maimonides, *Mishneh Torah, Hilkhot De'ot*, 4:2.

15 Harvey Levenstein, *Paradoxes of Plenty: A Social History of Eating in Modern America* (New York and Oxford: Oxford University Press, 1993), Chap. 16. For further reflections on the contemporary Orthodox diet, see Brill, "Judaism in Culture," 3, and Stolow, "Aesthetics/Ascetics: Visual Piety and Pleasure in a Stricly Kosher Cookbook," *Postscripts* 2:1 (2006), 5-28 (some of which also appears in his *Orthodox by Design*). Levinson does not put as much emphasis as American general culture on the aesthetic aspects of weight loss, perhaps because he does not perceive looking attractive as a religious goal. In this, Zulberg's *The Life-Transforming Diet* comes closer to the general American concern with body-image and aesthetics.

16 Molly Worthen, "Housewives of God," *The New York Times Magazine*, November 12, 2010, available at http://www.nytimes.com/2010/11/14/magazine/14evangelicals-t. html, viewed November, 2010.

17 See, for example, *Shulhan 'Arukh, Yoreh De'ah*, 336:1. The ambivalence about seeking doctors, on the theory that divine providence governs illness and heath, was generally of theoretical import only, and usually did not have practical implications. See the commentary of the Taz, ibid.

18 Helen Hardcare, "The Impact of Fundamentalism on Women, the Family, and Interpersonal Relations," in *Fundamentalisms and Society*, Eds. Martin E. Marty and R. Scott Appleby (Chicago and London: University of Chicago Press, 1993), 129. On similar Christian conflation of modern notions of marriage with traditional ones, see James Davison Hunter, *Evangelicalism: The Coming Generation* (Chicago and London: University of Chicago Press, 1987), 76-93.

19   Avraham Pam and Tzvi Baruch Hollander, "The Jewish Family – In Its Glory and in Crisis," *The Jewish Observer* 29:4 (May, 1996), 6.

20   Yirmiyohu Abramov and Tehilla Abramov, *Two Halves of a Whole: Torah Guidelines for Marriage* (Southfield, MI: Targum/Feldheim, 1994), 158.

21   Jacob Katz, *Tradition and Crisis: Jewish Society at the End of the Middle Ages* (New York: Schocken, 1971), 141-142. Unfortunately, a systematic history of the Jewish family has yet to be written. But see, Elisheva Baumgarten, *Mothers and Children: Jewish Family Life in Medieval Europe* (Princeton: Princeton University Press, 2004); Chae-Ran Freeze, *Jewish Marriage and Divorce in Imperial Russia* (Hanover, NH: Brandies University Press, 2004); David Kraemer, Ed., *The Jewish Family: Metaphor and Memory* (New York and Oxford: Oxford University Press, 1989); Avraham Grossman, *Pious and Rebellious: Jewish Women in Medieval Europe*, Trans. Jonathan Chipman (Waltham, MA: Brandeis University Press, 2004), Chaps. 2-4.

22   David Biale, *Eros and the Jews* (New York: Basic Books, 1992), Chap. 3.

23   Meir Winkler, *Bayis Ne'eman b'Yisrael: Practical Steps to Success in Marriage* (Jerusalem and New York: Feldheim, 1988), 53, 57.

24   The expression comes from Christopher Lasch, *Haven in a Heartless World: The Family Besieged* (New York: Basic Books, 1977).

25   Ironically, in the early modern period, the Haskalah, rather than the tradition, called for marriages based on love and compatibility rather than socio-economic advantage, and called to protect women from the marketplace by carving out for them a domestic role in which they could spend more of their time and energy on child-rearing. The central Jewish polemic against marriage as a financial arrangement and against women's role in the workplace came from Haredi popular literature's rhetorical enemies, the *maskilim*. See Biale, *Eros and the Jews*, 159-161.

26   Lawrence Stone, *The Family, Sex, and Marriage in England 1500-1800* (New York: Harper and Row, 1977); Steven Mintz and Susan Kellogg, *Domestic Revolutions: A Social History of American Family Life* (New York: Free Press, 1988).

27   Mintz and Kellogg, *Domestic Revoluations*, 115, describing the particular model of companionate marriage advocated by early twentieth century progressives in America. Also see 186. Haredim, like these progressives, advocate "divorce by mutual consent... on the grounds of incompatibility," at least as an unfortunate consequence of the failure of the companionate marriage (ibid.). Yet, Haredim are less likely than these progressive to support free use of contraception and open sex-education. Haredim also remain attached to Victorian sensibilities that distinguish between the feminine/domestic/secure sphere and the masculine/public/dangerous sphere, a distinction against which progressives polemicized.

28   Katz, *Tradition and Crisis*, 141-142

29   Abramov and Abramov, *Two Halves*, 65.

30   Aharon Feldman, *The River, the Kettle and the Bird: A Torah Guide to Successful Marriage* (Israel: CSB Publications, 1987), 11; Radcliff, *Aizer K'negdo: The Jewish Woman's Guide to Happiness in Marriage* (Southfield, MI: Targum/Feldheim, 1988), 11. Abramov and Abramov, *Two Halves*, 19. Also see Malka Kaganoff, *Dear Kallah: A Practical Guide for the New Bride* (Jerusalem and New York: Feldheim, 1993), Winkler, *Bayis Ne'eman*.

31   Lawrence Kelemen, *To Kindle a Soul: Ancient Wisdom for Modern Parents and Teachers* (Southfield, MI: Targum Press and Leviathan Press, 2001), 19-21. Some of Kelemen's formulations, as well as two of the book's central metaphors – that parenting consists of "building" and "planting" – come from the parenting guide of the twentieth-century Haredi rabbi, Shlomo Wolbe, which Kelemen had been involved in translating into English. Wolbe's ideas themselves are influenced by modern psychological and cultural categories, though the influence of modern psychology on contemporary musarists

like Wolbe has yet to be studied, to the best of my knowledge. See R. Shlomo Wolbe, *Zeri'ah U'Vinyan BeHinnukh* (Jerusalem: Feldheim, 1995), 23-24, and his *Planting and Building: Raising a Jewish Child*, Trans. Leib [Lawrence] Kelemen (Jerusalem and New York: Feldheim, 2000).

32   See Peter N. Stearns, *Anxious Parents: A History of Modern Childrearing in America* (New York and London: New York University Press, 2003), and Ann Hulbert, *Raising America: Experts, Parents, and a Century of Advice About Children* (New York: Vintage Books, 2003), Chap. 11.

33   On the difficulties in determining ancient Jewish attitudes toward child rearing, see David Kraemer, "Images of Childhood and Adolescence in Talmudic Literature," in his Ed., *The Jewish Family*, 65-68.

34   Baumgarten, *Mothers and Children*, 155.

35   Kelemen, *To Kindle a Soul*, 129-152. Quotes from 109, 130, 132-133.

36   *Shemot Rabbah*, 1 s.v. *Ve'eleh Shemot*, quoting Proverbs 13:24

37   Also see B.T. *Makkot*, 8a, *Bava Batra* 21a; *Midrash Tehillim*, Buber, 6; *Midrash Tenaim*, *Devarim* 25:3; Rashi on *Mishlei* 13:24 and on 19:18; Maimonides, *Mishneh Torah*, *Hilkhot Talmud Torah*, 2:2; *Shulhan 'Arukh*, *Yoreh De'ah*, 240:20 and Rama, 245:10; *Sefer Hasidim*, 302, cited in Baumgarten, *Mothers and Children*, 162; R. Yeshayahu Horowitz, *Shenei Luhot HaBerit* (Jerusalem: n.p., 1975), Letter Daled, paragraph 23-32; The Gaon of Vilna, *Even Shelemah* (n.p.: n.d., n.d.), 6:4. When *Shulhan 'Arukh*, *Yoreh De'ah*, 240:20 insists that one not beat his older children (according to Rama, 22-24 years old), this is not due to any opposition to corporal punishment per se, but, following his source (BT *Mo'ed Qatan* 17a), because the son might retaliate and violate the serious prohibition of injuring one's parent.

38   R. Alexander Ziskind of Horodno in his ethical will, quoted in Simhah Asaf, *Meqorot LeToldot HaHinnukh BeYisrael* (New York and Jerusalem: Jewish Theological Seminary, 2002), Vol. 1, 688. Also see Yitzchak ben Eliakim, author of *Sefer Lev Tov* (published in Prague in 1620), who insists that parents "not reveal their love [of their children] in their presence because then the children would not fear them and would not obey them." Cited in Gershon David Hundert, "Jewish Children and Childhood in Early Modern East Central Europe," in Kraemer, Ed. *The Jewish Family*, 82. Also see the related sources quoted in Hundert, 83, and Ephraim Kanarfogel, "Attitudes Toward Childhood in Medieval Jewish Society," in *Approaches to Judaism in Medieval Times*, Ed. David R. Blumenthal (Chico, CA: Scholars Press, 1985), Vol. 2, 1-34.

39   Horowitz, *Shnei Luhot HaBerit*, Letter Daled, para. 23-25.

40   See Steven Mintz, *Huck's Raft: A History of American Childhood* (Cambridge, MA, and London: Harvard University Press, 2004), 227-229, 349. Quote from 228.

41   Winkler, *Bayis Ne'eman*, 53-55.

42   Moshe Spieser, *Questions You Thought We Were Afraid You'd Ask and Answers You've Been Waiting to Hear* (Southfield, MI: Targum/Feldheim, 2004), 97-108. Gila Manolson, *The Magic Touch* (Jerusalem: Har Nof Publications, 1992).

43   See Yehudah Lebovits, *Shidduchim and Zivvugim: The Torah's Perspective on Choosing Your Mate* (Southfield, MI and New York: Targum/Feldheim, 1987). Lebovitz seems less enthusiastic than other Haredi works about dating as a means for choosing a spouse, and he adopts aspects of the pre-modern model of marriage as a financial arrangement when he compares choosing a spouse to purchasing a car (5-7). Yet, Lebovitz also coalesces the modern and pre-modern. He uses language borrowed from the modern conception of the companionate marriage to defend high levels of parental and communal input in choosing a spouse. Singles may get too caught up in the emotional high of falling in love to realistically assess with whom they are most emotionally compatible. Only parents, rabbis, and community members have enough

perspective to help the couple determine with whom they are most likely to enjoy a lifelong, satisfying relationship.

44   Abramov and Abramov, *Two Halves*, 220, 28-29.

45   Another example of the combination of coalescence and filtering involves Haredi images of masculinity, which combine some of the outgoing bold worldliness of the ideal contemporary American man with traditional Jewish images of the male scholar-sissy. The topic of Haredi visions of masculinity and how they compare to mainstream American images, evangelical and Fundamentalist Christian images, and images from the Jewish tradition requires further analysis and study. In the interim, examine Abramov and Abramov, *Two Halves*, which, in addition to notions of men as quiet scholars, also describes ideal men in other ways: strong, physical, detached, unemotional, and worldly (49, 177-178, 183, 186) as well as sensitive, warm, and caring (188-192, 203-207). The section of the book written by and for women describes husbands also as bumbling, lazy, uncooperative, immature, and emotionally needy (34, 44, 52-53, 58, 96, 109, 146). On American images of masculinity, see Michael Kimmel, *Manhood in America: A Cultural History* (New York: The Free Press, 1996). On the scholar-sissy in the Jewish tradition, see Daniel Boyarin, *Unheroic Conduct: The Rise of Heterosexuality and the Invention of the Jewish Man* (Berkeley, Los Angeles, and London: University of California Press, 1997).

46   Take, for example, Modern Orthodox historian Marc B. Shapiro, who wrote a book arguing that not all canonized Jewish sources accept the truth of Maimonides' famous thirteen articles of faith. He defined this canon on the basis of an "ArtScroll test." That is, if ArtScroll's editors consider a rabbi or text as part of the canon, he includes it. See his *The Limits of Orthodox Jewish Theology: Maimonides' Thirteen Principles Reappraised* (Oxford: Littman Library of Jewish Civilization, 2004), 27-29.

47   Malka Schaps, "The One-Way Mirror: Israel and the Diaspora in Contemporary Orthodox Literature," *Shofar* 16:2 (1998), 32-47.

48   Ruthie Pearlman, *Against the Wall* (Southfield, MI: Targum/Feldheim, 2004). In contrast, two studies of those who abandon Haredi identity link sexual frustration with those life changes. Regarding Hasidim in America, see Hella Winston, *The Unchosen: The Hidden Lives of Hasidic Rebels* (Boston: Beacon Press, 2005). On Israeli Haredim, see Sarit Barzilai, *Lifrotz Me'ah She'arim: Mas'a El 'Olamam Shel HaYotze'im LeShe'elah* (Tel Aviv: Yedi'ot Aharonot and Sifrei Hemed, 2004). Also cf. the professional and therapeutic discussion of Haredi dropouts, which does deal with sexual activity. See Yohanan Danziger, *The Incidence of At-Risk Youth in the Orthodox Jewish Community of Brooklyn, New York* (New York: New York City Department of Youth and Community Development and The Metropolitan Coordinating Council on Jewish Poverty, n.d.), and *Teenage Orthodox Jewish Girls At-Risk: Study and Recommendations* (New York: Metropolitan Council on Jewish Poverty and Jewish Board of Family and Children's Services, 2003).

49   From the secular market, see for example Judith Viorst's chapter, "Married Sex," in her *Grown-Up Marriage* (New York, London, Toronto, Sydney: Free Press, 2003), Chapter 7; John Gray, *Mars and Venus in the Bedroom: A Guide to Lasting Romance and Passion* (New York: Harper Collins, 1995); or Patricia Love and Jo Robinson, *Hot Monogamy* (Plume: New York, 1991).

50   Abramov, *The Secret of Jewish Femininity*; S. Wagschal, *The New Taharas Am Yisroel* (Jerusalem and New York: Feldheim, 1994); Shimon D. Eider, *The Halachos of Niddah* (Lakewood, NJ: Feldheim, 1981). A search of the Bar-Ilan University responsa database reveals that the term "*taharat hamishpahah*" did not appear in halakhic literature until the twentieth century. The euphemism for the laws of *niddah* has become so commonplace that some Haredi authors assume it to be traditional and ancient. One

51   book, for example, mistakenly refers to Maimonides' "*Hilkhot Taharat HaMishpacha*," a section of his Code that does not exist. See Hirshman, *One Above and Seven Below*, 115. Also see Abramov, *The Secret of Jewish Femininity*, 50. For a discussion of American Orthodox apologetics about the laws of *niddah*, see Jonah Steinberg, "From a 'Pot of Filth' to a 'Hedge of Roses' and Back: Changing Theorization of Menstruation in Judaism," *Journal of Feminist Studies in Religion* 13:2 (1997), 5-26.

51   Abramov and Abramov, *Two Halves of a Whole*, 193. Winkler, *Bayis Ne'eman*, 96-97.

52   Kaganoff, *Dear Kallah*. Also see the ambiguity created by one book's attempt to avoid speaking of the female orgasm. Yehudah Levi, *The Science of Torah: The Scientific Knowledge of the Talmudic Sages* (Jerusalem and New York: Feldheim, 2004), 13-14.

53   There are good reasons to suspect that these efforts meet with limited success and result in various kinds of inconsistencies and hypocricies. See Margaret Talbot, "Red Sex, Blue Sex," *The New Yorker*, November 3, 2008, available at http://www.newyorker.com/reporting/2008/11/03/081103fa_fact_talbot, viewed July, 2010.

54   Hendershot, *Shaking the World*, Chap. 3. Flake *Redemptorama*, 80-85. As Hendershot points out, the publication of Christian sex-guides for married couples is tied up with the attempt to create an image of an idyllic monogamous marriage so that the notion of chastity prior to marriage will be more compelling. On sexuality in Fundamentalist Christian discourse, see Barbara Ehrenreich, *Re-Making Love: The Feminization of Sex* (New York: Doubleday, 1986), Chap. 5.

55   On this ambivalent Haredi relationship with psychology, see Meir Winkler, "Halacha and Psychotherapy: Conflict or Compatibility?" *The Jewish Observer* 16:3 (May, 1982), 8-11, and Moshe Y'chiail Friedman, "In Search of a Torah Psychology," *The Jewish Observer* 16:6 (October, 1982), 13-15.

56   Cited in Heinze, "The Americanization of Mussar," 458.

57   See Miriam Adahan's self-help book, *Appreciating People (Including Yourself)* (Jerusalem: Feldheim and Gefen, 1988), which is based on Isabel Briggs Myers and Peter B. Myers, *Gifts Differing: Understanding Personality Types* (Palo Alto, CA: Davies Black, 1995). Adahan's influence and importance is reflected not only in her prolific writings, but also in her authorship of a *haskamah* [approbation] for Moshe Gans's parenting guide, *Make Me Don't Break Me* (Brooklyn: Mesorah, 1994). This may be the first example of a woman authoring a *haskamah* in Jewish literary history, an event that marks a significant development in the role of women in modern Judaism in general, and in the Haredi community in particular.

58   Miriam Adahan, *Awareness: The Key to Acceptance, Respect, Forgiveness, and Growth* (Jerusalem and New York: Feldheim, 1994), 5.

59   Adahan, *Appreciating People*, 6.

60   From the subtitle and book jacket of Don Riso and Russ Hudson, *The Wisdom of the Enneagram* (New York: Bantam, 1999).

61   See Riso and Hudson, *The Wisdom of the Enneagram*, 19-25; Moore, *Selling God*, 251-263.

62   For the Catholic critique, see Ralph Rath, *The New Age: A Christian Critique* (South Bend, IN: Greenlawn, 1996), and Mitch Pacwa, *Catholics and the New Age: How Good People are Being Drawn into Jungian Psychology, the Enneagram, and the Age of Aquarias* (Ann Arbor, MI: Servant Publications, 1991). Despite the claim that the Enneagram is ancient, the copyright page of Riso and Hudson goes out of its way to emphasize that their profits are protected by copyright laws. "No body of Enneagram material has been passed on in a preexisting 'oral tradition' in the public domain," and therefore the use of the book and its content requires the payment of royalties.

63   Adahan, *Awareness*, 3.

64   For a more detailed discussion of these tensions in the Christian book market, see

Cordero, "The Production of Christian Fiction." The forces in the Christian book market seem parallel to those in the Haredi market.

65 Nosson Slifkin, *The Science of Torah* (Southfield, MI: Targum/Feldheim, 2001), 90.

66 Ibid., 143.

67 For journalistic discussions of the ban, see Jenny Rothenberg, "The Heresy of Nosson Slifkin," *Moment* (October, 2005), 40, and Alex Mindlin, "Religon and Natural History Clash Among the Ultra-Orthodox," *The New York Times*, March 22, 2005, http://www.nytimes.com/2005/03/22/science/22rabbi.html, viewed April, 2011.

68 Zootorah.com/controversy/cherem.pdf, viewed July, 2006. Most of the texts and primary sources related to the ban and controversy are available at www.zootorah.com.

69 A partial transcript available at www.zootorah.com/controversy/ravreich.pdf.

70 From "The Slifkin Affair: Issues and Perspectives," by R. Aharon Feldman of Baltimore's Ner Yisrael yeshiva, available at http://www.zootorah.com/controversy/SLIFKINARTICLE.doc.

71 Feldman is quoted as saying, "We rarely can converge with Christians on anything, so I doubt we agree with them on this matter" [rejecting Darwinism and believing in a 6000 year old universe] (quoted in Rothenberg, "The Heresy," 42). This rhetoric might be helpful in Haredi attempts to deny their own acculturation, which we will deal with at length in Chapter 3, but in fact the controversy has much in common with Christian controversy regarding creationism and science. For more on the Orthodox Jewish tendency to deny similarity to Christians on matters of science, see Ira Robinson, "'Practically I'm a Fundamentalist': Twentieth Century Orthodox Jews Contend with Evolution and its Implications," and Shai Cherry, "Crisis Management via Biblical Interpretation: Fundamentalism, Modern Orthodoxy, and Genesis," both in *Jewish Tradition and the Challenge of Darwinism*, Eds. Geoffrey Cantor and Marc Swetlitz (Chicago: University of Chicago Press, 2006), 77-88, 166-187.

72 Rothenberg, "The Heresy of Nosson Slifkin," 40. When researching this book, I had to order his books from Bar-Ilan University's rare-books collection.

73 Personal communication, July 20, 2007. Controversial books "are sold in the big Judaica stores in every neighborhood, but sometimes behind the counter so only people who ask for it can get it." At least one rather well-known Haredi book store "has in their computer system a category BTC [behind the counter] for [such] books."

74 One Toronto rabbi essentially admitted that the ban was not intended to influence those outside the sphere of influence of the banning rabbis. It was meant more to shore up the oppositional attitude of those who already possessed such an attitude. "When one hears words of heresy, one should not contend with them.... To ourselves we should respond with words of encouragement." An open letter by R. Shlomo Miller, available at http://zootorah.com/controversy/controversy.html, viewed July, 2006.

75 www.zootorah.com/controversy, viewed February, 2008.

76 http://www.geocities.com/y_berkovits/Slifkin-Ban.html, viewed February, 2008; http://failedmessiah.typepad.com/failed_messiahcom/2005/12/rabbi_shmuel_ka.html, viewed February, 2008. For a few among very many examples, see the pseudonymous Meir Ben-Tzvi, "A Response to Rabbi Aharon Feldman's Article," http://www.zootorah.com/controversy/Feldman,%20Rav%20Aharon,%20Second%20Version%20Response.rtf, viewed December, 2010.

77 The internet contains, for example, venues for open and anonymous Haredi discussions of sexuality and even for the planning of prohibited sexual encounters between otherwise observant Jews. See, for example, the now defunct www.shaindy.com, which helped arrange adulterous affairs between Orthodox or Haredi Jews, or the quite explicit discussion of "intimate matters" on www.calmkallahs.com, viewed June, 2009.

78 See the *Jewish Observer's* special issue, "www.ensnared.com," 36:9 (November, 2003), quote from Aaron Twerski, "A Ubiquitous Challenge: An Insidious Trap," 14.

79 For a discussion of the controversy regarding Kook and exercise, see Bezalel Naor, *Orot: An Annotated Translation of Rabbi Abraham Isaac Kook's Seminal Work* (Northvale, NJ: Jason Aronson, 1993), 35- 44. *The Jewish Observer* 40:8 (November, 2007).

80 Joseph Schick, "Sports and the Orthodox Jewish Fan," *The Jewish Press*, January 30, 2008, available at, http://www.jewishpress.com/displaycontent_new.cfm?contentid= 29361&contentname=Sports%20and%20the%20Orthodox%20Jewish%20Fan&sect ionid=14&mode=a&recnum=0, viewed February, 2008.

81 See Jeffrey Gurock, *Judaism's Encounter with American Sports* (Bloomington and Indianapolis: Indiana University Press, 2005), particularly Chapter 4. Kosher food is available in several professional sports venues in North America. In *The Jewish Observer* and other publications, advertisements for Haredi summer camps, particular those for boys, advertise the camps' sports programs. For example, one celebrates the camp's "basketball and hockey clinics," and shows a photograph of male teens in basketball shorts, tee shirts, and *tzitzit* [ritual fringes] standing on a basketball court, all juxtaposed with a description of the camp's "enhanced [Torah] learning program" and the "air conditioned Shul [synagogue] and Bais Hamedrash [study hall]." See *The Jewish Observer* 41:2 (March, 2008), 33 and *Mishpacha* 141 (January 10, 2007), 43.

82 Max Anteby, *The Jewish Theory of Everything: A Behind-the-Scenes Look at the World* (Brooklyn: Shaar, 2002); Hurwitz, *Being Jewish*, 51.

83 Though he does not use the term monopolization, Sivan's conception of the enclave culture focuses on the way in which the enclave is to be as self-contained as possible while surrounded by a threatening general culture. See Sivan, "The Enclave Culture."

84 On the "shelf value" of these books, see Stolow, *Orthodox by Design*, 167-170.

85 See Barzilai, *Me'ah She'arim*, passim, where discovery of values and meaning outside the Haredi community was a first step toward rebellion for many former Haredi Jews in Israel.

86 Yehudah Lebovitz, *The B'nei Torah Edition of the Lebovitz System: The Revolutionary Breakthrough for Smokers* (Jerusalem: Feldheim, 1989). Searches on amazon.com, barnesandnoble.com, google.com, and several used-book sites were unable to find a non-"*B'nei Torah*" edition of this work.

87 Ibid., 247-249.

88 Tammy Poltsek, *Aristocratic Fruits: The Art of Transforming Fruit into Art* (Brooklyn: Aristocratic Party Design, 2003); Fishbein, *Kosher by Design*, 210, and idem, *Kosher by Design Entertains* (Mesorah: Brooklyn, 2005). These books are also involved in coalescence. *Kosher by Design* combines its religious messages about the holidays with suggestions for Americanizing the home, such as instructions for a "beer tasting evening to celebrate the husband's birthday" in which the housewife is to create a "rugged" and "masculine" look in the color scheme and table settings (*Kosher by Design Entertains*, 47). For a close reading of the aesthetics of *Kosher by Design*, as well as the book's popularity among Christian readers, see Stolow, *Orthodox by Design*, 120-132, and idem, "Aesthetics/Ascetics."

89 Hyman Goldberg, *Our Man in the Kitchen* (New York: Odyssey Press, 1964), and *The America's Test Kitchen Family Cookbook* (Brookline, MA: America's Test Kitchen, 2006). On gender in American cookbooks, see Jessamyn Neuhaus, *Manly Meals and Mom's Home Cooking: Cookbooks and Gender in Modern America* (Baltimore: Johns Hopkins University Press, 2003).

90 Fishbein, *Kosher by Design*, 3.

91 Finkelstein and Finkelstein, *Nine Wonderful Months: B'Sha'ah Tovah*. The expression *besha'ah tovah* [at a good time] is a formulaic Hebrew response to news that someone

is pregnant, borrowed into modern Hebrew from the Yiddish. Cf. Eilene Eisenberg, Heidi Murkoff, and Sandee Eisenberg, *What to Expect When You're Expecting* (New York: Workman, 1991). *What to Expect* is reportedly "read by 93 percent of [contemporary American] women who consult a guidebook during their pregnancies" (Hulbert, *Raising America*, 360). Also see Aviva Rappaport, *A Jewish Woman's Guide to Childbirth* (Jerusalem: Jerusalem Publications, 2004).

92   Finkelstein and Finkelstein, *Nine Wonderful Months*, 1, 43, xxvii, emphasis mine. Whether Haredi women actually experience pregnancy and childbirth in this way, and how they negotiate the dissonance that might be created in reading this book if they do not, has yet to be studied.

93   Eisenberg, Murkoff, and Eisenberg, *What to Expect*, 28.

CHAPTER THREE

1   Kelemen, *To Kindle a Soul*, 13, 198.

2   Haredi parenting guides often do quote the educational writings of R. Samson Raphael Hirsch (nineteenth century), whose modern middle-class sensibilities make his ideas particularly compatible with contemporary Haredi concerns. See, for example, Miriam Levi, *Effective Jewish Parenting* (New York and Jerusalem: Feldheim, 1986), and Aharon Pollak, *Torah Powerhouse: Insights into the Theory and Practice of Torah Parenting* (Jerusalem and New York: Feldheim, 1996).

3   "One who avoids making his son suffer and striking him when he deserves it, but protects him, he hates his child, who will eventually go off to a bad culture.... The greater his love [for his son] the greater he rebukes him. The same is true of girls.... If they do not [act properly] one must hit them and not have mercy on them at all." See the Gaon of Vilna, *Even Shelemah*, 6:1-4.

4   Kelemen, *To Kindle a Soul*, 142-143; Wolbe, *Building and Planting*, 34-36; idem, *Zeri'ah U'Vinyan*, 23-24.

5   Also see Kelemen's evidence that Judaism advocates eating a healthy and early breakfast, cited on 83 and 48. In fact, his prooftexts suggest eating a very late morning meal, something more akin to a late breakfast or early lunch than the breakfast to which he refers. These sources assume that people eat two meals a day, rather than the three that are standard in the contemporary West. Also see his claim that the widespread use in yeshivas of the *shtender* – a lectern that allows one to sit or stand while reading – exemplifies traditional Jewish commitment to differentiated education for individual students (48). He neglects to mention that the curriculum in yeshivas where the *shtender* is popular involves an almost exclusive diet of Talmud, hardly the stuff of differentiated education.

6   Noach Orlowek, *Raising Roses Among the Thorns* (Jerusalem and New York: Feldheim, 2002), xxiv. Also see Pollak, *Powerhouse*, jacket cover, which explains that the book "is based entirely on Torah sources... [and is] free from secular influences." This book advocates a more isolationist form of parenting than most other English-language Haredi works, though its assumptions about the family are more Victorian than ancient.

7   Kelemen, *To Kindle a Soul*, 22.

8   Everett Mendelsohn, "Religious Fundamentalism and the Sciences," in Marty and Appleby, Eds., *Fundamentalisms and Society*, 23-41.

9   See, in particular, Ann Hulbert, *Raising America*, who pays close attention to the scientific authority claimed by parenting experts in twentieth-century America.

10   Also see Kelemen's books of theology, *Permission to Believe: Four Rational Approaches to*

God's Existence and *Permission to Receive: Four Rational Approaches to the Torah's Divine Origin* (Southfield, MI: Targum/Feldheim, 1990 and 1996), which also cite extensively from scientific and academic literature (some of it considerably out of date). Similarly, Shmuel Waldman cites scientific evidence for the truths of Jewish dogma in his *Beyond a Reasonable Doubt: Convincing Evidence of the Truths of Judaism*, Ed. Ya'akov Astor (Jerusalem and New York: Feldheim, 2002). See below, Chapter 5, for a further discussion of these theology books and their relationships to science.

11 Neve Yerushalayim, where he teaches, is a Torah-study institution for college-age women that also offers degree-granting programs in counseling and psychology. See www.nevey.org, viewed July, 2010.

12 Kelemen, *To Kindle a Soul*, 15.

13 http://www.lawrencekelemen.com/about.asp, viewed January, 2008.

14 My exploration in January, 2008 of www.lawrencekelmen.com did not find the *haskamot*.

15 See Abraham J. Twerski, *Getting Up When You Are Down* (Brooklyn: Shaar Press, 1997), 8-9, and idem and Ursula Schwartz, *Positive Parenting: Developing Your Child's Potential* (Brooklyn: Mesorah, 1996), xv. On Twerski, see Heinze, "The Americanization of *Mussar*" and Stolow, *Orthodox by Design*, 138-140.

16 Miriam Adahan, *Raising Children to Care* (Jerusalem and New York: Feldheim, 1988), xvi.

17 Adahan, *Appreciating People*, 4; Myers and Myers, *Gifts Differing*; Adahan, *Awareness*.

18 Adahan, *Raising Children*, 273-275; *Awareness*, 529.

19 Adahan, *Raising Children*, xx. Adahan does not quote those sources or explain why those sources are not valid or relevant.

20 Adahan, *Appreciating People*, 6, and idem, *Awareness*, 5. Compare this to the more developed Modern Orthodox advocacy of general education: Aharon Lichtenstein, "Torah and General Culture: Confluence or Conflict?" in *Judaism's Encounter with Other Cultures*, Ed. Jacob J. Schacter (Northvale, NJ: Aronson, 1997), 217-292.

21 On women's secular education, see Shaul Stampfer, "Gender Differentiation and Education of the Jewish Woman in Nineteenth-Century Eastern Europe," *Polin* 7 (1992), 63-87.

22 Christian Smith and Melinda Lundquist Denton, *Soul Searching: The Religious and Spiritual Lives of American Teenagers* (Oxford and New York: Oxford University Press, 2005), 168. Eva S. Moskowitz, *In Therapy We Trust: America's Obsession with Self-Fulfillment* (Baltimore and London: Johns Hopkins University Press, 2001).

23 Soloveitchik, "Rupture and Reconstruction," 80-81.

24 Adahan, *EMETT: A Step-by-Step Guide to Emotional Maturity Established Through Torah* (Jerusalem and New York: Feldheim, 1987), xiii.

25 Ibid., xiii, 19.

26 Adahan, *Raising Children*, xviii.

27 Ibid., v, xvii, 182, 131.

28 Adahan, *EMETT*, 77, quoting Psalms 23:1.

29 Noach Orlowek, "Avoiding the Risks of Unthinking Parenting," *The Jewish Observer* 37:7 (September, 2004), 36. Also see Shmuel Yaakov Klein, "What Happened to Corporal Punishment?" *HaModia Magazine* (August 17, 2005), 7, and Dov Brezak, *Chinuch in Turbulent Times: Practical Strategies for Parents and Educators* (Brooklyn: Mesorah, 2002), 386. This is consistent with Orthodox approaches to change in halakhah, which often define Jewish law as immutable and comprehensive. Change derives exclusively from the fact that decisors must apply the immutable rules to changing conditions.

30 Twerski and Schwartz, *Positive Parenting*, xvi.

31 Wolbe, *Building and Planting*, 36.

32   Benzion Sorotzkin, "The Damaging Fallout of Competitiveness," *The Jewish Observer* 40:9 (December, 2007), 6.

33   Pinchos Jung, "Heads or Tails? Maximizing Your Child's Benefit," *The Jewish Observer* 41:1 (January/February, 2008), 8.

34   Benzion Sorotzkin, "Dr. Sorotzkin Responds," *The Jewish Observer* 41:1 (Janurary/February, 2008), 8.

35   Leah Steinberg, "Accomodating Children With Special Needs," *The Jewish Observer* 37:7 (Summer, 2004), 21.

36   Nisson Wolpin, "The Great Public School Rainbow," *The Jewish Observer* 8:9 (December, 1972), 3.

37   Shalom Noah Borozovski, *Kuntres Netivei Olam HaYeshiva* (Jerusalem: Yeshivat Beit Avraham, 1991), 76. This attitude might help explain why his followers, Hasidim from the Slonim group, became involved in the spring of 2010 in significant controversy. The Supreme Court of Israel viewed their practice of excluding from their school in the city of Emanuel all but the most strictly observant families as a thinly veiled racist attempt to exclude girls of Sephardic background.

38   On Yudel Rosenberg and his literary activity, see Ira Robinson, "Literary Forgery and Hasidic Judaism: The Case of Rabbi Yudel Rosenberg," *Judaism* 40:1 (1991), 61-78, and Shnayer Z. Leiman, "The Adventures of The Maharal of Prague in London: R. Yudel Rosenberg and the Golem of Prague," *Tradition* 36:1 (2002), 26-58. On genre developments in Haredi fiction, see Malka Schaps, "The One-Way Mirror: Israel and the Diaspora in Contemporary Orthodox Literature," *Shofar* 16:2 (1998), 32-47, and "The Filtered Voice: Genre Shifts in Orthodox Women's Fiction," in *To Be a Jewish Woman*, Ed. Margalit Shilo (Jerusalem: Urim, 2003), 116-128. Schaps, a professor of mathematics by profession, has authored several Haredi novels.

39   Asher Sabo, "Judaica vs. the Classics in the Yeshiva English Department," *The Jewish Observer* 22:9 (December, 1989), 27. Emphasis in the original. Also see Faiga Diskind, "Finding a Way When There is No Choice," *The Jewish Observer* 20:2 (March, 1987), 34; idem, "General Studies in the Yeshiva: Benefits and Booby Traps," *The Jewish Observer* 19:7 (October, 1986), 45-51; Yitzchak Kasnett, "'Rebbe, That Was Great!': Yeshiva English Studies, Another Dimension," *The Jewish Observer* 19:7 (October, 1986), 53-58; Shalva Mintz, untitled essay, *The Jewish Observer* 20:2 (March, 1987), 31. Also see Bernard Fryshman, "On Losing One's Mind," *The Jewish Observer* 15:6 (May, 1981), 50-51; the responses in letters to the editor, 15:9 (November, 1981), 32-35; and Fryshman's "So He's Reading a Book," 16:10 (November, 1983), 34.

40   Jacobs, "The Drama of Orthodox Life," 8. Also see below, n. 54, on the role of the Haskalah in creating modern Hebrew fiction.

41   Alyse Fisher Roller, *The Literary Imagination of Ultra-Orthodox Jewish Women: An Assessment of a Writing Community* (Jefferson, NC: McFarland, 1999), 84. This polemic about the inherent falsehood of fiction echoes some of the parallel evangelical Protestant arguments against parochial fiction. See Jan Blodgett, *Protestant Evangelical Literary Culture and Contemporary Society* (Westport, CT and London: Greenwood Press, 1997), 20-23.

42   Diskind, "Finding a Way," 47.

43   Yair Weinstock, *Eye of the Storm*, Trans. Libby Lazewnik (Brooklyn: Shaar Press, 1999), 52.

44   Schaps, "One-Way Mirror," 33-34.

45   Jung, "Let the Reader Beware," *The Jewish Observer* 33:9 (November, 2000), 43.

46   On Haredim as quietistic, see Samuel Heilman, "Jews and Fundamentalism," *Jewish Political Studies Review* 17:2 (Spring, 2005), 183-189, available at http://www.jcpa.org/cjc/cjc-heilman-s05.htm, viewed April, 2010.

47 Diskind, "Finding a Way," 34.

48 Roller, *Literary Imagination*, 142. Also see Yaffa Ganz, "You Can't Sell a Book by Its Cover (But It's a Good Place to Start): The Complexities of Religious Juvenile Publishing," *The Jewish Observer* 21:4 (May, 1988), 31-34.

49 Jacobs, "The Drama," 9.

50 Mintz, untitled essay, *The Jewish Observer* 20:2 (March, 1987), 31.

51 Diskind, "Finding a Way," 35.

52 Richard Altabe, "General Studies in the Yeshivos: A Neglected Frontier," *The Jewish Observer* 37:5 (May, 2004), 7.

53 See, for example, Ian Watt, *The Rise of the Novel: Studies in Defoe, Richardson, and Fielding* (Hardmonsworth: Penguin Books, 1970).

54 Robert Alter, *The Invention of Hebrew Prose: Modern Fiction and the Language of Realism* (Seattle: University of Washington Press, 1988).

55 Ganz, "Can't Sell a Book," 31.

56 Ibid., 32-33.

57 Pollak, *Powerhouse*, 64-65.

58 Chana Siegel, "Where Have All the Writers Gone? In Search of Jewish Fiction," *Bat Kol* 5 (Cheshvan/Kislev, 5757), 3-4.

59 For examples of novels that work to raise social and religious issues to the public agenda, and which include more than a small dose of internal Haredi criticism, see Rachel Pomerantz, *A Time to Rend, A Time to Sew* (Jerusalem: Feldheim, 1996), and her *As Mountains Around Jerusalem* (Jerusalem and New York: Feldheim, 1999); Libby Lazewnik, *Give Me the Moon* (Southfield, MI: Targum/Feldheim, 1996); Pearlman, *Against the Wall*; Chaim Eliav, *The Runaway*, Trans. Libby Lazewnik (Brooklyn: Shaar Press, 1998), and idem, *The Spider's Web*, Trans. Miriam Zakon (Brooklyn: Shaar Press, 1996). Yair Weinstock, *Blackout*, Trans. Miriam Zakon (Brooklyn: Shaar Press, 1998). In light of these and other novels, Roller's claim that "subversive narrative strategies in this [Haredi women's] fiction are unlikely and unintentional," seems inaccurate (*Literary Imagination*, 147).

60 In an article in the Israeli daily *Ha'aretz*, Tamar Rotem drew this conclusion from the non-prominent placement of Sarah Shapiro's works of fiction on the shelf in her own home. See "Their Language, Their Soul," June 13, 2005. In an unpublished letter to the editor, Shapiro responded that her writing matters to the community a great deal. (The editor agreed to publish only a short response. Shapiro was kind enough to share her more lengthy letter with me.)

61 Schaps, "The Filtered Voice," 118.

62 Pomerantz, *A Time to Rend, a Time to Sew*.

63 Yael Shenkar, "*Al Mah Sarah HaLashon? Siyyagim U'Migbalot BaSifrut HaHaredit HaNashit*," paper delivered at a conference on "Politics and Literature," June 2004, Hebrew University of Jerusalem, and "*Ezrat Nashim Mishelakh: 'Al Efsharut HaKetivah BaHavrah HaHaredit HaNashit*," *Mehqarei Yerushalayim BeSifrut Ivrit* 22 (2008), 177-188. For these reasons, we should not accept Roller's assertion (*Literary Imagination*, 1-2) that the Haredi women's literature which she studies "*is* the insider's voice" (emphasis Roller's) or that it is "an unmediated view of how ultra-Orthodox Jews talk to one another, how they see themselves."

64 Perlman, *Against the Wall*, and Riva Pomerantz, *Breaking Point* (Southfield, MI: Targum, 2004). Cf. Blodgett, *Protestant Evangelical Literary Culture*, 1-3, 69-70. Blodgett emphasizes the ways in which the ideologies of publishers, authors, and readers of contemporary evangelical popular fiction work to moderate each other. I imagine that much publishing operates with related kinds of internal censorship, and that the differences between Haredi publishers and secular publishers is a matter of degree rather

than of kind.

65 For a fuller discussion of Weinstock and his thriller novels, see Finkelman, "Medium and Message." Another author of Haredi adventure novels argued in conversation with me that the ideological messages in Weinstock's novels are too apparent and obvious.

66 *Calculated Risk*, 102-107.

67 On Haredi ambivalence regarding the internet, see Neri Horowitz, "*HaHaredim Ve-haInternet*," *Kivvunim Hadashim* 3 (2000), 7-30; Karine Barzilai-Nahon and Gad Barzilai, "Cultured Technology: Internet and Religious Fundamentalism," *The Information Society* 21:1 (2005), 25-40; Aharon Rose "*Ha'Im Anu Hozim BeAviv Shel Prague Ba'Olam HaHaredi*," and his "*Sone'im: Sippur Ahavah*," both in *Eretz Aheret* 41 (August-October, 2007), 38-42, 42-49. Also see *The Jewish Observer* 36:9 (November, 2003), 8-27 and 37:2 (February, 2004), 19-31.

68 *Calculated Risk*, 200.

69 Ibid., 80-81, 119.

70 R. Yaakov Perlow, "The Clash Between Modernity and Eternity," *The Jewish Observer* 26:10 (January, 1994), 10.

71 Weinstock, *Eye of the Storm*, 120. "Stop the World – I Want to Get Off" is, in fact, the title of a musical comedy that opened on Broadway in 1962.

72 See Michael Silber, "The Emergence of Ultra-Orthodoxy: The Invention of a Tradition," in *The Uses of Tradition: Jewish Continuity in the Modern Era*, Ed. Jack Wertheimer (New York and Jerusalem: Jewish Theological Seminary, 1992), 23-84. Silber points to ways in which complete rejection of change is internally contradictory and impossible to implement.

73 *Calculated Risk*, 103-106.

74 Ibid., 68.

75 *Blackout*, 142, 170; *Calculated Risk*, 68.

76 Chaim Eliav, *Ketonet Pasim* (Jerusalem: Pesher, 1997) and Weinstock, *The Runaway*.

77 Cf. the Hebrew version, *Bilti Hafikh* (Jerusalem: Or Zahav, 1997), 108, 159ff, 210-211, 216-217 to *Blackout*, 101, 153ff, 200-201, 207.

78 Pinchos Jung, "Let the Reader Beware," 42-43. Both *The Runaway* and *Blackout* appeared in English well before this article did.

79 I was not able to find references to the debate in the Hebrew Haredi press, though I thank Garylak, Weinstock, and Zakon for their assistance in looking for it (interviews in July, 2003). According to Weinstock, most of the debate did not make it to print, occurring in face-to-face conversations between educators, librarians, parents, youth, and authors.

80 I have no way of verifying these numbers. According to Schaps, "One-Way Mirror," the first printing of Haredi novels in Israel usually includes 1,500-2,000 copies.

81 *Calculated Risk*, 78.

82 Cf. Weinstock's use of play-acting in *Calculated Risk* with Annette Kuhn's discussion of cross dressing in Hollywood films, "Sexual Disguise and Cinema," in Bennet, Ed. *Popular Fiction*, 169-207. Just as films with cross-dressed characters allow viewers temporary "release from the ties of sexual difference that bind us" (170), so too the characters in *Calculated Risk* allow Haredi readers temporary freedom from the ties of religious affiliation that bind them to certain non-adventurous social relations and modes of behavior.

83 Though, as I have suggested in Chapter 1, generally Haredi elite religion does not oppose Haredi popular religion.

84 For more on the tension between ideological purity and profit in the religious book and product market, see Borden, "Making Money, Saving Souls"; Moore, *Selling God*; Einstein, *Brands of Faith*.

85   On this tension, see Hendershot, *Shaking the World*, Chap. 1. On Haredi films, see Vered BaGad-Elimelekh, "*Min He'Avar HaRahok Ve'Ad HaHoveh: Demuyot Rabbanim Be-Seratim Harediim*," in *Manhigut VeSamkhut BaHevrah HaHaredit BeYisrael*, Eds. Kimmy Caplan and Nurit Stadler (Jerusalem: Van Leer Institute and Hakkibutz HaMe'uhad, 2009), 99-126.

86   Sabo, "Judaica vs. the Classics," 27. Similarly, Haredi "rebbe cards" were produced to mimic the baseball cards so popular among American youth. Play, too, could be sanctified, training children to lionize the Torah giants rather than the San Francisco Giants. Some oppose these cards, seeing it inappropriate to trade, "flip," or compare the relative value of the community's holy rabbinic leadership (http://realjewish.blogspot.com/2005/09/rebbe-cards.html, viewed August, 2010).

87   Flake, *Redemptorama*.

88   Goldin, "Jewish Music World," 37, emphasis in original. One critic points out that the non-Haredi rock performers make better music than the Haredi ones. Writing in 1975, a Haredi musician explains that "If I like Tom Jones, I would choose to listen to the original, not a pale, pseudo-Jewish imitation." See Schiller, "Chasidus in Song," 21.

89   See http://www.israelnationalnews.com/News/News.aspx/123256; http://blogindm.blogspot.com/2008/02/its-beautiful-day-for-ban.html; http://www.theyeshivaworld.com/article.php?p=14875, all viewed May, 2010.

90   In an April 2003 interview, one author, who prefers to remain anonymous, said that publishers have no ideological limits on what they are willing to publish. Their self-censorship derives entirely from economic considerations of what would or would not sell and what will protect their reputations. Schaps, in a private correspondence of November, 2003, explained that she "strongly disagree[s]" with this assessment.

CHAPTER FOUR

1   Edward Shils, *Tradition* (Chicago and London: University of Chicago Press, 1981), 195.

2   Yael Zerubavel, *Recovered Roots: Collective Memory and the Making of Israeli National Tradition* (Chicago and London: University of Chicago Press, 1995), 8.

3   On the construction of collective memory and its role in building group identity, see ibid.; Eviatar Zerubavel, *Time Maps: Collective Memory and the Social Shape of the Past* (Chicago and London: University of Chicago Press, 2003); Maurice Halbwachs, *On Collective Memory*, Trans. Lewis Coser (Chicago: University of Chicago Press, 1992); Paul Connerton, *How Societies Remember* (Cambridge: Cambridge University Press, 1989).

4   On Orthodox historiography, see Ada Rapoport-Albert, "Hagiography with Footnotes: Edifying Tales and the Writing of History in Hasidism," *History and Theory* 27:4 (1988), 119-159; Israel Bartal, "'True Knowledge and Wisdom': On Orthodox Historiography," *Studies in Contemporary Jewry* 10 (1994), 178-192; Haim Gertner, "*Reishitah Shel Ketivah Historit Ortodoksit be-Mizrah Eropah: Ha'arakhah Mehudeshet*," *Zion* 67 (2002), 293-336; Kimmy Caplan, "Have 'Many Lies Accumulated in the History Books'? The Holocaust in Ashkenazi 'Haredi' Historical Consciousness in Israel," *Yad Vashem Studies* 29 (2001), 321-375; Caplan, "'Absolutely Intellectually Honest': A Case Study of American Jewish Modern Orthodox Historiography," in *Creation and Re-Creation in Jewish Thought*, Eds. Rachel Elior and Peter Schaefer (Tubingen: Mohr Siebeck, 2005), 339-361; and David Asaf, *Ne'ehaz BaSevakh: Pirqei Mashber Umevukhah BeToldot HaHasidut* (Jerusalem: Zalman Shazar Center, 2006); Zohar, "*VaYivra Artscroll et Haleb Betzalmo.*"

5   Anonymous, "Jewish History from a Torah Perspective," *The Jewish Observer* 22:4 (May, 1989), 33. For more on the *Jewish Observer*'s interest in ideologically supportive historiography, see Kimmy Caplan, "Innovating the Past: The Emerging Sphere of the

'Torah-True Historian' in America," *Studies in Contemporary Jewry* 21 (2005), 270-287.

6   On the challenges of modern historiography in helping to create identity, see Yosef Hayim Yerushalmi, *Zakhor: Jewish History and Jewish Memory* (New York: Schocken, 1989), Chap. 4.

7   Schacter, "Facing the Truths of History."

8   There is a very intensive discussion of the Holocaust in Haredi historiography, which requires separate discussion. Kimmy Caplan has begun such a project regarding Israeli Haredim in his, "Many Lies," and his "The Holocaust in Contemporary Israeli Haredi Popular Religion," *Modern Judaism* 22:2 (2002), 142-168.

9   One author refers to "Eastern European society" as "virtually unchanged from the Vilna Gaon's day [eighteenth century] until the twentieth century." See Yonoson Rosenblum, *They Called Him Mike: Reb Elimelech Tress, His Era, Hatzalah, and the Building of American Orthodoxy* (Brooklyn: Mesorah, 1995), 36.

10 Eastern European yeshiva students generally wore lighter colored hats, while only the rabbis wore black. In the contemporary Haredi community, all wear black ones.

11 On how contemporary Orthodox Jews construct a sense of continuity with the Beis Ya'akov schools of Poland, see Shani Bechhofer, "Ongoing Constitution of Identity and Educational Mission of Bais Yaakov Schools: The Structuration of an Organizational Field as the Unfolding of Discursive Logics," (PhD thesis, Northwestern University, 2005).

12 For the suggestion that communities construct their memories through ritual and practice, see Connerton, *How Societies Remember*.

13 On nostalgia, see Fred Davis, *Yearning for Yesterday: A Sociology of Nostalgia* (New York: Free Press, 1979), and Malcom Chase and Christopher Shaw, "The Dimensions of Nostalgia," in *The Imagined Past: History and Nostalgia*, Eds. Malcom Chase and Christopher Shaw (Manchester and New York: Manchester University Press, 1989), 1-17. Nostalgic Haredi historiography should modify Chase and Shaw's claim that nostalgia is fundamentally secular in nature.

14 See Zelig Schachnowitz, *The Light from the West: The Life and Times of the Chasam Sofer*, Trans. Joseph Leftwich (Jerusalem and New York: Feldheim, 2007).

15 Yitzchok Kassnett, *The World that Was: Lithuania* (Cleveland Heights: Hebrew Academy of Cleveland, 1996); idem, *The World that Was: Poland* (Cleveland Heights: Hebrew Academy of Cleveland, 1997); idem, *The World that Was: Hungary/Romania* (Cleveland Heights: Hebrew Academy of Cleveland, 1998). Quote from Kasnett, *Poland*, xii. That the series continues with a coffee-table book on Orthodox immigrants to the United States reinforces the centrality of the immigration narrative, to be discussed below. See A. Leib Scheinbaum, *The World that Was: America, 1900-1945* (Brooklyn: Shaar Press, 2004). The series further continued with A. Leib Scheinbaum, *The World that Was, Ashkenaz: The Legacy of German Jewry, 843-1945* (Cleveland Hights, OH and Brooklyn: The Hebrew Academy of Cleveland and Shaar Press, 2010).

16 Similarly, Devorah Rubin, *Daughters of Desinty* (Brooklyn: Mesorah, 1988) began as a school project to interview elderly women who had once been part of the Beis Ya'akov educational system in Poland. Also see Kasnett's description of an English writing-project for a Haredi high school, which would include "one *Devar Torah* [homily], one *Devar Musar* [ethical homily], and an interview or report focusing on some aspect of Orthodox Jewish life in Europe before World War II." Kassnet, "The Write Stuff," *The Jewish Observer* 31:4 (April, 1998), 23.

17 Kassnet, *Poland*, ix-xi.

18 A book reviewer suggests that an ideal way to transmit proper images of femininity to Haredi readers would be "to cull from what has been written about outstanding Torah personalities the vast amount of information on the women in their lives." Anony-

mous, "Jewish History from a Torah Perspective," 36. Ideal women are ones whose lives revolve around the "Torah personality" of their male loved ones.

19   Yitzchok Dershowitz, *The Legacy of Maran Rav Aharon Kotler* (Lakewood, NJ: M.H. Living 'Mishnas Rav Aharon,' 2005), 12.

20   Non-Orthodox Jews also often present nostalgic images of the *shtetl*. See David Roskies, *The Jewish Search for a Useable Past* (Bloomington, IN: Indiana University Press, 1999), Chap. 4, and Antony Polonsky, "The Shtetl: Myth and Reality," *Polin* 17 (2004), 3-33.

21   Rubin, *Daughters of Destiny*, 66.

22   Kasnett, *Poland*, 4-5. At times, Haredi historiography critiques its own tendency to idealize the past and view it in mythical terms. "It is so easy to romanticize the past, to create a past of pure nostalgia and wallow in a world of pure delight that never was.... We must remember, at all costs, that the Jewry of that time and place lived in a world of utter reality." Yehoshua Baumel, *A Blaze in the Darkening Gloom: The Life of Rav Meir Shapiro*, Trans. Charles Wengrov (Jerusalem and New York: Feldheim, 1994), xvi. The book still suffers from a considerable amount of romanticism and nostalgia.

23   See Shaul Stampfer, *HaYeshiva HaLitait BeHithavutah* (Jerusalem: Zalman Shazar Center, 2005), 226-232, 295-302; Immanuel Etkes, "*Samkhut VeOtonomiah: Rosh HaYeshiva HaLitait VeTalmidav*," in his Ed., *Yeshivot U'Vatei Midrashot* (Jerusalem: Zalman Shazar Center and Dinur Center, 2007), 209-242; Mordechai Breuer, *Ohalei Torah: HaYeshivah, Tavnitah VeToldotehah* (Jerusalem: Zalman Shazar Center, 2004), 378-383.

24   Stampfer, *HaYeshiva HaLitait*, 171-181.

25   Rubin, *Daughters of Destiny*, 72.

26   Celia Heller suggests that only about a third of interwar Polish Jews were observant. See her *On the Edge of Destruction: The Jews of Poland Between the Two World Wars* (Detroit: Wayne State University Press, 1994), 144. Paula Hyman and Gershon Bacon suggest that this estimate is probably low. See Hyman, *Gender and Assimilation in Modern Jewish History: The Roles and Representations of Women* (Seattle: University of Washington Press, 1995), 71-72; Bacon, "*HaHevrah HaMesoratit BeTemurat Ha'Itim: Hebetim BeToldot HaYahadut HaOrtodoksit BePolin UveRusiah, 1850-1939*," in *Qiyyum VaShever: Yehudei Polin LeDoroteihem*, Eds. Yisrael Bartal and Israel Guttman (Jerusalem: Zalman Shazar Center, 2001), 459.

27   On non-Orthodox life in Mir, see *Encyclopedia Judaica*, new edition, 14:304-305, or old edition, 12:17; and *Sefer Mir*, Ed. N. Blumental (Jerusalem: Entzyklopediah Shel Galuyot, 1962). The suggestion that all the doctors and lawyers in Mir were "*frum*" seems unlikely, but I was unable to verify or deny it. For a survey of social, religious, and cultural diversity in interwar Jewish Poland, see Ezra Mendelsohn, *The Jews of East Central Europe Between the World Wars* (Bloomington: Indiana University Press, 1983), 11-84.

28   Mitnagdic rabbis advocated this way of dividing time, but it was not economically feasible for the majority. See Immanuel Etkes, *Rabbi Yisrael Salanter and the Mussar Movement: Seeking the Torah of Truth* (Philadelphia and Jerusalem: Jewish Publication Society, 1993), 47, and R. Hayyim of Volozhin, *Ruah Hayyim* (Wickliffe, OH: n.p., 1998), 1:8, 2:2, and 2:4.

29   Berel Wein, *Triumph of Survival* (Brooklyn: Shaar Press, 1990), 156.

30   Chaim Leib Balgley, "The Brisker Legacy," in *The Torah Personality: A Treasury of Biographical Sketches*, Ed. Nisson Wolpin (Brooklyn: Mesorah and Agudath Israel of America, 1980), 27.

31   Brill, "Judaism in Culture," 13.

32   Kasnett, *Poland*, 33.

33   Marc B. Shapiro, *Between the Yeshiva World and Modern Orthodoxy: The Life and Works of Rabbi Jehiel Jacob Weinberg* (London and Portland, OR: Littman Library of Jewish Civilization, 1999).

34   On some of these and like rabbis, see Yosef Salmon, "Enlightened Rabbis as Reformers in Russian Jewish Society," in *New Perspectives on the Haskalah*, Eds. Shmuel Feiner and David Sorkin (London and Portland, OR: Littman Library of Jewish Civilization, 2001), 166-183. Given the Haredi investment in boundary maintenance and the Modern Orthodox interest in shifting and/or blurring those boundaries, it is not surprising that Modern Orthodox historiography has painted a different historical picture that is more supportive of its own religious commitments (and, in general, more historically accurate). Modern Orthodox authors and journals have published studies pointing to errors in Haredi historiography, particularly regarding the inclusion of secular studies in the Volozhin yeshiva. They have identified middle ground between Haskalah and Orthodoxy, particularly in the works of such figures as R. David Tzvi Hoffman and R. Yehiel Ya'akov Weinberg, and worked to present the Eastern European rabbinic heroes of Haredi historiography like the Netziv of Volozhin as being more nuanced in their relationship to Zionism, modernity, and their non-observant coreligionists. Modern Orthodox writers also mined the writings of religious-Zionist leaders, like R. Kook or the idiosyncratic Hasidic rabbi, Yissachar Teichtel, for their visions, which match Modern Orthodox sensibilities more closely.

35   On this incident and the public letter, see Jacob J. Schacter, "Haskalah, Secular Studies and the Close of the Yeshiva of Volozhin in 1892," *The Torah U-Madda Journal* 2 (1990), 76-133.

36   Noson Kamenetsky, *The Making of a Godol* (Jerusalem: HaMesorah Publications, 2002). On the ban of the first edition, see Marc B. Shapiro, "Of Books and Bans," *The Edah Journal* 3:2 (2003), 1-16. Available at www.edah.org/backend/JournalArticle/3_2; _Shapiro.pdf, viewed November, 2007. Also see Yohai Hakak, "Holy Amnesia: Remembering Religious Sages As Super Humans or As Simply Human," *Contemporary Jewry* 29:3 (December 2009), 215-240. Kamenetsky has collected the materials related to the ban in a self-published book entitled *The Anatomy of a Ban* (Israel: PP Publishers, 2003), which he circulated among family members and friends. The book, accompanied by extensive primary sources, traces at least Kamenetsky's version of the tale. (I thank Chaim I. Waxman for allowing me to read his copy, with permission of the author).

37   Kamentsky, *Anatomy of a Ban*, 38, from the first public letter banning the book.

38   Ibid., 125.

39   Shimon Finkelman, *The Story of Reb Elchonon* (Brooklyn: Mesorah, 1984), 126.

40   Devorah Greenblatt, "Making Our 'Bayis' a Mobile Home," *The Jewish Observer* 32:9 (November, 1999), 49.

41   For a less idealized image of the Eastern European Jewish family, including documentation of a high divorce rate, see Freeze, *Jewish Marriage and Divorce in Imperial Russia*.

42   Scheinbaum, *America*, 3. Similarly, "In the *shtetls* of Eastern Europe... basics of *emunah* [faith] and a complete Jewish worldview... were absorbed as a matter of course.... Not so in America, where... the broader American society impinged daily on every boy's consciousness in countless ways." Yonoson Rosenblum, *Reb Shraga Feivel* (Brooklyn: Mesorah, 2001), 123.

43   Amos Bunim, *A Fire in His Soul: Irving M. Bunim, 1901-1980, The Man and His Impact on American Orthodox Jewry* (Jerusalem and New York: Feldheim, 1989), 21-23. On Ridbaz, see Aaron Rakeffet-Rothkoff, "The American Sojourns of Ridbaz: Religious Problems Within an Immigrant Community," *American Jewish Historical Quarterly* 57 (1968), 557-572, and Abraham J. Karp, "The Ridwas: Rabbi Jacob David Wilowsky,

1845-1913," in *Perspectives on Jews and Judaism: Essays in Honor of Wolf Kelman*, Ed. Arthur A. Chiel (New York: The Rabbinical Assembly, 1978), 215-237. On rabbinic opposition to immigration to America, see Arthur Hertzberg, "'*Treifene Medine*': Learned Opposition to Emigration to the United States," *Proceedings of the 8ᵗʰ World Congress of Jewish Studies* (1984), Vol. 6, 1-30.

44   Aharon Sorasky, *Reb Elchonon: The Life and Ideals of Rabbi Elchonon Bunim Wasserman of Baronovich* (Brooklyn: Mesorah, 1982), 239.

45   Bunim, *Fire*, 21. Also see 26; Rosenblum, *Reb Shraga Feivel*, 98-99.

46   Rosenblum, *Reb Shraga Feivel*, 99.

47   Jonathan Sarna, *American Judaism: A History* (New Haven and London: Yale University Press, 2004), 156-157.

48   R. Shimon Schwab, *Selected Writings* (Lakewood, NJ: CIS, 1988), 234. Also see the critique of this position by Kamenetsky, *The Making of a Godol*, Vol. 1, xxiv-xxv.

49   Moshe Shoshan suggested to me in conversation that the manipulation of history for didactic ends relates to the flowering of works on the laws of *lashon hara* [forbidden speech]. These works, which expand the details of these laws well beyond the precedent in Jewish law, require community members to disbelieve negative stories told about others or to reinterpret such stories in a positive light. Following these laws would create habits of mind that make this kind of historiography plausible to writers and readers. If readers absorb this hermeneutic, they would hardly ask questions about the "truth" regarding people and events, focusing instead on meaning-making. Furthermore, these laws identify heretics and the non-observant as exceptions to at least some of these laws. To the extent that Haredi Jews follow these laws, they will learn to distinguish between members of the in-group, where the discourse is exclusively positive, and the out-group, about whom at least some negative discourse is allowed or encouraged. See Zelig Pliskin, *Guard Your Tongue: A Practical Guide to the Laws of Loshon Hora* (Brooklyn: Weissman, 1977), 82-83, 100-101, and Yisroel Greenwald, *We Want Life!* (Jerusalem and New York: Feldheim and The Chofetz Chaim Heritage Foundation, 1996), Chaps. 4-5. On the expansion of *lashon hara* into hard-and-fast laws, see Benjamin Brown, "From Principles to Rules and from Musar to Halakhah: The Hafetz Hayyim's Rulings on Libel and Gossip," *Dinei Yisrael* 25 (2008), 171-256.

50   Hindy Krohn, *The Way It Was: Touching Vignettes about Growing Up Jewish in the Philadelphia of Long Ago* (Brooklyn: Mesorah, 1989).

51   Wein, *Triumph*, 430-431.

52   Dershowitz, *Kotler*; Yonoson Rosenblum, *Reb Yaakov: The Life and Times of HaGaon Rabbi Yaakov Kamenetsky* (Brooklyn: Mesorah, 1993); Alter Pekier, *Reb Aharon: Moreinu HaRav Aharon Kotler* (New York, London, and Jerusalem: CIS, 1995); Shimon Finkelman, *Reb Moshe: The Life and Ideals of HaGaon Rabbi Moshe Feinstein* (Brooklyn: Mesorah, 1986). Rosenblum, *Reb Shraga Feivel*; Bunim, *Fire*. Also see Laura Deckelman and Chana Rubin, *The Final Solution is Life: A Chasidic Dynasty's Story of Survival and Rebuilding* (Brooklyn: Mesorah, 2000).

53   Dovid Silber, *Noble Lives, Noble Deeds*, Vols. 1-3 (Brooklyn: Mesorah, 2002-2004). This series is more diverse, including biographies of a wider range of figures than Scheinbaum, *America* or Chaim Dovid Zwiebel and Nisson Wolpin, Eds, *Daring to Dream: Profiles in the Growth of the American Torah Community* (New York: Agudath Israel of American, 2003), which focus exclusively on figures, immigrants in particular, who had an impact in America. Nisson Wolpin, the editor of *The Jewish Observer*, has edited *The Torah Personality*, as well as *Torah Lives: A Treasury of Biographical Sketches* (Brooklyn: Mesorah and Agudath Israel of America, 1995), and *Torah Leaders: A Treasury of Biographical Sketches* (Brooklyn: Mesorah and Agudath Israel of America, 2002), which includes Eastern European immigrant figures as well as others. Also see Rubin,

Daughters of Destiny; Yitzchok Gluestein, "Who Can Forget 'Mr. Shatnez'?" *The Jewish Observer* 39:8 (November, 2006), 36-37.

54   For a collective biography of such rabbis, see Kimmy Caplan, *Ortodoksiah Ba'Olam HaHadash: Rabbanim VeDarshanut BeAmerikah (1881-1924)* (Jerusalem: Zalman Shazar Center, 2002).

55   Scheinbaum, *America*, 174-175. Also see Shmuel Singer, "A Chief Rabbi for New York [Rabbi Jacob Joseph]," in Wolpin, *The Torah Personality*, 270-278, which also fails to mention the riot. On Joseph, see Abraham J. Karp, "New York Chooses a Chief Rabbi," *Publication of the American Jewish Historical Society* 44 (1954-1955), 129-198, and Kimmy Caplan, "HaRav Ya'akov Yosef, HaRav HaKollel LeYehudei New York: Hebetim Hadashim," *Hebrew Union College Annual* 47 (1996), 1-39.

56   Berel Wein, *Echoes of Glory* (Brooklyn: Shaar, 1995); *Herald of Destiny* (Brooklyn: Shaar, 1993); *Triumph of Survival*. Also see Chaim Schloss, *2000 Years of Jewish History* (Jerusalem and New York: Feldheim, 2002).

57   Feldheim Publisher's Chanukah Catalog, 2005 (in possession of the author).

58   Scheinbaum, *America*, xvii. Also see the numerous approbations for these biographies, which focus on the religious message to be derived from these works. For example, see Bunim, *Fire*, v-xii, and Dershowitz, *Kotler*, v-vii.

59   See, for example, the discussion of twentieth-century Orthodoxy in Sarna, *American Judaism*, Chap. 6.

60   Generally, this literature uses interview material uncritically. Despite acknowledging that "people in their 70s and 80s were asked to recall with precision events that occurred 50 or even 60 years ago," one author simply quotes these interviews as sources of accurate fact. See Rosenblum, *Mike*, xii.

61   Hanoch Teller, *Builders* (Jerusalem: New York City Publishing Company, 2000), xxii.

62   Dershowitz, *Kotler*, 1-2, 365.

63   Nisson Wolpin, "The Torah Personality," in his *The Torah Personality*, 14.

64   Aharon Feldman, "*Gedolim* Books and the Biography of Reb Yaakov Kamenetsky," *The Jewish Observer* 28:8 (November, 1994), 32.

65   Eliyahu E. Dessler, *Strive for Truth!* (New York and Jerusalem: Feldheim, 1988), Vol. 1, 217.

66   Cited in Kamentsky, *Anatomy of a Ban*, 32.

67   Scheinbaum, *America*, 191. For related reflection of continuity with Eastern European Jewry from an Israeli Haredi spokesman, see Moshe Garylak, *HaHaredim: Mi Anahnu BeEmet?* (Jerusalem: Keter, 2002), 17-24. Regarding such issues in American Hasidic circles, see Fader, *Mitzvah Girls*, 121-125.

68   Scheinbaum, *America*, xv-xvi. Also see Dershowitz, *Kotler*, 12, "Europe had been blessed with Yeshivos and Gedolei Torah [great Torah scholars] until its destruction. It would seem that Hashem planned that America take its place."

69   Zwiebel and Wolpin, *Daring to Dream*, 178. Elipses in original. Also see Rosenblum, *Reb Shraga Feivel*, 18.

70   Wein, *Faith and Fate: The Story of the Jewish People* (Brooklyn: Shaar, 2001), 228.

71   Wein, *Triumph*, 429-430. Also see Wein, *Faith and Fate*, 228-229.

72   Dershowitz, *Kotler*, 48. Also see Pekier, 158-160, and the more moderate tone of Wein, *Triumph*, 437.

73   Wein, *Triumph*, 436.

74   Jonathan Rosenblum, "Anatomy of a Slander," *The Jewish Observer* 38:6 (Summer, 2005), 30. This statement was part of a larger and rather aggressive debate that followed the publication of Efraim Zuroff, *The Response of Orthodox Jewry in the United States to the Holocaust: The Activities of the Vaad ha-Hatzala Rescue Committee, 1939-1945* (New York: Yeshiva University Press, 2000). Some Orthodox and Haredi read-

ers took offense at the book's questioning of some of the Orthodox rescue group's decisions and the implication that Orthodox refusal to cooperate with non-Orthodox groups weakened both groups. See David Kranzler, "Orthodoxy's Finest Hour," *Jewish Action* 63:1 (Fall, 2002), 27-36, and the responses in Efraim Zuroff and David Kranzler, "Orthodox Rescue Revisited," *Jewish Action* 63:3 (Spring, 2003), 32-39. For more Haredi celebration of rescue and relief work, see Rosenblum, *Mike*, 232-383; Rosenblum, *Shraga Feivel*, 277-285; Pekier, *Reb Aharon*, 97-117.

75 See Schacter, "Haskalah," and "Facing the Truths of History."

76 Cited in Shapiro, "Books and Bans," 6. As Shapiro points out, *The Making of a Godol* does not, in fact, emphasize this theme greatly, which only highlights just how important the absence of secular studies is for those who banned the book.

77 Rosenblum, *Reb Shraga Feivel*, 202. Also see 143, 167, 224.

78 Ibid., 78.

79 One source indicates that in 1947 Mendlowitz publicly debated R. Yehezkel Levenstein of the Mir Yeshiva, recently arrived on American shores, urging the latter to include secular studies in the yeshiva's curriculum. Levenstein refused. See the letter from Moshe Yehudah HaCohen Blau to *Otzrot Yerushalyim*, 291 (1981), final page, available at http://www.hebrewbooks.org/13333 (My thanks to Marc Shapiro for pointing me to this and several other sources; viewed September, 2010).

80 Joseph Kaminetsky and Alex Gross, "Shraga Feivel Mendlowitz," in *Men of Spirit*, Ed. Leo Jung (New York: Kymson Publishing Company, 1964), 563.

81 Rosenblum, *Shraga Feivel*, 147.

82 Ibid., 90.

83 Ibid., 94.

84 Ibid., 198. The biography does not explain how this approach of "balancing" differs from "compromise," which, as we have seen, Mendlowitz supposedly rejected. Also see Rosenblum, *Shraga Feivel*, 225, where the biography apologizes for Mendlowitz's close relationship with the Religious-Zionist Mizrahi party. It seems likely that Mendlowitz adopted a more positive attitude toward college, given his role in trying to create a private college for yeshiva students. See Schacter, "Facing the Truths of History," 222-223. Also see the hint at Mendlowitz's role in arranging for students to attend Brooklyn College in Ze'ev Lev, "Teshuvah LaBiqoret," *HaMa'ayan* 32:4 (Summer, 1992), 49.

85 Rosenblum, *Shraga Feivel*, 103-104. For more on this group, see Bernard Zvi Sobel, "The M'lochim: A Study of a Religious Community," (M.A. thesis, The New School of Social Research, 1956), and Jerome R. Mintz, *Hasidic People: A Place in the New World* (Cambridge, MA and London: Harvard University Press, 1992), 21-26. Rosenblum reports that Mendlowitz preferred to keep them in the school, but that older students made them so uncomfortable that they left. In fact, Mendlowitz expelled the students, who refused to leave the school. Mendlowitz turned to a local halakhic authority who determined that Mendlowitz was permitted to expel them, and they were subsequently required to leave. See Yehoshua Baumel, *Shut 'Emeq Halakhah* (Jerusalem: n.p, 1976), Vol. 2, No. 28, 272-275.

86 Rosenblum, *Reb Shraga Feivel*, 95. The same paragraph appears in Rosenblum, *Mike*, 20.

87 E. Zerubavel, *Time Maps*, 19.

88 Halbwachs, *On Collective Memory*, 93-96.

89 Y. Zerubavel, *Recovered Roots*, 7-8.

90 Ibid., 10. Halbwachs, *On Collective Memory*, 94. Also see Roskies, *The Jewish Search for a Usable Past*, 3.

91 Halbwachs, *On Collective Memory*, Chap. 4.

92 See the similar suggestion by Haredi historian Tzvi Veinman, *MiKatovitz 'Ad Heh*

BeIyyar: Perakim BeToldot Agudat Yisrael VehaYahadut HaHaredit, Prospektivot Hadashot (Jerusalem: Vatikin, 1995), 9-11. Thanks to my father, Eliezer Finkelman, for some of the formulations in these last paragraphs.

CHAPTER FIVE

1   Shmuel Waldman, *Beyond a Resonable Doubt: Convincing Evidence of the Truths of Judaism* (Jerusalem and New York: Feldheim, 2004); Hurwitz, *Being Jewish*; Yaakov Weinberg, *Fundamentals and Faith: Insights Into Rambam's 13 Principles*, Ed. Mordechai Blumenfeld (Southfield, MI: Targum Press, 1991). The text is, in fact, Blumenfeld's reconstruction of R. Weinberg's oral lectures. It does not matter in this context how accurate a rendering it is. Noah Weinberg and Yaakov Salomon, *What the Angel Taught You: Seven Keys to Life Fulfillment* (Brooklyn: Shaar Press, 2003); Akiva Tatz, *Living Inspired* (Southfield, MI: Targum/Feldheim, 1991).

2   See, for example, Mary Douglas, *Natural Symbols* (London: Barrie and Rockliff, 1970), and H. Richard Niebuhr, *The Social Sources of Denominationalism* (New York: H. Holt and Co., 1929).

3   Binyamin Brown, "Shuvah Shel 'HaEmunah HaTemimah': Tefisat HaEmunah HaHaredit U'Tzmihatah BeMe'ah HaEsrim," in *'Al HaEmunah: Iyyunim BeMusag HaEmunah Uve-Toldotav BaMasoret HaYehudit*, Eds. Moshe Halbertal, David Kurzweil, and Avi Sagi (Jerusalem: Keter, 2005), 403-443.

4   Binyamin Brown, "VeEin Lanu Shiur Rak HaTorah HaZot," *Eretz Aharet* 41 (August-October, 2007), 56-65. Some of this fideistic approach may have its roots in Hasidic rejection of attempts to rationalize faith. See, for example, a handful of relevant primary sources in Norman Lamm, Alan Brill, and Shalom Carmy, *The Religious Thought of Hasidism: Text and Commentary* (New York: Yeshiva University Press, 1999), Chap. 3.

5   On "*hashkafah*" see Brown, "*VeEin Lanu.*" Due to its unconscious nature, Haredi implicit theology often flies under the radar of outsiders, who expect theology to look somewhat different than it does within Haredi literature. See, for example, Brown's critique of Dov Schwartz's claim that Haredim lack theology: "*Pareshat Derakhim LeLo Motza,*" *Akdamot* 2 (1997), 85-99. In this earlier and polemical essay, Brown seems to argue that Haredi theology is more systematic than he presents it in his later and less polemical essays.

6   Cf. Boaz Huss "The New Age of Kabbalah: Contemporary Kabbalah, the New Age and Postmodern Spirituality," *Journal of Modern Jewish Studies* 6:2 (2007), 107-125.

7   Women's writings are, of course, full of "unconscious theology." On occasion, women address the theological sides of "women's issues," such as feminism. See for example Sara Tikva Kornbluth and Doron Kornbluth, Eds., *Jewish Women Speak about Jewish Matters* (Southfield, MI: Targum/Feldheim, 2000). Women's non-fiction inspirational literature sometimes drifts in the direction of explicit theology. See, for example, Tzipporah Heller, *This Way Up: Torah Essays on Spiritual Growth* (Jerusalem and New York: Feldheim, 2000). After completion of this manuscript, Shira Smiles' book, *Torah Tapestries* (New York and Jerusalem: Feldheim, 2010) appeared. These essays on the weekly Torah portion qualify as explicit theology authored by a woman, though she is not concerned with proofs for Torah dogmas.

8   Kelemen, *Permission to Believe* and his *Permission to Receive*; Moshe Speiser, *Questions You Thought We Were Afraid You'd Ask, and Answers You've Been Waiting to Hear* (Southfield, MI: Targum/Feldheim, 2004); Yitzchak Coopersmith, *The Eye of a Needle: Aish Hatorah's Kiruv Primer* (Jerusalem: Feldheim, 1993); Waldman, *Beyond a Resonable Doubt*, 2004.

9   Waldman, 2002, 3.

10   Waldman, *Beyond a Reasonable Doubt*, 2004. Also see Dovid Sapirman, *A Mechanech's Guide on Why and How to Teach Emunah* (Brooklyn: Torah Umesorah, 2009).

11   This claim has its roots in the thought of several early twentieth-century Haredi rabbis. See Hazon Ish, *Emunah UVitahon* (Jerusalem: n.p., 1954), Chap. 1. Cf. R. Elhanan Wasserman, *Kovetz Ma'amarim VeIggarot* (Jerusalem: Makhon Or Elhanan, 2001), Vol. 1, 3-12, and R. Aharon Kotler, *Mishnat Rabbi Aharon* (Lakewood, NJ: Makhon Mishnat Rabbbi Aharon, 1996), Vol. 1, 3-7.

12   Weinberg and Salomon, *Angel*, 8.

13   Gershon Robinson, *The Obvious Proof* (New York: CIS Publishers, 1993).

14   Sapirman, *A Mechanech's Guide*, 48.

15   For a poorly argued attack on these works of theology, see R. D. Gold, *Bondage of the Mind* (Menlo Park, CA: Aldus Books, 2008) and a critique of Gold by Yoel Finkelman, "The Jewish God Delusion: Orthodoxy and the New Atheism," available at http://www.atid.org/resources/survey/column3.asp, viewed July, 2008.

16   Chaim Kupperwasser, "Sixty Years Since Churban Europa," *The Jewish Observer* 38:5 (May, 2005), 11.

17   Waldman, *Reasonable Doubt*, 2002, 4.

18   Dovid Gottlieb, *Living Up... to the Truth* (Jerusalem, 1995), available at http://www.dovidgottlieb.com/works/RabbiGottliebLivingUpToTheTruth.pdf (viewed July, 2010; all references will be to the pdf internet edition).

19   I will leave aside the issue of the so-called "Torah-codes," since they do not seem to be in the Haredi consensus, and are often conspicuously left out of many of these books.

20   He states explicitly that his goal is not "proof" but rather "*high probability vis-à-vis* the alternatives" (18). Still, he makes it clear that he considers his arguments valid based on the "scientific method," and that his are the only reasonable conclusions.

21   Here, I use the term "strong" to modify religion differently than do Almond, Appleby, and Sivan in their book *Strong Religion*, where they refer to a militant and aggressive force to be reckoned with. Instead, I refer to a commitment perceived as strong, unwavering, and solid by its adherents. See their *Strong Religion*, 2.

22   Akiva Tatz, *The Thinking Jewish Teenager's Guide to Life* (Southfield, MI: Targum Press, 1999), 136-138. Also see Weinberg, *Fundamentals and Faith*, 74-75, and Waldman, *Reasonable Doubt*, 2002, 3-4. This is virtually identical to some devout Chistian apologetics, which claim that "Christianity is *not* a blind faith. It is the *only* religion that can prove itself" (emphasis in original). See http://www.clarifyingchristianity.com/b_proof.shtml (viewed April, 2011). A Google search in January of 2010 for the words "proof, truth, Christianity" reveals some 5 million links.

23   Ezriel Tauber, *Choose Life!* (Monsey, NY: Shalheves, 1991), 41.

24   Kelemen, *Permission to Believe*, 99. Also see Gottlieb, *Living Up*, 18, and Waldman, *Beyond a Reasonable Doubt*, 2004, 2-4.

25   Speiser, *Questions*, 10.

26   Sapirman, *A Mechanech's Guide*.

27   Gevirtz, *Lehovin UleHaskil: A Guide to Torah Hashkofoh, Questions and Answers on Judaism* (New York: Jewish Educational Program, 1980), Table of Contents.

28   Waldman, *Beyond a Reasonable Doubt*, 2004, 4.

29   See, for example, Maimonides, *Guide of the Perplexed*, 2:32-48

30   Waldman, *Beyond a Reasonable Doubt*, 2004, 268.

31   Tauber, *Choose Life!*, particularly 40-41.

32   Speiser, *Questions*, 44, 64.

33   Coopersmith, *Eye*, 39-40. Coopersmith is not correct here. "Biblical Christianity is one of the very few religions which claims to be capable of experimental verification."

A mid-twentieth-century representative of the Moody Institute of Science, cited in Hendershot, *Shaking the World*, 155.

34 Gottlieb, *Living Up*, 22-23.

35 See Thomas Nagle, *The View from Nowhere* (Oxford: Oxford University Press, 1986). Nagle argues that no such perspective exists for humans, despite science's attempts to limit the conditionality of knowledge.

36 Hendershot, *Shaking the World*, Chap. 5.

37 Kelemen, *Permission to Believe*, 103, 60-61. Also see Gevirtz, *Guide to Torah Hashkofoh*, 48. Waldman also quotes extensively from anti-evolutionary scientists, such as Michael Behe and Michael Denton.

38 Gottlieb, *Living Up*, 26.

39 Colin Grant, *Myths We Live By* (Ottowa: University of Ottowa Press, 1998), 30, cited in Robinson, "Practically, I'm a Fundamentalist," 72.

40 Chaim Dov Keller, "The Cosmic Question: Random Evolution or Intelligent Design?" *The Jewish Observer* 39:4 (May, 2006), 10.

41 Peter J. Bowler, *Monkey Trials and Gorilla Sermons: Evolution and Christianity from Darwin to Intelligent Design* (Cambridge: Harvard University Press, 2007), 11.

42 Ibid.

43 Waldman, *Reasonable Doubt*, 2002, 240, 249, 252, 255.

44 Yonoson Rosenblum, "The Myth of Scientific Objectivity," *The Jewish Observer* 39:4 (May, 2006), 27-34, quote from 27-28. See Thomas Kuhn, *The Structure of Scientific Revolutions* (Chicago: University of Chicago Press, 1962). Also see Gevirtz, *Guide to Torah Hashkofoh*, 58-60.

45 Robinson, *The Obvious Proof*, 11ff.

46 Waldman, *Reasonable Doubt*, 2004, 240.

47 Nosson Slifkin, *The Science of Torah: The Reflection of Torah in the Laws of Science, the Creation of the Universe, and the Development of Life* (Southfield, MI: Targum Press, 2001), 13.

48 Ibid.

49 Nosson Slifkin, *The Camel, the Hare, and the Hyrax: A Study of the Laws of Animals with One Kosher Sign in Light of Modern Zoology* (Southfield, MI: Targum Press, 2004). Those who banned Slifkin's books regularly insisted that the Talmudic rabbis could not err in matters of science, since their scientific knowledge came from God. See many of the documents available at http://www.zootorah.com/, viewed July, 2010. Also see Zamir Cohen, *Science Outscienced: How Torah Outpaced Science by 3300 Years* (Jerusalem: Kest-Lebovitz Jewish Heritage and Roots Library, 1997).

50 Street-poster quoting R. Eliya Weintraub from September of 2004, available at http://www.zootorah.com/controversy/cherem.pdf, viewed July, 2010.

51 Waldman, *Reasonable Doubt*, 68

52 Weinberg and Solomon, *Angel*, 95-97.

53 Max Anteby, *The Jewish Theory of Everything* (Brooklyn: Shaar Press, 2002), 30.

54 Gottlieb, *Living Up*, 7, 13. Gottlieb offers a somewhat idiosyncratic definition of the scientific method, in that he excludes controlled experimentation or replicability. Also see 11. "From the philosopher's point of view... there is no truth to be had."

55 Kelemen, *Permission to Believe*, 21. Gottlieb, *Living Up*, 49, echoing a sentiment expressed by the twelfth-century R. Yehudah Halevi in *Sefer HaKuzari*, 5:14. Also see Waldman, *Reasonable Doubt*, 2002, 68.

56 Levi, *The Science in Torah*, 75-76.

57 According to Peter Byrne, the assumption that someone or something must *make* morality binding places Kelemen in the "crude argument" for God's existence. See his "Moral Arguments for the Existence of God," *Stanford Encyclopedia of Philosophy*, avail-

able at http://plato.stanford.edu/entries/moral-arguments-god/, viewed November, 2009.

58   Sa'adia Gaon, *The Book of Beliefs and Opinions*, Trans. Samuel Rosenblatt (New Haven and London: Yale University Press, 1948), 3:1; also see BT Sotah 67b.

59   Avi Sagi and Daniel Statman, *Religion and Morality* (Amsterdam and Atlanta: Rodopi, 1995), 7.

60   Waldman, *Beyond a Reasonable Doubt*, 2004, 1. This passage appears only in the preface of the edition of this book for the non-observant, not the original edition for the already observant but struggling.

61   Speiser, *Questions*, 54-55. Also see Weinberg and Solomon, *Angel*, 145-146.

62   Kelemen, *Permission to Believe*, 11.

63   Robinson, *The Obvious Proof*, 35, and see the longer discussion on 15-48. Also see Waldman, *Reasonable Doubt*, 2002, 5, and Speiser, *Questions*, 46. No doubt, the discussion relates to the ongoing attempt in the Eastern European *musar* movement to eliminate self-interest (*negios*) from a person's decision-making. Also see R. Elhanan Wasserman's claim that belief in God and in the divine revelation of Torah should be obvious to even a simpleton, and that those who reject faith do so in order to flee from the obligations that observance requires. *Kovetz Ma'amarim VeIggarot*, Vol 1, 3-12.

64   Avraham Baharan, *The Two-Way Channel: Society and the Individual* (Southfield, MI: Targum/Feldheim, 1999), 46.

65   Kelemen, *Permission to Believe*, 17.

66   Jeremy Kagan, *The Jewish Self: Recovering Spirituality in the Modern World* (Jerusalem: Feldheim, 1998), 40-41. He also combines this with Hegelian notions about the dialectical progress of history. He does not seem aware that the philosophical positions that he combines seem diametrically opposed to one another.

67   *Bereishit Rabbah*, 1:1.

68   Kagan, *Jewish Self*, 97-98.

69   Ibid., 43.

70   Ibid., 41-42.

71   Tatz, *Teenager*, 147-148. Also see Tauber, *Choose Life*, 31-32.

72   Weinberg and Solomon, *Angel*, 102.

73   Tatz, *Teenager*, 12.

74   Speiser, *Questions*, 55.

75   Tatz, *Teenager*, 86, 88.

76   For the most part, Haredi popular literature does not consider the possibility that an emphasis on objective rationality could lead to constantly rethinking one's identity and commitment, since one would have to constantly re-evaluate changing evidence and new discoveries. Ironically, this is part of the reason why rationalism is *not* appealing to some Modern Orthodox theologians.

77   Tauber, *Choose Life*, 43.

78   Coopersmith, *Eye of the Needle*, 8.

79   Ammiel Hirsch and Yosef Reinman, *One People, Two Worlds* (New York: Schocken, 2002), 5, 11, 216. The book gained some notoriety in the Haredi community when a book tour with the two authors was called off because Haredi rabbis were opposed to giving the impression of accepting the legitimacy of Reform.

80   Weinberg, *Fundamentals and Faith*, 28, 14.

81   Menachem Kellner suggests a link between Maimonides' principles and proper practice on the part of Jews, both because true belief is itself a halakhic requirement and because it serves as a prerequisite for other halakhic practices. See his *Dogma in Medieval Jewish Thought* (Oxford: Oxford University Press and Littman Library of Jewish Civilization, 1986), 34-49, 53-63.

82   Weinberg, *Fundamentals and Faith*, 73.

83   Ibid., 93.

84   Compare the Hebrew edition – Yehoshua Yeshayah Neuwith, *Shemirat Shabbat Ke-Hilkhetah* (Jerusalem: Feldheim, 1965) – with the 1984 English version.

85   Shimon D. Eider, *Halachos of Niddah* (Lakewood, NJ: n.p., 1981). Also see Simcha Bunim Cohen, *The Sanctity of Shabbos* (Brooklyn: Mesorah, 2000), or his other books of halakhah, which follow the same pattern. Not translating the notes was a deliberate policy. See Benny Kraut, *The Greening of American Orthodoxy: Yavneh in the Nineteen Sixties* (Cincinnati: Hebrew Union College Press, 2011), 84.

86   Chris Gowans, "Moral Relativism," *The Stanford Encyclopedia of Philosophy*, available at http://plato.stanford.edu/entries/moral-relativism/, viewed June, 2008. Strictly speaking, moral skepticism differs from relativism. Skepticism admits that one cannot know what is morally binding, while relativism argues that morals may be knowable and binding, but only from the situated perspective of a particular individual or group.

87   Gottlieb, *Living Up*, 7.

88   See Maimonides, *Guide*, 2:15.

89   R. Yosef Albo, *Sefer HaIqqarim* (Jerusalem: n.p., 1987), 1:7-8, partially translated in *Medieval Political Philosophy: A Sourcebook*, Eds. Ralph Lerner and Muhsin Mahdi (Ithaca, NY: Cornell University, 1993), 242-249.

90   Maharal of Prague, *Tifferet Yisrael* (Israel: n.p., 1980), Chap. 17. On the idea of the Torah's permanence and unchanging nature, see Chap. 58.

91   While I am not familiar with a canonized Jewish source that explicitly adopts this position on theological matters, Menachem Fish has claimed that the sages of the Talmud adopted such an attitude toward halakhic reasoning. See his *Rational Rabbis: Science and Talmudic Culture* (Bloomington: Indiana University Press, 1997). Menaham Kellner suggests that Maimonides adopted a fallibilist position regarding human knowledge of science. See his "Maimonides on the Science of the *Mishneh Torah*: Provisional or Permanent?" *AJS Review* 18:2 (1993), 169-194, and his "Maimonides' Allegiances to Science and Judaism," *The Torah u-Madda Journal* 7 (1997), 88-104. Rav Kook also suggested a certain fallibilistic attitude toward truth claims, given his notion of evolutionary development of theology. See, for example, David Shatz, "Thoughts on the Integration of Torah and Culture: Its Scope and Limits in the Thought of Rav Kook," in his *Jewish Thought in Dialogue: Essays on Thinkers, Theologies, and Moral Theories* (Boston: Academic Studies Press, 2009), 93-117.

92   This is a position at the very least suggested by R. Joseph B. Soloveitchik's essay "Confrontation," *Tradition* 6:2 (1964), 5-27, according to which a member of one religious group cannot understand the language and faith commitments of another religious group. Soloveitchik expands on the theme of the incommensurability of certain kinds of truth claims in *The Halakhic Mind*, where he argues for epistemological pluralism, the idea that there are different legitimate ways of examining the same phenomena, and that those ways are potentially legitimate even when they are mutually exclusive.

93   Nahmanides, Introduction to *Milhamot Hashem*, which appears as an appendix to standard editions of BT *Berakhot*.

94   For an example of such a position, see R. Nissim Gerondi (the Ran), *Derashot HaRan* (Jerusalem: Makhon Shalem, 1977), 198. The Torah "gave the generation's wise men the task of deciding... [because] for the most part this will lead to improvement and right justice, for great wise men are less likely to make a mistake then those with lesser wisdom.... And even though in a rare and occasional fashion they will make a mistake about something... it is worth suffering that, for this generally leads to improvement."

95   Rabbi Aryeh Leib HaKohen Heller's *Ketzot HaHoshen*, (Jerusalem: Oraita, 2002), Introduction. He goes on to explain that human input into the law means that the study

and interpretation of the law is an exercise in falsehood. For a fuller analysis of these themes, see Avi Sagi, *Eilu VeEilu: Mashma'uto Shel HaSiah HaHilkhati* (Israel: HaKibbutz HaMe'uhad, 1996), and William Kolbrener, "Chiseled from All Sides: Hermeneutics and Dispute in the Rabbinic Tradition," *AJS Review* 28:2 (2004), 273-295.

96   Moshe Feinstein, *Sefer Iggerot Moshe* (New York: Noble Book Press, 1959), *Orah Hayyim*, Vol. 1, Introduction.

97   Hurwitz, *Being Jewish*, 77.

98   Weinberg and Solomon, *Angel*, 102.

99   Hirshman, *One Above and Seven Below*, 51.

100   Rosenblum, *Reb Shraga Feivel*, 126.

101   Weinbeg, *Fundamentals and Faith*, 14.

102   Aryeh Carmell, *Masterplan: Judaism: Its Programs, Meanings, and Goals* (Jerusalem: Jerusalem Academy Publications, 1991), xii.

103   Rosenblum, *Reb Shraga Feivel*, 172.

104   Tatz, *Living Inspired*, 11-12.

105   Weinberg and Solomon, *Angel*, 178-179.

106   Carmell, *Masterplan*, ix.

107   Gottlieb, *Living Up*, 6.

108   Hirschman, *One Above*, 32.

109   See Yonason Rosenblum, "*Torah Umadda*: A Critique of Rabbi Dr. Norman Lamm's Book and its Approach to Torah Study," *The Jewish Observer* 25:2 (March, 1992), 27-40. Also see the presentation of R. S.R. Hirsch's *Torah 'Im Derekh Eretz* approach in Eliyahu Meir Klugman, *Rabbi Samson Raphael Hirsch: Architect of Torah Judaism for the Modern World* (Brooklyn: Mesorah, 1998), 200-217. This book downplays Hirsch's advocacy of general education as an intrinsic value and envisions Hirsch's advocacy of general education primarily as "the one possible antidote to the challenge posed to Jewish belief by exposure to secular society." According to this biography, Hirsch saw general education as a way to "inoculate Jewish youth against the enticements of the outside world," so that the "inevitable exposure to ideas directly or potentially at odds with the Torah should take place under the guidance of those well versed in Torah, who could point out how and why the Torah rejects those ideas" (205, 213). And, while Klugman does not argue, as other Haredi apologists have, that Hirsch considered *Torah Im Derekh Eretz* education a temporary measure, he does suggests that it "cannot be used as a paradigm for other eras and settings" (217). For a fuller discussion of Hirsch's approach to general education, see Shnayer Z. Leiman, "Rabbinic Openness to General Culture in the Early Modern Period," in Schacter, Ed. *Judaism's Encounter with Other Cultures*, 180-201.

110   Gevirtz, *Guide to Torah Hashkofoh*, xxi.

111   Kagan, *Jewish Self*, 37-38.

112   Gottlieb, *Living Up*, 6.

113   Tatz, *Worldmask*, 90-92.

114   Tatz, *Teenager*, 83-84.

115   Nesanel Kasnett, "'We are Israel': A Chanuka Essay," *The Jewish Observer* 21:8 (November, 1988), 27.

116   Zev Leff, "The Reality of Torah," *MDTorah Weekly* 4:18 (February 22, 2003), 3.

117   Pollak, *Powerhouse*, 111, 119.

118   Dessler, *Strive for Truth!*, Vol. 1, 195-196. Dessler's attitude toward the dangers of science are certainly related to his occasionalist approach to natural causation, in which scientific laws are illusions, since God directly causes each and every event in the world. Occasionalism undermines the epistemological grounds of contemporary science. On Dessler's occasionalism, see *Strive for Truth*, Vol. 2, 236-261; Eliezer Gold-

man, "Responses to Modernity in Orthodox Jewish Thought," *Studies in Contemporary Jewry* 2 (1986), 52-73; and David Shatz, "Divine Intervention and Religious Sensibilities," in his *Jewish Thought in Dialogue*, 179-208.

119 *Strive for Truth*, vol. 1, 170.

120 The quotes in this paragraph come from *Strive for Truth*, Vol. 1, 170-171, 176-177, 219, 223.

121 From an address before Agudath Israel's 82nd National Convention by R. Uren Reich. Available at http://www.zootorah.com/controversy/ravreich.pdf, viewed Sept, 2010.

122 Mendelsohn, "Religious Fundamentalism and the Sciences," 23-41.

123 For example, a young Israeli Haredi man received a negative reception when he began trying to address theological and religious questions using his intellect. See Shabtai Cor, *Nahag Hadash* (Jerusalem: Carmel, 2007).

124 Sapirman, *A Mechanech's Guide*, 17, 45.

125 Coopersmith, *Eye of the Needle*, 41.

126 Sa'adia Gaon, *Beliefs and Opinions*, Introductory Treatise, sec. iii, 10.

127 Ibid., sec. ii-iii.

128 Bahya ibn Paquda, *The Book of Directions to the Duties of the Heart*, Trans. Menahem Mansoor (London: Routledge and Kegan Paul, 1973), Introduction, 86.

129 See, among many other sources, Maimonides, *Guide* 3:51.

130 A full discussion of these themes in Modern Orthodox theology is beyond the scope of this study. As an example of some of these themes, see Shatz, *Jewish Thought in Dialogue*, as well as the numerous contributions by varying authors to Yeshiva University's *Torah U-Madda Journal* and the volumes of the Orthodox Forum series.

131 David Shatz, "The Overexamined Life is Not Worth Living," in his *Jewish Thought in Dialogue*, 387-412.

132 Aharon Lichtenstein, "The Source of Faith is Faith Itself," in his *Leaves of Faith: The World of Jewish Living* (Jersey City: Ktav, 2004), Vol. 2, 366; Shalom Carmy, *Forgive Us, Father-in-Law For We Know Not What to Think: Letter to a Philosophical Dropout From Orthodoxy* (Jerusalem: ATID, 2004), 14. Also see Marvin Fox's contribution to *Commentary*'s influential symposium, "The State of Jewish Belief," 42:2 (August, 1966), 89-92. Notice that Fox makes explicit the link between his "irrational" belief and his lack of interest in religious polemics or in "proving" either Judaism true or any other religion false.

133 Norman Lamm, *Torah Umadda: The Encounter of Religious Learning and Worldly Knowledge in the Jewish Tradition* (Northvale, NJ and London: Jason Aaronson, 1990), ix-x, Chap. 3.

134 Ibid., jacketcover.

135 Modern Orthodox intellectuals, with greater concern for individual autonomy, may also have a greater awareness and fear of scientific dystopias, in which scientific rationalism undergirds the authority of a totalitarian government.

136 Debra Renee Kaufman, *Rachel's Daughters: Newly Orthodox Jewish Women* (New Brunswick, NJ: Rutgers University Press, 1991), 8. Also see Lynn Davidman, *Tradition in a Rootless World: Women Turn to Orthodox Judaism* (Berkeley: University of California Press, 1991), 90-93, and Herbert Danzger, *Returning to Tradition: The Contemporary Revival of Orthodox Judaism* (New Haven: Yale University Press, 1989), Chap. 10. Danzger places more emphasis on truth in his analysis of returnees, but he describes nothing like the individual systematic search for abstract and provable objective truth. Both Davidman and Kaufman study women exclusively. I see no evidence that meaning-making matters more for women than for men.

137 Davidman, *Tradition*, 93. Without denying the validity of the proofs, Haredi author Gila Manolson describes her own journey to Haredi Judaism as occurring before there

were "classes for people... illustrating the historical accuracy of Biblical prophecies or the hidden codes in the Torah as revealed through modern computer research. My interest in Judaism was initially sparked *solely* by what I sensed to be its wisdom regarding how to live a meaningful life." Gila Manolson, *The Magic Touch: A Candid Look at the Jewish Approach to Relationships* (Jerusalem: Har Nof Publications, 1992), 8.

CHAPTER SIX

1   See http://abcnews.go.com/US/wireStory?id=8154675, viewed March, 2010.

2   http://www.vosizneias.com/35851/2009/07/29/borough-park-ny-spinka-rebbe-tells-legal-symposium-%E2%80%98we%E2%80%99ve-learned-things-the-hard-way%E2%80%99/,viewed August, 2009.

3   http://daashedyot.blogspot.com/2009/08/breaking-news.html#links, viewed August, 2009.

4   Eviatar Zerubavel, *The Elephant in the Room: Silence and Denial in Everyday Life* (Oxford and New York: Oxford University Press, 2006), 40-41, 76-78. Needless to say, every community will explain in altruistic terms the desire to limit self-criticism, claiming for example that airing dirty laundry will undermine group unity or put weapons in the hands of enemies. See, for example, Daren Lenard Hutchinson, "Beyond the Rhetoric of 'Dirty Laundry': Examining the Value of Internal Criticism within Progressive Social Movements and Oppressed Communities," *Michigan Journal of Race and Law* 5 (1999-2000), 185-199.

5   Kimmy Caplan, "'Yesh Riqavon Retzini BaHevrah Shalanu VeTzrikhin LeHakir Et HaEmet': Biqqoret 'Atzmit BaSiah HaPenimi Shel HaHevrah HaHaredit BeYisrael," in *Mi'utim, Zarim VeShonim: Kevutzot Shulayim BaHistoriah*, Ed. Shlomit Volkov (Jerusalem: Zalman Shazar Center, 2000), 299-330.

6   Zerubavel, *The Elephant in the Room*. For example, Haredi print media almost never speak of the role of leading rabbis in protecting perpetrators of sexual abuse in Haredi education, such that discussion of the topic appears primarily in internet venues or the non-Haredi press, out of Haredi editorial oversight. Not accidentally, when a Hasidic woman published a novel about the covering up of sexual abuse in the Haredi community, it was not published by a mainstream Haredi publisher. See the pseudonymous Aishes Chayil, *Hush* (New York: Walker Press, 2010). The role of rabbis in hiding and perpetuating sexual abuse in Jewish religious schools appears in several articles in Amy Neustein, Ed., *Tempest in the Temple: Jewish Communities and Child Sex Scandals* (Lebanon, NH: University Press of New England, Brandeis University Press, 2009). Also see Robert Kolker, "On the Rabbi's Knee: Do the Orthodox Jews Have a Catholic Priest Problem?" *New York Magazine*, May 14, 2006, available at http://nymag.com/news/features/17010/, viewed February, 2010.

7   Dilip Gaonkar and Charles Taylor, "Block Thinking and Internal Criticism," *Public Culture* 18:3 (2006), 454.

8   Caplan, "*Yesh Rikavon*."

9   As an example of the latter approach, see Uri Zohar, *Waking Up Jewish* (Jerusalem: Hemesorah Publications, 1985).

10   A nearly identical analysis could have been based on *Mishpacha*, a competing Haredi weekly magazine. No doubt, competition from *Mishpacha* and from the internet helps explain Agudath Israel's decision to close *The Jewish Observer* in 2009.

11   Michael Walzer, *The Company of Critics: Social Criticism and Political Commitment in the 20ᵗʰ Century* (New York: Basic Books, 2002, 226).

12   Ignazio Silone, *Bread and Wine* (New York: Harper and Brothers, 1937), 157, quoted

in Michael Walzer, *Interpretation and Social Criticism* (Cambridge and London: Harvard University Press, 1987), 42.

13   Marvin Schick, "The Orthodox Community's Confused Priorities," *The Jewish Observer* 40:5 (June/Summer, 2007), 31-35.

14   Golding, "Jewish Music," 37. Cf. Hendershot, *Shaking the World*, Chap. 2, and Romanowski, "Evangelicals and Popular Music" for similar issues in the Christian music scene.

15   Sara Medwed, "Shalom Bayis Like It Was Not Too Long Ago," *The Jewish Observer* 40:7 (October, 2007), 15-17. Also see her article in *The Jewish Observer* 38:3 (March, 2005), 40-42.

16   See Abramov and Abramov, *Two Halves of a Whole*, and John Gray, *Men are from Mars, Women are from Venus* (London: Thorsons, 1992).

17   See, for example, www.theyeshivaworld.com and www.vosizneias.com. In December, 2009, after publication of *The Jewish Observer*'s article, several prominent Haredi rabbis attempted to ban even Haredi-organized websites. See http://abcnews.go.com/Technology/wireStory?id=9664125, viewed March, 2010.

18   Zvi Frankel, "Blogs: Transgressing a Major Sin 'In the Name of Heaven'," *The Jewish Observer* 40:9 (December, 2007), 32-33.

19   See the discussion of the role of the internet in bringing issues of sexual abuse to the public agenda in Kolker, "On the Rabbi's Knee."

20   Frankel, "Blogs," 32-33.

21   http://www.jewishmediaresources.com, viewed March, 2010.

22   Yonoson Rosenblum, "Growing Pains," *The Jewish Observer* 41:2 (March, 2008), 18-21.

23   Yonoson Rosenblum, "Real Jews: Noah Efron's Research and the Chareidi Image," *The Jewish Observer* 37:3 (March, 2004), 14-18. Noah Efron, *Real Jews: Secular Versus Ultra-Orthodox and the Struggle for Jewish Identity in Israel* (New York: Basic Books, n.d).

24   Anonymous, "Introduction," *The Jewish Observer*, March 2000, 6.

25   Michael Apple, *Education and Power* (Boston, London, Melbourne, and Henley: Routledge and Kegal Paul, 1982), 13. While I share Apple's concern with the way hidden aspects of education help to reproduce the existing social (and in this case, religious) power structure, my analysis differs from Apple's in significant ways. He focuses on the macro-economic ideological work of education, while I focus on more micro-ideological and social matters. I also do not share his progressive, Marxist-influenced ideology.

26   Prominent Israeli journalist Yisrael Segal and author Dov Elbaum, for example, eventually became very successful no-longer-Haredi Jews. Also see Barzilai's discussion of different kinds of people who leave the Israeli Haredi world in her *Lifrotz Me'ah She'arim*.

27   November, 1999, 10. Also see the *haskamah* of another parenting guide, which explains that "only in the path of Torah will he [the child] be successful all the days of his life." Gans, *Make Me, Don't Break Me*. Cf. November, 1999, 67, a rare voice who considers the possibility that a dropout might remain non-observant but overcome an addiction or return at least to psychological health.

28   Nisson Wolpin, "Rx: For Yeshiva Dropouts," *The Jewish Observer* (May, 1964), 16-19.

29   On the state of Orthodoxy in those years, with a prescient prediction of the eventual rise of a more isolationist Orthodoxy, see Liebman, "Orthodoxy in American Jewish Life," 21–92.

30   Yakov Horowitz, "Report from Ground Zero," 32:9 (November, 1999), 51.

31   Shmuel Kamenetsky, "Dealing with the Dilemmas of Kids-At-Risk," November, 1999, 25; Horowitz, "Ground Zero," 52-53; Norman Blumenthal and Shimon Russell, "Help-

ing the 'At-Risk' Child: A Guide to Therapy," November, 1999, 59.

32   Miriam Levi, *Effective Jewish Parenting*, (New York and Jerusalem: Feldheim, 1986), 205.

33   Shimon Schwab, "The New Horizon in Education," in *Timeless Parenting: Raising Children in Troubled Times*, Ed. Nisson Wolpin (Brooklyn: Mesorah, 2000), 191. For more on parent-home cooperation in Haredi discourse, see Yoel Finkelman, "Relationships Between Schools and Parents in Haredi Popular Literature in the United States," in *Jewish Day Schools, Jewish Communities*, Eds. Alex Pomson and Howard Deitcher (Oxford and Portland: Littman Library of Jewish Civilization, 2009), 237-254.

34   Eliyahu Meir Klugman, "Introduction," November, 1999, unpaginated front cover.

35   November, 1999, 12.

36   November, 1999, 15.

37   Joseph Elias, "Bechira/Freedom of Choice and Psychology," November, 1999, 55.

38   Wolbe, "Parenting," November, 1999, 16-17.

39   Aharon Kaufman, "Of Growth and Belonging," November, 1999, 38.

40   See for example "L'emaan Hashem – What Will it Take?" (http://www.rabbihorowitz.com/PYes/ArticleDetails.cfm?Book_ID=1041&ThisGroup_ID=262&Type=Article) and "They Do Not Represent Us," (http://www.rabbihorowitz.com/PYes/ArticleDetails.cfm?Book_ID=904&ThisGroup_ID=262&Type=Article) or any number of his articles at www.rabbihorowitz.com, viewed April, 2011.

41   Horowitz, "Report from Ground Zero," November, 1999, 51-54.

42   Alman Lachman, "When Conventional Parenting is Not Enough," November, 1999, 62-65; Blumenthal and Russell, "Helping the 'At-Risk Child'," November, 1999, 57-61.

43   David Pelcovitz and Shimon Russel, "The 'At Risk Child': Early Identification and Intervention," November, 1999, 43-46.

44   Ahron Kaufman, "Of Growth and Belonging," November, 1999, 38.

45   The quote comes from the table of contents.

46   Anonymous, "Thoughts of a Mother," November, 1999, 10.

47   Anonymous, "Introduction," *The Jewish Observer* 33:3 (March, 2000), 6.

48   Rabbi Jeruchom L. Shapiro, an administrator of a girls' school, March, 2000, 23.

49   Anonymous, "Introduction," March, 2000, 6.

50   Letter to the editor, March, 2000, 7.

51   Anonymous, "The Chinuch Scene," March, 2000, 17.

52   Ibid.

53   Ibid. Other authors support this idea. "To put the blame on the system in *yeshivos* and *mechanchim* is unfair and inaccurate" (Yisroel Wolpin, himself an educator, in "Some Kids on the Brink Can Be Saved," March, 2000, 18). Oddly enough, the article then goes on to suggest several things that educators and schools should be doing differently, such as offering individualized education in the form of tutoring for weaker students, implying some criticism of the existing educational system.

54   M. Birnbaum, March, 2000, 25-26.

55   A Mother in Flatbush, March, 2000, 27.

56   Anonymous letter, March, 2000, 26.

57   Nisson Wolpin, "Introduction," March, 2000, 6.

58   Moshe Schapiro, "Drawing Lines in a Moving Field," March, 2000, 53.

59   *The Jewish Observer*, November, 1999, inside cover.

60   "Pushing the Conformity Envelope Too Far," March, 2000, 36-37.

61   "Editors' Response," March, 2000, 37. Generally, as a matter of policy, yeshiva students wear white dress-shirts and dark dress-pants.

62   See Yohanan Danziger, *The Incidence of At-Risk Youth in the Orthodox Jewish Community of Brooklyn, New York* (New York: New York City Department of Youth and Community

Development and The Metropolitan Coordinating Council on Jewish Poverty, n.d.); The Metropolitan Coordinating Council on Jewish Poverty and Jewish Board of Family and Children's Services, *Teenage Orthodox Jewish Girls At-Risk: Study and Recommendations* (New York, 2003).

63 See Blumenthal and Russel, "Helping the At-Risk Child."

64 *The Jewish Observer*, March, 2000, 7.

65 See http://www.themarker.com/tmc/article.jhtml?ElementId=tle20100211_06, viewed April, 2010, as well as Nathaniel Deutsch, "The Forbidden Fork, the Cell Phone Holocaust, and Other Haredi Encounters with Technology," *Contemporary Jewry* 29:1 (2009), 4-19.

66 http://abcnews.go.com/Technology/wireStory?id=9664125, viewed April, 2010.

67 See above, p. 165.

68 See Rose, "*Halm Anahnu Hozim Be'aviv Shel Prague.*" Andrea Lieber has found less subversiveness then I suggest here in her study of blogs by Orthodox Jewish women. See her "Domesticity and the Home (Page): Blogging and the Blurring of Public and Private among Orthodox Jewish Women," in *Jews at Home: The Domestication of Identity*, Ed. Simon Bronner (Oxford: Littman Library of Jewish Civilization, 2010), 257-282.

CHAPTER SEVEN

1 Cynthia Ozick, "Literature as Idol: Harold Bloom," in *Art and Ardor* (New York: Alfred A. Knopf, 1983), 178-199.

2 Or, in more theoretical terms: "Narrators build shared representations about who they are by creating story-worlds in which identities are characterized in common ways and routinely related to specific actions and reactions.... These [narrative] schemas allow members of the group to answer questions on who they are, what their criteria for membership in the group are, how they relate to members of other groups and what their goals and values are." Anna de Fina, "Group Identity, Narratives, and Self-Representations," in *Discourse and Identity*, Eds. Anna De Fina, Deborah Schiffrin, and Michael Bamberg (Cambridge: Cambridge University Press, 2006), 350, 356.

3 Cf. Benedict Anderson's reflections on the role of mass-produced newspapers in creating national identity by distributing a shared narrative in easily accessible format. Benedict Anderson, *Imagined Communities: Reflections on the Origins and Spread of Nationalism* (London and New York: Verso, 1983).

4 Martin Lockshin, "Dueling Prayerbooks: ArtScroll, Koren and Contemporary Orthodox Values," presentation at the conference of the Association of Jewish Studies, Los Angeles, December, 2010.

5 This is the main claim of the so-called Katz thesis regarding Orthodoxy, set out in Jacob Katz, "Orthodoxy in Historical Perspective," *Studies in Contemporary Jewry* 2 (1986), 3-17. This thesis has been questioned on both historical and conceptual grounds, particularly in articles in Joseph Salmon, Aviezer Ravitzky, and Adam Ferziger, *Ortodoksiah Yehudit: Hebetim Hadashim* (Jerusalem: Magnes Press, 2006), particularly in the articles by Ravitzky, Sagi, and Rosenberg. Despite these criticisms, I find that thesis essentially compelling.

6 Shlomo Gottesman, "Reflections on Kevod Shamayim: Travels with Rabbi Aaron Leib Steinman," *The Jewish Observer* 38:1 (January, 2005), 6.

SELECTED BIBLIOGRAPHY

Abramov, Tehilla. *The Secret of Jewish Femininity: Insights into the Practice of Taharat HaMishpachah.* Southfield, MI: Targum/Feldheim, 1988.

Abramov, Yirmiyohu and Tehilla Abramov. *Two Halves of a Whole: Torah Guidelines for Marriage.* Southfield, MI: Targum/Feldheim, 1994.

Adahan, Miriam. *EMETT: A Step-by-Step Guide to Emotional Maturity Established Through Torah.* Jerusalem and New York: Feldheim, 1987.

Adahan, Miriam. *Raising Children to Care.* Jerusalem and New York: Feldheim, 1988.

Adahan, Miriam. *Appreciating People (Including Yourself).* Jerusalem: Feldheim and Gefen, 1988.

Adahan, Miriam. *Awareness: The Key to Acceptance, Respect, Forgiveness, and Growth.* Jerusalem and New York: Feldheim, 1994.

Albo, Yosef. *Sefer HaIqqarim.* Jerusalem: n.p., 1987.

Almond, Gabriel A., R. Scott Appleby, and Emmanuel Sivan. *Strong Religion: the Rise of Fundamentalisms around the World.* Chicago and London: University of Chicago Press, 2003.

Altabe, Richard. "General Studies in the Yeshivos: A Neglected Frontier." *The Jewish Observer* 37:5 (May, 2004): 6-7.

Alter, Robert. *The Invention of Hebrew Prose: Modern Fiction and the Language of Realism.* Seattle: University of Washington Press, 1988.

Anderson, Benedict. *Imagined Communities: Reflections on the Origins and Spread of Nationalism.* London and New York: Verso, 1983.

Anonymous. "Jewish History from a Torah Perspective." *The Jewish Observer* 22:4 (May, 1989): 31-34.

Anteby, Max. *The Jewish Theory of Everything: A Behind-the-Scenes Look at the World.* Brooklyn: Shaar, 2002.

Apple, Michael. *Education and Power.* Boston, London, Melbourne, and Henley: Routledge and Kegal Paul, 1982.

ArtScroll Publishers, *The Schottenstein Edition of the Talmud.* Brooklyn: Mesorah, 1990-2004, 72 volumes.

Asaf, Simhah. *Meqorot LeToldot HaHinnukh BeYisrael.* New York and Jerusalem: Jewish Theological Seminary, 2002.

Baharan, Avraham. *The Two-Way Channel: Society and the Individual.* Southfield, MI: Targum/Feldheim, 1999.

Barzilai, Sarit. *Lifrotz Me'ah She'arim: Mas'a El 'Olamam Shel HaYotze'im LeShe'elah.* Tel Aviv: Yedi'ot Aharonot and Sifrei Hemed, 2004.

Baumel, Yehoshua. *Shut 'Emeq Halakhah.* Jerusalem: n.p, 1976.

Baumgarten, Elisheva. *Mothers and Children: Jewish Family Life in Medieval Europe.* Princeton: Princeton University Press, 2004.

Bennett, Tony, ed. *Popular Fiction: Technology, Ideology, Production, Reading.* London and New York: Routledge, 1990.

Benor, Sarah B. "Second Style Acquisition: The Linguistic Socialization of Newly Ortho-dox Jews." Ph.D diss., Stanford University, 2004.

Ben-Tzvi, Meir. "A Response to Rabbi Aharon Feldman's Article." Accessed February, 2010. http://www.zootorah.com/controversy/Feldman,%20Rav%20Aharon,%20 Second%20Version%20Response.rtf.

Berger, Joseph. "An English Talmud for Daily Readers and Debaters." *New York Times*, February 10, 2005. Accessed November, 2010. http://www.nytimes. com/2005/02/10/books/10talm.html?pagewanted=all&position.

Berry, John W. "Immigration, Acculturation, and Adaptation." *Applied Psychology: An International Review* 46 (1997): 7.

Biale, David. *Eros and the Jews.* New York: Basic Books, 1992.

Blodgett, Jan. *Protestant Evangelical Literary Culture and Contemporary Society.* West-port, CT and London: Greenwood Press, 1997.

Borozovski, Shalom N. *Kuntres Netivei Olam HaYeshiva.* Jerusalem: Yeshivat Beit Avra-ham, 1991.

Bowler, Peter J. *Monkey Trials and Gorilla Sermons: Evolution and Christianity from Dar-win to Intelligent Design.* Cambridge: Harvard University Press, 2007.

Breuer, Mordechai. *Ohalei Torah: HaYeshivah, Tavnitah VeToldotehah.* Jerusalem: Zal-man Shazar Center, 2004.

Brezak, Dov. *Chinuch in Turbulent Times: Practical Strategies for Parents and Educators.* Brooklyn: Mesorah, 2002.

Brill, Alan. "Judaism in Culture: Beyond the Bifurcation of Torah and Madda." *The Edah Journal* 4:1 (2004):1-26. Accessed July, 2010. http://www.edah.org/backend/Jour-nalArticle/4_1_brill.pdf.

Brown, Binyamin. "*Shuvah Shel 'HaEmunah HaTemimah': Tefisat HaEmunah HaHaredit U'Tzmihatah BeMe'ah HaEsrim.*" In *'Al HaEmunah: Iyyunim BeMusag HaEmunah Uve-Toldotayv BaMasoret HaYehudit*, edited by Moshe Halbertal, David Kurzweil, and Avi Sagi, 403-443. Jerusalem: Keter, 2005.

Brown, Binyamin. "*VeEin Lanu Shiur Rak HaTorah HaZot.*" *Eretz Aharet* 41 (August-October, 2007): 56-65.

Bunim, Amos. *A Fire in His Soul: Irving M. Bunim, 1901-1980, The Man and His Impact on American Orthodox Jewry.* Jerusalem and New York: Feldheim, 1989.

Byrne, Peter. "Moral Arguments for the Existence of God." *Stanford Encyclopedia of Philosophy.* Accessed November, 2009. http://plato.stanford.edu/entries/moral-arguments-god/.

Cantor, Geoffrey and Marc Swetlitz, eds. *The Jewish Tradition and the Challenge of Dar-winism.* Chicago: University of Chicago Press, 2006.

Caplan, Kimmy and Emmanuel Sivan, eds. *Haredim Yisraeliim: Hishtalvut BeLo Temi'a?* Jerusalem: Van Leer Institute and HaKibbutz HaMe'uhad, 2003.

Caplan, Kimmy and Nurit Stadler, eds. *Manhigut VeSamkhut BaHevrah HaHaredit BeYis-rael.* Jerusalem: Van Leer Institute and Hakkibutz HaMe'uhad, 2009.

Caplan, Kimmy. "'*Yesh Riqavon Retzini BaHevrah Shalanu VeTzrikhin LeHakir Et HaEmet': Biqqoret 'Atzmit BaSiah HaPenimi Shel HaHevrah HaHaredit BeYisrael.*" In *Mi'utim, Zarim VeShonim: Kevutzot Shulayim BaHistoriah*, edited by Shlomit Volkov, 299-330. Jerusalem: Zalman Shazar Center, 2000.

Caplan, Kimmy. "Haredim and Western Culture: A View from Both Sides of the Ocean." *Middle Eastern Societies and the West: Accommodation or Clash of Civilizations?*, edited by Meir Litvak, 269-288. Tel Aviv: The Moshe Dayan Center for Middle Eastern and African Studies, Tel Aviv University, 2006.

Caplan, Kimmy. *Besod HaSiah HaHaredi*. Jerusalem: Zalman Shazar Center, 2007.

Carmell, Aryeh. *Masterplan: Judaism: Its Programs, Meanings, and Goals*. Jerusalem: Jerusalem Academy Publications, 1991.

Carmy, Shalom. *Forgive Us, Father-in-Law, For We Know Not What to Think: Letter to a Philosophical Dropout From Orthodoxy*. Jerusalem: ATID, 2004.

Chait, Baruch. *The Lost Treasure of Tikkun HaMiddos Island*. Jerusalem: B and B Septimus Educational Publications, 2001.

Clark, Lynn Schofield, ed. *Religion Media and the Marketplace*. New Brunswick, NJ: Rutgers University Press, 2007.

Cohen, Anthony P. *The Symbolic Construction of Community*. London and New York: Tavistock Publications, 1985.

Connerton, Paul. *How Societies Remember*. Cambridge: Cambridge University Press, 1989.

Coopersmith, Yitzchak. *The Eye of a Needle: Aish Hatorah's Kiruv Primer*. Jerusalem: Feldheim, 1993.

Cordero, Jonathan. "The Production of Christian Fiction." *Journal of Religion and Popular Culture*, 6 (2004). Accessed September, 2008. www.usak.ca/relst/jrpc/art6-xianfiction-print.html.

Danzger, Herbert. *Returning to Tradition: The Contemporary Revival of Orthodox Judaism*. New Haven: Yale University Press, 1989.

Danziger, Yohanan. *The Incidence of At-Risk Youth in the Orthodox Jewish Community of Brooklyn, New York*. New York: New York City Department of Youth and Community Development and The Metropolitan Coordinating Council on Jewish Poverty, n.d.

Davidman, Lynn. *Tradition in a Rootless World: Women Turn to Orthodox Judaism*. Berkeley: University of California Press, 1991.

Dershowitz, Yitzchok. *The Legacy of Maran Rav Aharon Kotler*. Lakewood, NJ: M.H. Living 'Mishnas Rav Aharon,' 2005.

Dessler, Eliyahu E. *Strive for Truth!* New York and Jerusalem: Feldheim, 1988.

Diamond, Etan. *And I Will Dwell in Their Midst: Orthodox Jews in Suburbia*. Chapel Hill and London: University of North Carolina Press, 2000.

Diskind, Faiga. "General Studies in the Yeshiva: Benefits and Booby Traps." *The Jewish Observer* 19:7 (October, 1986): 45-51.

Diskind, Faiga. "Finding a Way When There is No Choice." *The Jewish Observer* 20:2 (March, 1987): 31-38.

Douglas, Mary. *Natural Symbols*. London: Barrie and Rockliff, 1970.

Efron, Noah J. *Real Jews: Secular Vs. Ultra-Orthodox and the Struggle for Jewish Identity in Israel*. New York: Basic Books, n.d.

Eider, Shimon D. *The Halachos of Niddah*. Lakewood, NJ: Feldheim, 1981.

Einstein, Mara. *Brands of Faith: Marketing Religion in a Commercial Age*. London and New York: Routledge, 2008.

Eisenberg, Eilene, Heidi Murkoff, and Sandee Eisenberg. *What to Expect When You Are Expecting*. New York: Workman, 1991.

Eliav, Chaim. *Ketonet Pasim*. Jerusalem: Pesher, 1997.

Eliav, Chaim. *The Runaway*, translated by Libby Lazewnik. Brooklyn: Shaar Press, 1998.

Fader, Ayala. *Mitzvah Girls: Bringing Up the Next Generation of Hasidic Jews in Brooklyn.* Princeton and Oxford: Princeton University Press, 2009.

Falk, Pesach E. *Modesty: An Adornment for Life.* Jerusalem: Feldheim, 1998.

Feinstein, Moshe. *Sefer Iggerot Moshe.* New York: Noble Book Press, 1959.

Feldman, Aharon. *The River, the Kettle and the Bird: A Torah Guide to Successful Marriage.* Israel: CSB Publications, 1987.

Feldman, Aharon. "*Gedolim* Books and the Biography of Reb Yaakov Kamenetsky." *The Jewish Observer* 28:8 (November, 1994): 32-34.

Feldman, Aharon. "The Slifkin Affair: Issues and Perspectives." Accessed February, 2011. http://www.zootorah.com/controversy/SLIFKINARTICLE.doc.

Finke, Roger and Laurence Iannacone. "Supply-Side Explanations for Religious Change." *Annals of the American Academy of Political and Social Science* 527 (1993): 27-39.

Finkelman, Shimon. *The Story of Reb Elchonon.* Brooklyn: Mesorah, 1984.

Finkelman, Yoel. "Medium and Message in Contemporary Haredi Adventure Fiction." *The Torah U-Madda Journal* 13 (2005): 50-87.

Finkelman, Yoel. "Relationships Between Schools and Parents in Haredi Popular Literature in the United States." In *Jewish Day Schools, Jewish Communities*, edited by Alex Pomson and Howard Deitcher, 237-254. Oxford and Portland, OR: Littman Library of Jewish Civilization, 2009.

Finkelman, Yoel. "It's a Small, Small World: Secular Zionism through the Eyes of a Contemporary Religious Zionist *Parshat Hashavua* Pamphlet." In *The Relationship of Orthodox Jews with Believing Jews of Other Religious Ideologies and Non-Believing Jews*, edited by Adam Mintz, 313-350. New York: Yeshiva University Press, 2010.

Finkelman, Yoel. "Ultra-Orthodox/Haredi Education." In *The International Handbook of Jewish Education*, edited by Helena Miller, Alex Pomson, and Lisa Grant, Vol 2, 1063-1080. Dordrecht, Heidelberg, London, and New York: Springer, 2011.

Finkelstein, Baruch and Michal Finkelstein. *Nine Wonderful Months: B'Sha'ah Tovah.* New York and Jerusalem: Feldheim, 1993.

Fishbein, Susie. *Kosher By Design: Picture Perfect Foods for the Holidays and Everyday.* Brooklyn: Mesorah, 2003.

Fishbein, Susie. *Kosher by Design Entertains.* Mesorah: Brooklyn, 2005.

Fishman, Sylvia Barack. *Jewish Life and American Culture.* Albany, NY: State University of New York Press, 2000.

Flake, Carol. *Redemptorama: Culture, Politics, and the New Evangelicalsim.* n.p.: Penguin, 1984.

Frankel, Zvi. "Blogs: Transgressing a Major Sin 'In the Name of Heaven.'" *The Jewish Observer* 40:9 (December, 2007): 32-33.

Freedman, Samuel G. *Jew vs. Jew: The Struggle for the Soul of American Jewry.* New York: Touchstone, 2000.

Freeze, ChaeRan. *Jewish Marriage and Divorce in Imperial Russia.* Hanover, NH: Brandies University Press, 2004.

Friedman, Murray I. "What is Our Historical Imperative? On the Function of Torah-True Literature in Our Times." *The Jewish Observer* 1:1 (September, 1963): 19-20.

Frykholm, Amy J. *Rapture Culture: Left Behind in Evangelical America.* New York: Oxford University Press, 2004.

Fryshman, Bernard. "On Losing One's Mind." *The Jewish Observer* 15:6 (May, 1981): 50-51.

Fryshman, Bernard. Letters to the editor. *The Jewish Observer* 15:9 (November, 1981): 32-35.

Fryshman, Bernard. "So He's Reading a Book." *The Jewish Observer* 16:10 (November, 1983): 34.

Gans, Moshe. *Make Me Don't Break Me*. Brooklyn: Mesorah, 1994.

Ganz, Yaffa. "You Can't Sell a Book by Its Cover (But It's a Good Place to Start): The Complexities of Religious Juvenile Publishing." *The Jewish Observer* 21:4 (May, 1988): 31-34.

Gaon of Vilna. *Even Shelemah Tosfa'ah*. n.p.: n.p., n.d.

Gaonkar, Dilip and Charles Taylor. "Block Thinking and Internal Criticism." *Public Culture* 18:3 (2006): 453-455.

Gevirtz, Eliezer. *Lehovin UleHaskil: A Guide to Torah Hashkofoh, Questions and Answers on Judaism*. New York: Jewish Educational Program, 1980.

Goldberg, Hyman. *Our Man in the Kitchen*. New York: Odyssey Press, 1964.

Golding, Yosef C. "How to Get the Entire Jewish Music World Angry at Me... Or a Parents' Guide to What Your Children Listen To." *The Jewish Observer* 40:4 (May, 2007): 36-37.

Gormly, Eric. "Evangelizing through Appropriation: Toward a Cultural Theory on the Growth of Contemporary Christian Music." *Journal of Media and Religion* 24:4 (2003): 251-65.

Gottesman, Shlomo. "Reflections on Kevod Shamayim: Travels with Rabbi Aaron Leib Steinman." *The Jewish Observer* 38:1 (January, 2005): 6-14.

Gottlieb, Dovid. *Living Up to the... Truth*. Jerusalem, 1995. Accessed July, 2010. http://www.dovidgottlieb.com/works/RabbiGottliebLivingUpToTheTruth.pdf.

Gray, John. *Men are from Mars, Women are from Venus*. London: Thorsons, 1992.

Greenblatt, Devorah. "Making Our '*Bayis*' a Mobile Home." *The Jewish Observer* 32:9 (November, 1999): 49-50.

Greenwald, Yisroel. *We Want Life!* Jerusalem and New York: Feldheim and The Chofetz Chaim Heritage Foundation, 1996.

Grossman, Avraham. *Pious and Rebellious: Jewish Women in Medieval Europe*, translated by Jonathan Chipman. Waltham, MA: Brandeis University Press, 2004.

Gurock, Jeffrey. "The Winnowing of American Orthodoxy." In *American Jewish Orthodoxy in Historical Perspective*, edited by Jeffrey Gurock, 299-312. Hoboken, NJ: Ktav, 1996.

Gurock, Jeffrey. *Judaism's Encounter with American Sports*. Bloomington and Indianapolis: Indiana University Press, 2005.

Gurock, Jeffrey. *Orthodox Jews in America*. Bloomington and Indianapolis: Indiana University Press, 2009.

Halbwachs, Maurice. *On Collective Memory*, translated by Lewis Coser. Chicago: University of Chicago Press, 1992.

Hall, Stuart. "Encoding, Decoding." In *The Culture Studies Reader*, edited by Simon During, 507-517. London: Routledge, 1990.

Hayyim of Volozhin. *Ruah Hayyim*. n.p.: Wickliffe, OH, 1998.

Hazon Ish, *Emunah u-Vittahon*. Jerusalem, 1954.

Heilman, Samuel. *Sliding to the Right: The Contest for the Future of American Jewish Orthodoxy*. Berkeley: University of California Press, 2006.

Heinze, Andrew R. "The Americanization of 'Mussar': Abraham Twerski's Twelve Steps." *Judaism* 48:4 (1999): 450-469.

Heller, Aryeh L. *Ketzot HaHoshen.* Jerusalem: Oraita, 2002.

Helmreich, William B. *The World of the Yeshiva: An Intimate Portrait of Orthodox Jewry.* New Haven and London: Yale University Press, 1982.

Hendershot, Heather. *Shaking the World for Jesus: Media and Conservative Evangelical Culture.* Chicago: University of California Press, 2004.

Herberg, Will. *Protestant-Catholic-Jew: An Essay in American Religious Sociology.* Garden City, NY: Anchor Books, 1955.

Hirsch, Ammiel and Yosef Reinman. *One People, Two Worlds.* New York: Schocken, 2002.

Hirshman, Yechezkel. *One Above and Seven Below: A Consumer's Guide to Orthodox Judaism from the Perspective of the Chareidim.* Jerusalem: Mazo, 2007.

Horowitz, Yeshayahu. *Shnei Luhot HaBerit.* Jerusalem: n.p., 1975.

Hulbert, Ann. *Raising America: Experts, Parents, and a Century of Advice about Children.* New York: Vintage Books, 2003.

Hurwitz, Shimon. *Being Jewish.* Jerusalem: Feldheim, 1979.

ibn Paquda, Bahya. *The Book of Directions to the Duties of the Heart,* translated by Menahem Mansoor. London: Routledge and Kegan Paul, 1973.

Jung, Pinchos. "Let the Reader Beware." *The Jewish Observer* 33:9 (November, 2000): 42-43.

Jung, Pinchos. "Heads or Tails? Maximizing Your Child's Benefit." *The Jewish Observer* 41:1 (January/February, 2008): 8.

Kagan, Jeremy. *The Jewish Self: Recovering Spirituality in the Modern World.* Jerusalem: Feldheim, 1998.

Kaganoff, Malka. *Dear Kallah: A Practical Guide for the New Bride.* Jerusalem and New York: Feldheim, 1993.

Kamenetsky, Noson. *The Making of a Godol.* Jerusalem: HaMesorah Publications, 2002.

Kamenetsky, Noson. *The Anatomy of a Ban.* Israel: PP Publishers, 2003.

Kaminetsky, Joseph and Alex Gross. "Shraga Feivel Mendlowitz." In *Men of Spirit,* edited by Leo Jung. New York: Kymson Publishing Company, 1964.

Kanarfogel, Ephraim. "Attitudes Toward Childhood in Medieval Jewish Society." In *Approaches to Judaism in Medieval Times,* edited by David R. Blumenthal, 1-34. Chico, CA: Scholars Press, 1985.

Kaplan, Lawrence. "Daas Torah: A Modern Conception of Rabbinic Authority." In *Rabbinic Authority and Personal Autonomy,* edited by Moshe Sokol, 1-60. Northvale, NJ: Aaronson, 1992.

Kasnett, Nesanel. "'We are Israel': A Chanuka Essay." *The Jewish Observer* 21:8 (November, 1988): 23-27.

Kasnett, Yitzchak. "'Rebbe, That Was Great!': Yeshiva English Studies, Another Dimension." *The Jewish Observer* 19:7 (October, 1986): 53-58.

Kassnett, Yitzchok. *The World that Was: Lithuania.* Cleveland Heights: Hebrew Academy of Cleveland, 1996.

Kassnett, Yitzchok. *The World that Was: Poland.* Cleveland Heights: Hebrew Academy of Cleveland, 1997.

Kassnet, Yitzchak. "The Write Stuff." *The Jewish Observer* 31:4 (April, 1998): 23-27.

Kassnett, Yitzchok. *The World that Was: Hungary/Romania*. Cleveland Heights: Hebrew Academy of Cleveland, 1998.

Katz, Jacob. *Tradition and Crisis: Jewish Society at the End of the Middle Ages*. New York: Schocken, 1971.

Kaufman, Debra R. *Rachel's Daughters: Newly Orthodox Jewish Women*. New Brunswick, NJ: Rutgers University Press, 1991.

Kelemen, Lawrence. *Permission to Believe: Four Rational Approaches to God's Existence*. Southfield, MI: Targum/Feldheim, 1990.

Kelemen, Lawrence. *Permission to Receive: Four Rational Approaches to the Torah's Divine Origin*. Southfield, MI: Targum/Feldheim, 1996.

Keleman, Lawrence. *To Kindle a Soul: Ancient Wisdom for Modern Parents and Teachers*. Southfield, MI: Targum Press and Leviathan Press, 2001.

Keller, Chaim D. "The Cosmic Question: Random Evolution or Intelligent Design?" *The Jewish Observer* 39:4 (May, 2006): 6-21.

Kimball, Christopher. *The America's Test Kitchen Family Cookbook*. Brookline, MA: America's Test Kitchen, 2006.

Klitsner, Judy. *Subversive Sequels in the Bible: How Biblical Stories Mine and Undermine Each Other*. Philadelphia: The Jewish Publication Society, 2009.

Klitsner, Shmuel, Judy Klitsner, and Ehud Tokatly. *The Lost Children of Tarshish*. Southfield, MI and Lakewood, NJ: Targum Press and CIS, 1989.

Klitsner, Shmuel. *Wrestling Jacob: Deception, Identity and Freudian Slips in Genesis*. Jerusalem and New York: Urim Publication, 2006.

Klugman, Eliyahu M. *Rabbi Samson Raphael Hirsch: Architect of Torah Judaism for the Modern World*. Brooklyn: Mesorah, 1998.

Kraemer, David, ed. *The Jewish Family*. New York and Oxford: Oxford University Press, 1989.

Kranzler, David. "Orthodoxy's Finest Hour." *Jewish Action* 63:1 (Fall, 2002): 27-36.

Krohn, Hindy. *The Way It Was: Touching Vignettes about Growing Up Jewish in the Philadelphia of Long Ago*. Brooklyn: Mesorah, 1989.

Kupperwasser, Chaim. "Sixty Years Since Churban Europa." *The Jewish Observer* 38:5 (May, 2005): 11-13.

Lamm, Norman. *Torah Umadda: The Encounter of Religious Learning and Worldly Knowledge in the Jewish Tradition*. Northvale, NJ and London: Jason Aaronson, 1990.

Lamont, Michele and Virag Molnar. "The Study of Boundaries in the Social Sciences." *Annual Review of Sociology* 28 (2002): 167-195.

Lasch, Christopher. *Haven in a Heartless World: The Family Besieged*. New York: Basic Books, 1977.

Lebovits, Yehudah. *Shidduchim and Zivvugim: The Torah's Perspective on Choosing Your Mate*. Southfield, MI and New York: Targum/Feldheim, 1987.

Lebovitz, Yehudah. *The B'nei Torah Edition of the Lebovitz System: The Revolutionary Breakthrough for Smokers*. Jerusalem: Feldheim, 1989.

Leff, Zev. "The Reality of Torah." *MDTorah Weekly* 4:18 (February 22, 2003): 3.

Leizerson, Breindy. "Set the Record Straight." *The Jewish Observer* 20:4 (May, 1987): 40-41.

Levenstein, Harvey. *Paradoxes of Plenty: A Social History of Eating in Modern America*. New York and Oxford: Oxford University Press, 1993.

Levi, Miriam. *Effective Jewish Parenting*. New York and Jerusalem: Feldheim, 1986.

Levi, Yehudah *The Science of Torah: The Scientific Knowledge of the Talmudic Sages*. Jerusalem and New York: Feldheim, 2004.

Levinson, Yaakov. *The Jewish Guide to Natural Nutrition*. Jerusalem and New York: Feldheim, 1995.

Levy, B. Barry. "ArtScroll: An Overview." In *Approaches to Modern Judaism*, edited by Marc Lee Raphael, 111-140. Chico, CA: Scholars Press, 1983.

Levy, B. Barry. "Our Torah, Your Torah and Their Torah: An Evaluation of the ArtScroll Phenomenon." In *Truth and Compassion: Essays on Religion in Judaism*, edited by H. Joseph, et al., 137-189. Waterloo, Ontario: Wilfrid Laurier University Press, 1983.

Levy, B. Barry. "Contemporary Jewish Booklore: The Exegetical and Editorial Work of Rabbi Meir Zlotowitz and Rabbi Nosson Scherman (or The ArtScroll Phenomenon, 2005)." Unpublished manuscript.

Lichtenstein, Aharon. "The Source of Faith is Faith Itself." In *Leaves of Faith: The World of Jewish Living*, edited by Aharon Lichtenstein. Jersey City: Ktav, 2004.

Liebman, Charles. "Orthodoxy in American Jewish Life." *American Jewish Year Book* 66 (1967): 21-92.

Lockshin, Martin. "Dueling Prayerbooks: ArtScroll, Koren and Contemporary Orthodox Values." Presentation at the conference of the Association of Jewish Studies, Los Angeles, December, 2010.

Lynch, Gordon. *Understanding Theology and Popular Culture*. Oxford: Blackwell, 2005.

Lynch, Gordon, ed. *Between Sacred and Profane: Researching Religion and Popular Culture*. London and New York: I.B. Taurus, 2007.

Maharal of Prague. *Tifferet Yisrael*. Israel: n.p., 1980.

Manolson, Gila. *The Magic Touch: A Candid Look at the Jewish Approach to Relationships*. Jerusalem: Har Nof Publications, 1992.

Marty, Martin E. and R. Scott Appleby, eds. *Fundamentalisms and Society*. Chicago and London: University of Chicago Press, 1993.

Marty, Martin E. and R. Scott Appleby, eds. *Fundamentalisms Observed*. Chicago and London: University of Chicago Press, 1994.

McDannell, Colleen. *Material Christianity: Religion and Popular Culture in America*. New Haven and London: Yale University Press, 1995.

Medwed, Sara. "Shalom Bayis Like It Was Not Too Long Ago." *The Jewish Observer* 40:7 (October, 2007): 15-17.

Metropolitan Council on Jewish Poverty and Jewish Board of Family and Children's Services, *Teenage Orthodox Jewish Girls At-Risk: Study and Recommendations*. New York, 2003.

Miller, Shlomo. "A Letter of Admonishment Regarding N. Slifkin's Opinions." Accessed July, 2006. http://www.zootorah.com/controversy/SLIFKINARTICLE.doc.

Mintz, Shalva. Untitled essay. *The Jewish Observer* 20:2 (March, 1987): 31.

Mintz, Steven and Susan Kellogg. *Domestic Revolutions: A Social History of American Family Life*. New York: Free Press, 1988.

Mintz, Steven. *Huck's Raft: A History of American Childhood*. Cambridge, MA and London: Harvard University Press, 2004.

Moore, R. L. *Selling God: American Religion in the Marketplace of Culture*. New York and Oxford: Oxford University Press, 1994.

Myers, Isabel B. and Peter B. Myers. *Gifts Differing: Understanding Personality Types*. Palo Alto, CA: Davies Black, 1995.

Nagle, Thomas. *The View from Nowhere*. Oxford: Oxford University Press, 1986.

Neustein, Amy. *Tempest in the Temple: Jewish Communities and Child Sex Scandals*. Lebanon, NH: University Press of New England, Brandeis University Press, 2009.

Neuwirth, Yehoshua. *Shemirat Shabbat KeHilkhetah*. Jerusalem: Feldheim, 1965.

Neuwirth, Yehoshua. *Shemirath Shabbath: A Guide to the Practical Observance of the Sabbath*. Jerusalem and New York: Feldheim, 1984.

Orlowek, Noach. *Raising Roses Among the Thorns*. Jerusalem and New York: Feldheim, 2002.

Orlowek, Noach. "Avoiding the Risks of Unthinking Parenting." *The Jewish Observer* 37:7 (September, 2004): 34-37.

Ozick, Cynthia. "Literature as Idol: Harold Bloom." In *Art and Ardor*, 178-199. New York: Alfred A. Knopf, 1983.

Pam, Avraham and Tzvi Baruch Hollander. "The Jewish Family – In Its Glory and in Crisis." *The Jewish Observer* 29:4 (May, 1996): 6-9.

Pearlman, Ruthie. *Against the Wall*. Southfield, MI: Targum/Feldheim, 2004.

Pekier, Alter. *Reb Aharon: Moreinu HaRav Aharon Kotler*. New York, London, Jerusalem: CIS, 1995.

Perlow, Yaakov. "The Clash Between Modernity and Eternity." *The Jewish Observer* 26:10 (January, 1994): 9-13.

Pliskin, Zelig. *Gateway to Self-Knowledge*. Jerusalem: Aish Hatorah Publications, 1986.

Pollak, Aharon. *Torah Powerhouse: Insights into the Theory and Practice of Torah Parenting*. Jerusalem and New York: Feldheim, 1996.

Poltsek, Tammy. *Aristocratic Fruits: The Art of Transforming Fruit into Art*. Brooklyn: Aristocratic Party Design, 2003.

Pomerantz, Riva. *Breaking Point*. Southfield, MI: Targum, 2004.

Radcliff, Sara C. *Aizer K'negdo: The Jewish Woman's Guide to Happiness in Marriage*. Southfield, MI: Targum/Feldheim, 1988.

Rapoport-Albert, Ada. "Hagiography with Footnotes: Edifying Tales and the Writing of History in Hasidism." *History and Theory* 27:4 (1988): 119-159.

Riso, Don and Russ Hudson. *The Wisdom of the Enneagram*. New York: Bantam, 1999.

Robinson, Gershon. *The Obvious Proof*. New York: CIS Publishers, 1993.

Roller, Alyse F. *The Literary Imagination of Ultra-Orthodox Jewish Women: An Assesment of a Writing Community*. Jefferson, NC: McFarland, 1999.

Romanowski, William D. "Evangelicals and Popular Music: The Contemporary Christian Music Industry." In *Religion and Popular Culture in America*, edited by Bruce David Forbes and Jeffrey H. Mahan, 103-124. Berkeley and Los Angeles: University Of California Press, 2000.

Roof, Wade C. *A Generation of Seekers: The Spiritual Journeys of the Baby Boom Generation*. San Francisco: Harper, 1993.

Rose, Aharon. "Ha'Im Anu Hozim BeAviv Shel Prague Ba'Olam HaHaredi." *Eretz Aheret* 41 (August-October, 2007): 38-42.

Rosenblum, Yonoson. "*Torah Umadda*: A Critique of Rabbi Dr. Norman Lamm's Book and its Approach to Torah Study." *The Jewish Observer* 25:2 (March, 1992): 27-40.

Rosenblum, Yonoson. *They Called Him Mike: Reb Elimelech Tress, His Era, Hatzalah, and the Building of American Orthodoxy*. Brooklyn: Mesorah, 1995.

Rosenblum, Yonoson. *Reb Shraga Feivel*. Brooklyn: Mesorah, 2001.

Rosenblum, Yonoson. "Real Jews: Noah Efron's Research and the Chareidi Image." *The Jewish Observer* 37:3 (March, 2004): 14-18.

Rosenblum, Yonoson. "Anatomy of a Slander." *The Jewish Observer* 38:6 (Summer, 2005): 22-30.

Rosenblum, Yonoson. "The Myth of Scientific Objectivity." *The Jewish Observer* 39:4 (May, 2006): 27-34.

Rosenblum, Yonoson. "Growing Pains." *The Jewish Observer* 41:2 (March, 2008): 18-21.

Roskies, David. *The Jewish Search for a Useable Past*. Bloomington, IN: Indiana University Press, 1999.

Rothenberg, Jennie. "The Heresy of Nosson Slifkin." *Moment* (October, 2005): 37-43, 45, 58, 70, 72.

Rubin, Devorah. *Daughters of Desinty*. Brooklyn: Mesorah, 1988.

Sa'adia Gaon. *The Book of Beliefs and Opinions*, translated by Samuel Rosenblatt. New Haven and London: Yale University Press, 1948.

Sabo, Asher. "Judaica vs. the Classics in the Yeshiva English Department." *The Jewish Observer* 22:9 (December, 1989): 27-34.

Sagi, Avi and Daniel Statman. *Religion and Morality*. Amsterdam and Atlanta: Rodopi, 1995.

Sapirman, Dovid. *A Mechanech's Guide on Why and How to Teach Emunah*. Brooklyn: Torah Umesorah, 2009.

Sarna, Jonathan. *American Judaism: A History*. New Haven and London: Yale University Press, 2004.

Schachnowitz, Zelig. *The Light from the West: The Life and Times of the Chasam Sofer*, translated by Joseph Leftwich. Jerusalem and New York: Feldheim, 2007.

Schacter, Jacob J. "Haskalah, Secular Studies and the Close of the Yeshiva of Volozhin in 1892." *The Torah U-Madda Journal* 2 (1990): 76-133.

Schacter, Jacob J. "Facing the Truths of History." *The Torah U-Madda Journal* 8 (1998-1999): 200-276.

Schaps, Malka. "The One-Way Mirror: Israel and the Diaspora in Contemporary Orthodox Literature." *Shofar* 16:2 (1998): 32-47.

Schaps, Malka. "The Filtered Voice: Genre Shifts in Orthodox Women's Fiction." In *To Be a Jewish Woman*, edited by Margalit Shilo, 116-128. Jerusalem: Urim, 2003.

Scheinbaum, Leib. *The World that Was: America, 1900-1945*. Brooklyn: Shaar Press, 2004.

Schick, Marvin. "The Orthodox Community's Confused Priorities." *The Jewish Observer* 40:5 (June/Summer, 2007): 31-35.

Schiller, Mordechai. "Chassidus in Song – Not for the Record." *The Jewish Observer* 10:8 (March, 1975): 21-26.

Schwab, Shimon. *Selected Writings*. Lakewood, NJ: CIS, 1988.

Shapiro, Marc B. *Between the Yeshiva World and Modern Orthodoxy: The Life and Works of Rabbi Jehiel Jacob Weinberg*. London and Portland, OR: Littman Library of Jewish Civilization, 1999.

Shapiro, Marc B. "Of Books and Bans." *The Edah Journal* 3:2 (2003): 1-16. Accessed November 4, 2007. www.edah.org/backend/JournalArticle/3 _2; _Shapiro.pdf.

Shatz, David. *Jewish Thought in Dialogue: Essays on Thinkers, Theologies, and Moral*

Theories. Boston: Academic Studies Press, 2009.

Shenkar, Yael. *"Ezrat Nashim Mishelakh: 'Al Efsharut HaKetivah BaHavrah HaHaredit HaNashit."* Mehqarei Yerushalayim BeSifrut Ivrit 22 (2008): 177-188.

Shenkar, Yael. *"'Al Mah Sarah HaLashon? Siyagim U'Migbalot BaSifrut HaHaredit HaNashit."* Unpublished paper delivered at a conference on "Politics and Literature." June 2004, Hebrew University.

Shils, Edward. *Tradition.* Chicago and London: University of Chicago Press, 1981.

Siegel, Chana. "Where Have All the Writers Gone? In Search of Jewish Fiction." *Bat Kol* 5 (Cheshvan/Kislev, 5757): 3-4.

Silber, Dovid. *Noble Lives, Noble Deeds.* Brooklyn: Mesorah, 2002-2004.

Silber, Michael. "The Emergence of Ultra-Orthodoxy: The Invention of a Tradition." In *The Uses of Tradition: Jewish Continuity in the Modern Era,* edited by Jack Wertheimer, 23-84. New York and Jerusalem: Jewish Theological Seminary, 1992.

Sivan, Emmanuel. "The Enclave Culture." In *Fundamentalisms Comprehended,* edited by Martin E. Marty and R. Scott Appleby. Chicago and London: University Of Chicago Press, 1995.

Sklare, Marshall. *Conservative Judaism: An American Religious Movement.* Glencoe, IL: Free Press, 1955.

Slifkin, Nosson. *The Science of Torah: The Reflection of Torah in the Laws of Science, the Creation of the Universe, and the Development of Life.* Southfield, MI: Targum Press, 2001.

Slifkin, Nosson. *The Camel, the Hare, and the Hyrax: A Study of the Laws of Animals with One Kosher Sign in Light of Modern Zoology.* Southfield, MI: Targum Press, 2004.

Smith, Christian and Melinda Lundquist Denton. *Soul Searching: The Religious and Spiritual Lives of American Teenagers.* Oxford and New York: Oxford University Press, 2005.

Smith, Christian. *American Evangelicalism: Embattled and Thriving.* Chicago and London: University of Chicago, 1998.

Soloveitchik, Haym. "Rupture and Reconstruction: The Transformation of Contemporary Orthodoxy." *Tradition* 28:4 (1994): 64-130.

Sorasky, Aharon. *Reb Elchonon: The Life and Ideals of Rabbi Elchonon Bunim Wasserman of Baronovich.* Brooklyn: Mesorah, 1982.

Sorotzkin, Benzion. "The Damaging Fallout of Competitiveness." *The Jewish Observer* 40:9 (December, 2007): 6-7.

Sorotzkin, Benzion. "Dr. Sorotzkin Responds." *The Jewish Observer* 41:1 (Janurary/February, 2008): 8-9.

Spieser, Moshe. *Questions You Thought We Were Afraid You'd Ask and Answers You've Been Waiting to Hear.* Southfield, MI: Targum/Feldheim, 2004.

Stampfer, Shaul. *HaYeshiva HaLitait BeHithavutah.* Jerusalem: Zalman Shazar Center, 2005.

Stearns, Peter N. *Anxious Parents: A History of Modern Childrearing in America.* New York and London: New York University Press, 2003.

Steinberg, Leah. "Accomodating Children With Special Needs." *The Jewish Observer* 37:7 (Summer, 2004): 21.

Stolow, Jeremy. "Communicating Authority, Consuming Tradition: Jewish Orthodox Outreach Literature and Its Reading Public." In *Religion, Media and the Public Sphere,* edited by Brigite Meyers and Annelies Moors, 73-91. Bloomington: Indiana University Press, 2006.

Stolow, Jeremy. *Orthodox by Design: Judaism, Print Politics, and the ArtScroll Revolution.* Berkeley, Los Angeles, and London: University of California Press, 2010.

Stout, Daniel and Judith M. Buddenbaum, eds. *Religion and Popular Culture: Studies in the Interaction of Worldviews.* Ames, IO: Iowa State University Press, 2001.

Striks, Aryeh and Shimon Zehnwirth. *Pinnacle of Creation: Torah Insights into Human Nature.* Brooklyn: Mesorah, 2007.

Swatos, William H. and Kevin J. Christiano. "Secularization Theory: The Course of a Concept." *Sociology of Religion* 60:3 (1999): 209-28.

Tatz, Akiva. *Living Inspired.* Southfield, MI: Targum/Feldheim, 1991.

Tatz, Akiva. *Worldmask.* Southfield, MI: Targum/Feldheim, 1995.

Tatz, Akiva. *The Thinking Jewish Teenager's Guide to Life.* Southfield, MI: Targum Press, 1999.

Tauber, Ezriel. *Choose Life!* Monsey, NY: Shalheves, 1991.

Teller, Hanoch. *Builders.* Jerusalem: New York City Publishing Company, 2000.

The Jewish Observer. "A Healthy and Productive Life as a Torah Jew." 40:8 (November, 2007).

The Jewish Observer. "www.ensnared.com." 36:9 (November, 2003).

The Jewish Observer. "Children on the Fringe... and Beyond." 32:9 (November 1999).

The Jewish Observer. "Readers Respond." 33:3 (March 2000).

Twerski, Abraham J. and Ursula Schwartz. *Positive Parenting: Developing Your Child's Potential.* Brooklyn: Mesorah, 1996.

Twerski, Abraham J. *Getting Up When You're Down.* Brooklyn: Shaar Press, 1997.

United Jewish Communities, *American Jewish Religious Denominations.* New York: National Jewish Population Survey, n.d. Accessed August, 2010, http://www.jewishfederations.org/local_includes/downloads/7579.pdf.

Waardenburg, J.D.J. "Summaries of the Contributions." In *Official and Popular Religion: Analysis of a Theme for Religious Studies,* edited by Pieter H. Vrijof and Jacques Waardenburg, 636-637. The Hague: Mouton Publishers, 1979.

Waldman, Shmuel. *Beyond a Reasonable Doubt: Convincing Evidence of the Truths of Judaism,* edited by Ya'akov Astor. Jerusalem and New York: Feldheim, 2002/2004.

Walzer, Michael. *Interpretation and Social Criticism.* Cambridge and London: Harvard University Press, 1987.

Walzer, Michael. *The Company of Critics: Social Criticism and Political Commitment in the 20th Century.* New York: Basic Books, 2002.

Warner, R. Stephen. "Work in Progress: Toward a New Paradigm for the Sociological Study of Religion in the United States." *The American Journal of Sociology* 98:5 (1993): 1044-93.

Wasserman, Elhanan. *Kovetz Ma'amarim VeIggarot.* Jerusalem: Makhon Or Elhanan, 2001.

Wein, Berel. *Triumph of Survival.* Brooklyn: Shaar Press, 1990.

Wein, Berel. *Herald of Destiny.* Brooklyn: Shaar Press, 1993.

Wein, Berel. *Echoes of Glory.* Brooklyn: Shaar Press, 1995.

Wein, Berel. *Faith and Fate: The Story of the Jewish People.* Brooklyn: Shaar, 2001.

Weinberg, Noah and Yaakov Salomon. *What the Angel Taught You: Seven Keys to Life Fulfillment.* Brooklyn: Shaar Press, 2003.

Weinberg, Yaakov. *Fundamentals and Faith: Insights Into Rambam's 13 Principles*, edited by Mordechai Blumenfeld. Southfield, MI: Targum Press, 1991.

Weinstock, Yair. *Blackout*, translated by Miriam Zakon. Brooklyn: Shaar Press, 1998.

Weinstock, Yair. *Eye of the Storm*, translated by Libby Lazewnik. Brooklyn: Shaar Press, 1999.

Weiser, Chaim M. *Frumspeak: The First Dictionary of Yeshivish*. Northvale, NJ: Jason Aaronson, 1995.

Winkler, Meir. *Bayis Ne'eman b'Yisrael: Practical Steps to Success in Marriage*. Jerusalem and New York: Feldheim, 1988.

Wolbe, Shlomo. *Zeri'ah U'Vinyan BeHinnukh*. Jerusalem: Feldheim, 1995.

Wolbe, Shlomo. *Planting and Building: Raising a Jewish Child*, translated by Leib [Lawrence] Kelemen. Jerusalem and New York: Feldheim, 2000.

Wolfson, Yaakov. *All I Needed to Know I Learned in Yeshiva*. Southfield, MI: Targum Press, 1995.

Wolpin, Nisson. "Rx: For Yeshiva Dropouts." *The Jewish Observer* (May, 1964): 16-19.

Wolpin, Nisson. "The Great Public School Rainbow." *The Jewish Observer* 8:9 (December, 1972): 3.

Wolpin, Nisson, ed. *The Torah Personality: A Treasury of Biographical Sketches*. Brooklyn: Mesorah and Agudath Israel of America, 1980.

Wolpin, Nisson, ed. *The Torah Personality: A Treasury of Biographical Sketches*. Brooklyn: Mesorah and Agudath Israel of America, 1995.

Wolpin, Nisson, ed. *Torah Lives: A Treasury of Biographical Sketches*. Brooklyn: Mesorah and Agudath Israel of America, 1995

Wolpin, Nisson, ed. *Timeless Parenting: Raising Children in Troubled Times*. Brooklyn: Mesorah, 2000.

Wolpin, Nisson, ed. *Torah Leaders: A Treasury of Biographical Sketches*. Brooklyn: Mesorah and Agudath Israel of America, 2002.

Worthen, Molly. "Housewives of God." *The New York Times Magazine*, November 12, 2010. Accessed November, 2010. http://www.nytimes.com/2010/11/14/magazine/14evangelicals-t.html.

Zerubavel, Eviatar. *Time Maps: Collective Memory and the Social Shape of the Past*. Chicago and London: University of Chicago Press, 2003.

Zerubavel, Eviatar. *The Elephant in the Room: Silence and Denial in Everyday Life*. Oxford and New York: Oxford University Press, 2006.

Zerubavel, Yael. *Recovered Roots: Collective Memory and the Making of Israeli National Tradition*. Chicago and London: University of Chicago Press, 1995.

Zlotowitz, Meir, ed. *The Megillah*. Brooklyn: ArtScroll, 1976.

Zohar, Zvi. "VaYivra ArtScroll et Haleb Betzalmo: Itzuvah Shel Haleb KaKehilat Kodesh Haredit." In *Kehilat Yehudei Haleb*, edited by Miriam Frankel. Jerusalem: Makhon Ben Tzvi, forthcoming.

Zulberg, David J. *The Life-Transforming Diet: Based on the Health and Psychological Principles of Maimonides and Other Classical Sources*. Jerusalem and New York: Feldheim, 2007.

Zweibel, Chaim D. and Nisson Wolpin, eds. 2003. *Daring to Dream: Profiles in the Growth of the American Torah Community*. New York: Agudath Israel of America.

Index

CPSIA information can be obtained at www.ICGtesting.com
Printed in the USA
LVOW040635201011

251286LV00001B/1/P